The N

Shostakovich: the Man and his Music

edited
by

CHRISTOPHER NORRIS

LAWRENCE AND WISHART
LONDON

Lawrence and Wishart Ltd
39 Museum Stret
London WC1A 1LQ

First published 1982
Copyright © Lawrence and Wishart, 1982

Printed and bound in Great Britain at
The Camelot Press Ltd, Southampton

Contents

Christopher Norris

Introduction

For the artist to become 'a legend in his lifetime' is at best an ambiguous blessing, and at worst a painful test of creative endurance. Shostakovich was thrust into public prominence from the outset of his career, achieving the kind of representative status, as Soviet citizen-composer, which made his every work and utterance a topic of intense debate. Of modern composers, perhaps only Schoenberg created such a constant stir of partisan claims and counter-claims, and that (needless to say) for quite different reasons. Schoenberg indeed singled out Shostakovich – along with Sibelius – as one of the few modern symphonists who spoke with an authentic and original voice. Shostakovich was never able to fully reciprocate the compliment, although his attitude to Schoenberg – and to Western music generally – became more tolerant and receptive in later years.

In a sense these two composers represent the opposite sides of a single, uniquely modern predicament. Schoenberg the musical iconoclast, bearer of a new and (to many ears) intolerable message, looked forward all the same to a time when his music would be known and loved by the average concert-going listener. His messianic zeal involved, paradoxically, both a sense of extreme isolation and a craving for wider acclaim.

With Shostakovich the paradox is reversed, but the ultimate predicament not so very different. Shostakovich was quick to achieve a large-scale audience and popular fame which Schoenberg could hardly have hoped for in his wildest dreams. One can appreciate why Bartók, on an impulse of thinly-veiled resentment, worked a parody of the famous *Leningrad* march into the final scoring of his *Concerto for Orchestra*. At the time Shostakovich must have seemed to be riding a wave of fortuitous popular appeal, understandably galling to Western composers with no such opportunities for public display. But this was a brief and in many ways untypical phase in Shostakovich's career. Rarely was he able to match musical ideas with public occasion in so direct and acceptable a form as in the *Leningrad Symphony*. The price of Shostakovich's preëminence was that he became, willingly or not, the virtual embodiment of Soviet music in an age of fiercely competing ideologies. One can only guess at how a composer like Schoenberg – or indeed Bartók – might have borne up under such pressures of public commitment. At any rate it is impossible to separate Shostakovich, 'the man and his music', from the highly politicised culture in which he came to maturity. If Schoenberg's desire was to reach out beyond his devoted following to a wider, more varied audience, Shostakovich faced the opposite problem: how to reconcile the demands of socialist commitment with the search for an authentic and self-fulfilling language.

This means that questions of political import can never be far from the surface in any discussion of Shostakovich's music. These issues have been sharpened by the recent publication of *Testimony*, purportedly Shostakovich's 'memoirs' as related to, and edited by, the émigré Soviet musicologist Solomon Volkov. The authenticity of this document has been – and will no doubt continue to be – a topic of heated dispute. Its existence, however, can hardly be ignored by anyone discussing the political context or implied 'meaning' of Shostakovich's work.

On the other hand, even at their most tendentious, the *Memoirs* have a strangely familiar ring. They supply the same kind of retrospective slant on Shostakovich's life and music as Western ideologists have long been anxious to provide. Volkov presents the composer as a kind of anarchic saintly fool, a deceiver of infinite resource, using his music to mock at officialdom through a muttering undertow of satire and deliberate double-meaning. Such things had often enough been said by Western critics, especially in connection with the geared-up 'optimist' symphonic finales which do bear the marks of involuntary self-parody. What is suspect about the *Memoirs* is the way in which every such suggestive ambiguity is worked up into a more or less conscious gesture of private defiance. It is hard to credit Volkov's claim that these expertly barbed and slanted anecdotes were the product of a series of rambling monologues conducted (on Shostakovich's part) in a state of extreme nervous depression.

In other words the *Memoirs* are just too good to be true from an anti-Soviet propaganda viewpoint. The overall effect is of a cunning narrative tactician at work, creating an impression of vague, roundabout talk but in fact homing in on every loaded point with relish and impeccable timing. One certainly wouldn't guess at such qualities of mind from anything that Shostakovich published – or was quoted as saying – during his lifetime. Of course, as Volkov would no doubt argue, his public pronouncements were carefully vetted and could hardly be expected to display such a wittily subversive mind in action. But what of the music, which Volkov rightly appeals to as the intimate register and sounding-board of Shostakovich's feelings? Certainly there is humour of the stoical, resilient kind, as celebrated explicitly in the Thirteenth Symphony where 'humour' bounces back against all the assaults of fortune. Wit there is too, but of an edgily repetitive kind, and not in the vein of quick-thinking cleverness and mordant irony which the *Memoirs* consistently display. With many composers it might seem naïve to judge the character through the music in this way. With Shostakovich it is a natural, instinctive thing to do, mainly because the music is so much of a piece temperamentally, despite all the surface shifts of direction. The *Memoirs* seem no more true to the music than that other, official 'version' of Shostakovich which they try so hard to subvert. As I argue in my essay here, the music eludes any superimposed single order of meaning, whether of the orthodox or the Western-revisionist cast.

It is claimed that Shostakovich signed every page of the

Volkov transcript as a witness of its authenticity. The book
would certainly have carried more weight and silenced much
dispute if the publishers had troubled to reproduce at least a
few of those pages. Maxim Shostakovich, the composer's son,
has decisively rejected Volkov's claims to authenticity. His
account of how the book was most probably concocted may be
found in an interview in the *Sunday Times* (17 May 1981). 'A
book about my father rather than by him' is the mildest
statement in Maxim's vigorous rebuttal. Meanwhile one can
only regard *Testimony* as yet another phase in the struggle to
appropriate Shostakovich's music which has long been waged
by ideologues of various colour.

Some readers will probably want to reply that the essays in
this volume are themselves (or some of them) markedly
political in content and bearing. That this should be so –
properly and inevitably so – is the consequence of Shostakovich's own deep involvement in the cultural politics of his age.
The frequent *ambivalence* of that involvement should also be
clear from the different interpretations placed on it by (for
instance) Alan Bush and Robert Stradling. Shostakovich's
musical commitment was rarely of the straightforward, uncomplicated kind ideally demanded by the premises of Socialist
Realism. Neither can one seriously doubt, on the other hand,
that he met those demands with a genuine will to bring them
creatively into harness with his own musical temperament. The
problems he faced were real enough, and it is a measure of
Shostakovich's complex situation that the essays in this book
can take such widely divergent political views, and yet not seem
completely at odds. Taken altogether they acknowledge –
unlike Volkov – the irreducibility of music to any clear-cut
programmatic meaning.

I am indebted to my contributors one and all for their
cooperative attitude and promptness of response to various
problems and queries. To mention individuals is perhaps a
breach of editorial tact. All the same I should like to thank
Christopher Rowland and Alan George of the Fitzwilliam
Quartet for taking time off from a crowded schedule and
providing some unique interpretative insights. Readers familiar with their recordings of the quartet cycle will hardly need
persuading that they speak with a special authority and

knowledge. My thanks also to Jeff Skelley of Lawrence & Wishart for his firm but unobtrusive encouragement in bringing this book to press.

September 1981

Note

As originally planned, this volume was to have included an essay by Hugh Ottaway on the string quartets, providing a broadly 'analytical' approach to complement the aspects of performance discussed by Christopher Rowland and Alan George. Sadly this project never reached fruition: his work on the essay was cut short by an illness which swiftly proved fatal. The book hardly seems complete without a contribution from one of the most informed and deeply sympathetic commentators on Shostakovich's music.

Christopher Rowland and Alan George

Interpreting the String Quartets

Quartets 1–11   CHRISTOPHER ROWLAND

Fortunately there exists no such thing as *the* definitive performance; at least not in the performance of notated music. The very
act of committing a musical idea to paper, however precise the
notation, leaves the composer vulnerable to interpretation. No
matter how much rehearsal the performer has invested in, or
how many decisions he may have made independently or with
the composer, the spontaneity of each performance will reveal a
host of new highlights and emphases, both good and bad. The
decisions, however, must be made. One cannot rely solely on
the alchemy.

It would be churlish to ignore any source of insight into the
composer's mind, and with Shostakovich, besides the valuable
personal contact, there is a considerable legacy of recordings to
be considered. Composers are often the first to acknowledge
that they are not necessarily the best interpreters of their own
music, but much can be learnt from their performances. Not
least the manner in which they interpret their own metronome
marks.

Shostakovich's performances of his music reveal a great
flexibility of tempi and, if one is to generalise, a habit of
exaggerating the extremes of his metronome marks. As one

might expect the greatest freedom is heard in intimate chamber music and solo performances; with larger forces there is, of necessity, a tighter rhythmic discipline. In his recording of the second Piano Concerto, with Alexander Gauk, it is only in the slow movement, where the romantic shade of Rachmaninov is never far from the surface, that speeds differ radically from the printed score.

The members of the Beethoven String Quartet were life-long friends of Shostakovich and shared many informal chamber music soirées with the Composer besides premièring the Piano Trio, Piano Quintet and all the String Quartets save the first and the last. One would expect great understanding and flexibility in their performances and the recording of the Piano Quintet confirms just that. Tsyganov begins the Fugue considerably slower than indicated and each subsequent entry is marginally slower. Rather than picking up the tempo at the magical fifth entry the Composer is content to take even more time. Generally speaking, from the first episode there is a gradual increase in speed which is emphasised the louder the music becomes and the smaller the denomination of the notes. This propensity is even clearer in the *Scherzo* where there is a 'gear change' both at the G major quaver section and again at the piano's F natural pedal.

The effect is not of being unrhythmic, but of increasing drive and propulsion. There is a slight steadying for the G sharp minor second subject. The recording confirms an obvious misprint in the piano part which has puzzled so many interpreters. The *Intermezzo* dissolves on to a D minor chord and according to the published edition there is an immediate new marking of *Allegretto* with a *ritenuto* for the first three bars followed by a *poco-a-poco a tempo*. The *ritenuto* has obviously been displaced by three bars as the playing of the Composer demonstrates. He effects a *molto ritenuto* and a pause on the D minor chord before an immediate and gradual acceleration to the *A tempo*. The tendency to gain momentum through the movement is again predominant with Shostakovich pressing forward wherever he has continuous quavers. The dynamic climax also marks the point of maximum speed; thereafter as textures thin and dynamics reduce, the speed relaxes correspondingly.

Even greater freedom can be heard when Shostakovich joined his friend and colleague, Rostropovich, to record the Cello Sonata. (A work, incidentally, whose editions vary considerably on several tempo indications.) The *Scherzo* movement is marked *moderato con moto* and ascribed a metronome mark of ♩ = 152. Both are misleading. There have been various suggestions as to why Shostakovich continually shied away from designating movements *Allegro*. One has only to glance at a list of movements anywhere in his oeuvre to confirm the unusually high incidence of *Allegrettos* and *moderatos*. Sometimes his decision to include the teasing *moderato* tag seems connected with harmonic pace and much has been made of his unwillingness to label first movements *Allegro*. The Beethovenian *Allegro* archetype was a dear and elusive ideal for him. In this *Scherzo*, *moderato* seems a disarming understatement. Shostakovich and Rostropovich enjoy something closer to ♩ = 182. In any case, who is to say that another day would not have produced a radically slower or even faster performance. Shostakovich's performances possessed, by all accounts, one great consistency: they were inconsistent. Solomon Volkov confides in *Testimony* how Shostakovich expressed distress at musicians who mindlessly regurgitated peformances. There is always a fine line between being faithful to the spirit and the letter of the score.

Often too it is the intuitive rather than the deductive process which one must confide in. But as might be expected, Shostakovich retained great admiration for the disciplined, less romantic interpretations of his music. He criticised the distinguished Soviet pianist Yudina for her recording of his second Sonata . . . 'The tempi are wrong and there's a rather free approach to the text. . . .'

Shostakovich's widow Irina and son Maxim have confirmed that the Composer took great pains over choosing his metronome marks and for a large number of works they seem entirely appropriate. One would never expect there to be one precise speed for any piece of music. Shostakovich's performances of his Preludes and Fugues for piano certainly confirm this. The D major Prelude No. 5 marked *Allegretto* is played at ♩ = 166, as opposed to the printed ♩ = 120. Conversely, in the B flat minor Prelude No. 16 Shostakovich ignores his suggestion of ♩ = 152, beginning much slower and never exceeding ♩ = 126. One would anticipate great freedom in these enigmatic miniatures, especially the more atmospheric Preludes, but there are occasions when one wonders from Shostakovich's playing whether he might have committed himself to a few more interpretative guidelines. Perhaps in his lifelong struggle with rules and regulations himself he was wary of imposing them upon others.

The flexibility that marks Shostakovich's own interpretations is to be found in the performances of his closest colleagues; David Oistrakh, Rostropovich, Richter, the Beethoven Quartet and his son, Maxim. In the Violin Sonata, Richter and Oistrakh exaggerate the contrast of the slower cantabile dodecaphonic first subject material with the later scherzando music. There is no compunction about speeding up. But for all that it is reassuring that many of the great performances of his music, in all genres, are closely related to his suggested speeds. It is worth mentioning that Shostakovich had a penchant for wide, almost idiosyncratic variation even within his Classical performances and his critics have described his playing as rhythmically wilful. The starting point for the interpreter can only be the score and even when instructions are implicit there still remains a wealth of ambiguity.

The First String Quartet presents few interpretative problems and certainly the *Scherzo* and *Finale* are totally convincing played either at the suggested speed or slightly faster. The first two movements share the same metronome mark and the same desigation of *moderato*. It is tempting to play the first movement at a faster tempo but the pervading mood of a gentle lullaby can all too easily be lost. Shostakovich originally subtitled this Quartet 'Springtime'. It was for him a deliberate exercise in simplicity, unpretentious and relaxing – perhaps a personal antidote to the 'Winter of discontent' that Shostakovich had suffered at the hands of the Soviet censors in 1936.

The second movement is a set of variations on a theme of obvious Russian peasant stock. There is very little real thematic development; indeed, the theme's preservation creates a mood more akin to that of a *passacaglia*. The viola and first violin's variation in B flat minor has a sudden and ecstatic climax in the middle, but with a rather self-conscious balancing join which leaves the first violin alone with the problem of treading the difficult ground between being too literal or over-rhetorical in a movement of determined simplicity. (See Example 1)

Example 1

The second movement of the Second Quartet, *Recitative* and *Romance*, is a unique experiment in Shostakovich's output. Instrumental recitative becomes more and more a feature of his style and it is at its most telling when, as in the Fourteenth Quartet, it is totally integrated within a canvas of contrasting textures or in the Thirteenth Quartet where the viola's bleak soliloquy is painfully apposite. In the Second Quartet, the extended recitatives leave Shostakovich more vulnerable to the expressive eloquence of the performer than at any other time. Perhaps the reason for his constant recourse to recitative is the sublimation in instrumental terms of his strong dramatic vein. After the severe criticism of his opera 'Lady Macbeth of Mtsensk' in 1936, he never again had the confidence to complete another opera although he was attracted to several sources, particularly Chekhov's 'The Black Monk' and Gogol's 'The Gamblers'.

His designation of ♩ = 69 for the central *Romance* section would be considerably too slow were the melody to be sung. In the context of the whole Quartet, with three monumental movements containing much quick music, it is crucial to sustain this deliberate tread and Shostakovich emphasises this by writing *molto tenuto* under the first violin part. A few months after completing the Second Quartet, Shostakovich integrated much shorter, poignant phrases of recitative for solo bassoon into the *Largo* of his Ninth Symphony. Here the mood changes immediately into the 'Falstaff'-like swagger of the *Finale*. In the

Quartet the Valse is not marked *attacca*, but should follow as quickly as is practicable as the effect of the final recitative section, with its cadence in deliberately self-conscious oratorio style, is still one of anticipation.

The metronome mark for the third movement is impractical, especially bearing in mind the retake down-bows that are marked in the middle section. The E flat minor Valse, which brings to mind a similar movement from Rachmaninov's Symphonic Dances of 1940, should be restless and as swift as clarity allows. Most of the middle section is *fortissimo*, which creates an intended feeling of strain as the quartet is muted throughout. As with all of Shostakovich's dynamic climaxes, if the bows are used correctly there is no hint of miscalculation. Strain, in any case, and the sustaining of long passages at extreme dynamics had been a feature of quartet dialectic in Beethoven's visionary Grosse Fuge over a century earlier. Shostakovich's Quartets are not drawing-room affairs; they need space and reverberation. (Ironically, they sound ideal in good church acoustics!) It is no coincidence that every concert hall the Fitzwilliam Quartet has encountered in the Soviet Union, including less fashionable venues like Minsk and Gomel, proved ideal for Shostakovich.

Traditionally variation movements pose all kinds of recurring problems to the performer. If different variations are over-characterised by excessive contrasts in speed then, in certain movements, there is the obvious lack of accumulative flow and a sectionalisation which continually overstresses the shape and length of the theme. A traditional recipe for variation is to gradually increase the pace of the movement by using progressively smaller note values. Broadly speaking, this is what Shostakovich does here, and though the first section is nominally marked at one tempo ($\downarrow$ = 116), momentum can be gained as each player states the theme so that by the *Allegretto* variation the speed is closer to $\downarrow$ = 140, and it is a relatively smooth gear change into the *più mosso* $\downarrow$ = 160. (Exactly the process Shostakovich as pianist effects in microcosm in the B flat minor Prelude and a method that serves well in the first movement of the Piano Trio.) The feeling of accumulated momentum is effected at the next *più mosso* ($\downarrow$ = 168) by a change to triple time and from a basic quaver or semiquaver currency to a triplet pedal in the cello. This is subjectively the fastest music of the movement and from the mid-point in the variation where the violins take over the triplets and the cello and viola intone the theme from the movement's introduction, slow music and fast music exist simultaneously. It is not a case of papering over the Composer's joins; the performers must merely respond to the overall pattern of rhythmic directions. The crucial transition is into the ensuing *Allegro non troppo* ($\downarrow$. = 76), where the lower instruments play the main theme in augmentation against a hectic figure on the violins. Through-out this section and the *Allegro* which follows, the *crotchet* value is always faster but the effect, with the harmonic speed slowing down, the long pedals and the elimination of any note value greater than a quaver, is one of the gradual dissipation of energy marked by a basic dynamic level of *pianissimo*, the refining of textures and the brief use of the mute, solo, for each violin. The fact is that Shostakovich's *Allegro* sounds like a $\frac{2}{4}$ with triplet accompaniment (or a $\frac{6}{8}$), but the visual effect of doubled note values heightens the feeling of arch which the movement has created. He has a penchant for using larger denominations than is usual. The Eighth Quartet, for instance, could so easily have its second movement notated in quavers instead of crotchets. Perhaps as well as being easier to write down at the compositional stage longer note values give the psychological impression (to performers and score readers) of simpler music.

Virtually all of the exposition of the first movement of the Second Quartet is marked at a minimum dynamic of *forte* and there are plenty of examples in Shostakovich's chamber music of movements of unrelenting loudness, e.g. the second move-ments of the Eighth and Tenth Quartets and the Violin Sonata, and most of the third movement of the Third Quartet. Conversely, Shostakovich will write extended passages at very low dynamic levels; the 'will o' the wisp' Scherzo of the First Quartet, the slow movements from the Fifth, Sixth, Seventh and Eighth Quartets, and most significantly, as will be elaborated on later, large stretches of the Fifteenth Quartet and the finale of the Tenth Quartet. He is conscious both of the accumulative effect of such sections and of the heightened dramatic effect of long term juxtapositions.

Internal balancing by the performers is crucial, and Shostakovich often assists in any ambiguity by marking the *prima voce*
'solo' or 'espressivo'. The opening of the First Quartet is clearly
a simple melody for the first violin, but only in the context of a
perfectly balanced relationship with the cello, whose part is
marked *espressivo*. In the development section of the Third
Quartet, Shostakovich defines the individual lines in his double
fugue with contrapuntal dynamics. Much of the musical
characterisation in Shostakovich is achieved by the dynamic
aspect; a crucial platitude. The opening of the finale of the
Third Quartet loses its searching quality if projected too loudly,
and the subtle viola pizzicato harmonics only tell at a low
threshold. Shostakovich insisted dynamics were paramount.
The fact that the three main melodies of the movement are all
heard at initial dynamics of *piano* or *pianissimo*, despite the
amazing variety of their constituents, makes the climax, when
the passacaglia theme from the fourth movement reappears in
heroic canon between viola and cello, all the more majestic and
inexorable.

In the first movement of the Fourth Quartet, the dynamic
climax occurs after a mere 24 bars. Shostakovich utilises the
open D strings of the lower two instruments to add a supporting
pedal to the dovetailed octave doubling. Many of the most
vibrant climaxes in Shostakovich's Quartets rely on the
brilliance of octave doubling, often with the *first* violin in the
highest reaches of the E string. By contrast, he will often write
bare octaves in a quiet context, as in the muted scherzo of the
Fourth Quartet. Here, rather than concealing any problems of
tonal uniformity (or intonation) with excessive vibrato, the
ideal sound is best sought with a light and even right hand. The
last movement of the Tenth Quartet pits a bare and treacherous
tune in octaves against a strangely independent *pizzicato* line for
the first violin. (Example 2)

Example 2

The most testing of all octave doublings occurs in the recapitulation of the first movement of the Fourteenth Quartet where the top three instruments play the first subject in high octaves. Intonation is always a vital aspect of performance in Shostakovich's music; particularly critical as an essentially tonal or polytonal language emphasises (besides the octave) thirds, fourths and fifths; and duos or solos over extended pedals abound. The fourth is an interval associated, both melodically and harmonically, with Russian folk music, and to take but one instance, the first 18 bars of the Fourth Quartet contain 41 fourths between the two violins all over a revealing tonic pedal.

The Finale of this same Quartet has a critical metronome mark ($\downarrow$ = 144) which demands considerable rhythmic restraint from the performer. The movement is a heavy-footed dance, deliberately four beats to a bar and all the more exciting for being held back on the leash. If momentum is naturally gained in the massive climax then the ensuing declamatory unison can be the vehicle of a subtle return to the opening tempo for the cello's passionate statement of the main theme.

The slow movement of the Fifth Quartet is a perfect example of a movement whose characterisation demands imaginative control of vibrato. At the outset the viola and first violin's tune two octaves apart is muted and marked *pianissimo* and can have its bareness and resignation heightened by the virtual absence of vibrato. Shostakovich marks the second violin's chromatic countermelody *piano* and *espressivo*, further poignantly contrasted if played with a warm and telling vibrato. By the first *forte* in the movement the four parts are in closer harmony, all are *espressivo* and a rich, slower vibrato coupled with identical bow speeds seems appropriate; the mellow richness associated particularly with the Russian school of string playing and of bass singing. These are objective interpretative observations as Shostakovich never mentioned the use or abuse of vibrato, although he seemed very content with just this kind of differentiation made by the Fitzwilliam and Beethoven String Quartets.

In the Piano Trio Op. 67, the cello's opening tune is muted and in high, eerie harmonics, of necessity a disembodied timbre. The second voice is the violin in a normally rich *tessitura* on the D and A strings. The piano's entry is in bare *pianissimo* octaves low in the bass clef. If the violinist were to apply a projecting cantabile vibrato there would be a tension between his line and that of his partners. This would in effect deny the equality of Shostakovich's counterpoint, so a light floating bow with a minimum vibrato seems the best solution.

In Shostakovich's lifetime the USSR witnessed a great flowering of virtuoso string playing represented at its apogee by the talents of Heifetz, Elman, Kogan, Rostropovich and the Oistrakhs. Leopold Auer, the distinguished pedagogue, demanded the most flexible use of vibrato from his protegées and a wide, distinctive palate of sound based on the crucial ratio between vibrato speed, bow speed, distance from the bridge and pressure.

There are few specific references to vibrato in Shostakovich's chamber music, save the occasional marking of *non-espressivo* and a request for vibrato on the remote harmonics at the end of the Piano Trio, but there are many places where its application needs to be carefully considered. However, the Composer was most painstaking in his indications as to whether a note should be played short and off the string, or long and on the string. This is another crucial factor of characterisation. If, for example, the first violin part at the beginning of the scherzo of the Sixth Quartet is played off the string, the contrast between it and the legato octaves in the bass is too great and the emphasis on each beat too insistent. The movement's speed is governed largely by the technical exigency of the cello *pizzicato* at the return of the first theme. Shostakovich's nomination of ♩. = 80 is just a little too hopeful. The ensuing *Largo* has a dramatically wrong published metronome speed ♩ = 116. The Fitzwilliam String Quartet agreed with the composer a speed closer to ♩ = 116. There is a moment of critical balance in the middle of this serene *passacaglia* where the three part tread of repeated crotchets is maintained by virtue of one part double-stopping. The texture and harmonic integer is thus unchanged against the first violin's hauntng melody. The last movement follows with a weaving violin line which allows freedom in subtle rhythmic shaping and harmonic emphasis, in contrast to the deliberately prosaic and metric second tune in the cello. To define or calculate the exact phrasing of the violin part can easily rid the performance of a welcome improvisatory and spontaneous quality. At the climax of the movement there are no off the string markings. The same is true of much of the louder music in the outer movements of the Fourth and Fifth Quartets, *Allegro non troppo* of the Third Quartet, opening of the last movement of the Ninth Quartet, *Valse* of the Second Quartet, *Scherzo* of the Seventh Quartet and *Allegro molto* of the Eighth Quartet. These movements lack power and direction if interpreted with short, insistent notes. Even when the Composer indicates *marcato* or *marcatissimo*, his intention is that the music should be punched heavily *on* the string.

A glance at the score of the shortest quartet, the Seventh, reinforces the opinion that Shostakovich is absolutely explicit about note lengths and the mode of bowing. In the first movement, all the quavers which derive from the three quavers at the end of the cryptic opening phrase are played off the string (as indicated), as evenly as possible with just a slight emphasis on the bar line (three up bows work admirably!). All the semiquavers accompanying the second subject are off the string and meticulously dotted in the score. The first violin's version of the second subject is left undotted, a fact emphasised by the marking, *espressivo*. When the first subject returns at the end of the fugue in piled-up fourths, it is heavier and best executed *detaché* on the string, not clipped and off. Similarly the quaver accompaniments in the muted Waltz section should not be too short; the dots do not reappear until the violins recapitulate *arco* what was in any case a *pizzicato* sonority in the opening movement.

Shostakovich is equally careful about the placing of accents and stresses. [When, in the Eighth Quartet, the lower three instruments are intoning the revolutionary song 'Tormented by the weight of bondage' *fortissimo espressivo* in octaves, the first violin's independent part has accents on every note to help the balance. In the last movement the Composer cannot resist putting lines on many of the melodic dissonances emphasising painful discord and resolve.] His essentially tonal vocabularly relies heavily on the conflict between dissonance and consonance and the performer must respond with the appropriate fingering, stress, balance, rubato and vibrato, to highlight the patterns of tension and release. Sometimes a consonance or

dissonance occurs as an almost haphazard result of purely
horizontal lineality, but more often than not, the context is
deliberately tonal. In the following example from the first
movement of the Eighth Quartet, if the E natural is a crucial
note sounding as the first really positive major third in the
movement, so too is the contradicting A flat and D flat in the
second violin part. The players must capture these crucial
emphases. (Example 3).

Example 3

In the Ninth Quartet there are two critical decisions to make
about tempi. The third movement's metronome mark seems
too slow for the brilliance of the music. Many of the repeated
quavers beg to be thrown off the string in one bow and even
taken at a brisk speed, its solid sonata form structure is of
sufficient proportion to balance the slow music it both succeeds
and precedes. Shostakovich's habit of integrating duple and
triple time music within a single movement leaves the interpreter with a distinct problem in the last movement. In the
exposition the change from $\frac{3}{4}$ to $\frac{2}{4}$ is marked not with a
continuous crotchet pulse, but as bar equals bar. At the height
of the development section there is a ferocious fuge in triple
time. Shostakovich marks the return of the duple time at the
ensuing cello cadenza again with the instruction bar equals bar.
From that point on, virtually the whole movement is in $\frac{4}{4}$, a
rhythmic transformation of the Finale's opening theme and
quotations from other movements, notably the Scherzo. (As in
most of Shostakovich's large scale works, there are close
melodic relationships to be found between separate movements.) The performer can gradually increase the momentum
so that the final pages of the quartet balance the crotchet speed
of the opening of the *Allegro* or else in a passage where there is a

deliberate and gradual build-up of texture and dynamics, hold the tempo in defiant harness. To make sudden gear change at the recapitulation seems the least faithful solution.

If the metronome indication for the Scherzo of the Ninth Quartet seems below the mark, the designation of $\d$ = 100 for the *Allegretto furioso* of the Tenth is too fast. With semiquavers at this projected speed it is amazing that the Composer still persists with the *Allegretto* heading. This is the most brutal of all Shostakovich's *scherzi* and demands enormous stamina with unremitting *fortissimo*, his only recourse to unison writing for the two violins; open E strings clashing like cold steel, stabbed down bows, lines of fingered octaves for the first violin and savagely dissonant harmonies. The metronome mark for the *passacaglia* which follows is, if anything, a little on the fast side, though Shostakovich was insistent that the movement should maintain a constant flow. In the light of these observations it would seem difficult to justify a swifter tempo for the finale. If the movement is played too fast, the feeling of one in a bar reduces the effect of each chromatic note and makes the melody sound banal. Perhaps the image should be of a controlled and vital *trepak*. The first subject revolves continually around one note with a single pervading rhythmic figure, the second subject against a continuous drone is also replete with repetitions, both rhythmic and melodic. The third significant melody is a transformation of the Scherzo theme against a convoluting pizzicato line. (See Example 2) All these elements and their various derivatives should be heard at this steady and deliberate tempo and *all* at basic dynamics of *piano* and *pianissimo*. The effect is a controlled and studied monotony which provides an ideal launching pad for Shostakovich's brilliant and decisive climax. This canvas demands absolute rhythmic control from the performer, any idiosyncratic or exaggerated rubato, any pressing forward or over expressiveness, far from giving viable shape or liberation, positively detracts from this calculated and vital greyness. (It begs the similes of Asian steppes and Moscow apartment blocks.)

The Eleventh Quartet is in the nature of a suite with seven movements, all strongly contrasted yet unified thematically. Even the violin's opening refrain traces the Quartet's motto theme. The players must respond immediately to the essence, the single basic character of each movement, yet the gestures are all expressions on the same face. It is the face of the clown, at once tender (*Introduction*), enigmatic (*Scherzo*), severe (*Recitative*), quicksilver (*Étude*) and droll (*Humoresque*). Simplicity is delighted in – sometimes, as in the Scherzo's opening, actually to the point of banality: stony-faced and mechanical lines, where sophisticated phrasing would land the performers on their metaphorical backsides.

The piece was dedicated to the memory of Vasily Petrovich Shirinsky, the Beethoven Quartet's second violinist, apparently a man of mercurial moods, endearing, with a dry, engaging sense of humour. The emotional climax of the Quartet is in the *Elegy*, where textures and key bring to mind the fourth movement of the Eighth Quartet. The dotted rhythms must be played deliberately with the tread of a funeral march (perhaps an echo of the 'Eroica' for the Beethoven Quartet) and the violins' lament floated *pianissimo*. The finale recapitulates in a dream of childlike naïvety, which can only be rudely awakened if Shostakovich's rocking tempo is exceeded or personal sentiments indulged.

The Last Four Quartets   ALAN GEORGE

I well remember that day in 1972, when I first tried the opening viola solo of the Thirteenth Quartet in our rehearsal room. It was almost certainly the first time those sounds had ever come to life outside the USSR, and for a twenty-two-year-old, staring wide-eyed at those pages received directly from the hand of the most famous living composer in the world, this was a moment to cherish. The music itself was not unfamiliar – I knew how it 'went' having picked up a Soviet recording some weeks previously – and it wasn't just the fame of its creator which made it so special. From my earliest acquaintance with this piece I had felt that here was something tremendous and powerful; my resolve to perform it didn't really arise out of any desire to bring off a musical 'coup', as the papers rather cynically put it: rather my sense of responsibility was stirred by a feeling of incredulity and outrage that, two years after the quartet's composition, none of the more illustrious British ensembles had taken any notice of it – or even seemed aware of its existence. And so the situation remains today, eight years further on. What is it that prevents other groups from performing one of the finest and most original works this century has produced for our medium?

The Thirteenth Quartet is indeed a harrowing experience for all involved; many listeners have been truly frightened by it, and even the most resilient emotional temperament could hardly fail to be at least uncomfortably disturbed by it. For this reason it is important to be acutely sensitive when programming the work: the type of occasion, venue and audience needs to be selected with great care, as well as the other music to be included in the concert. It is too easy these days to throw together three or four string quartets into the usual stereotyped programme format, and this casual approach might well lead to musical disaster. We were made aware of the problem from our very first performance of the work, after which we received a letter from a member of the audience complaining at our decision to follow it (after an interval) with one of Beethoven's last quartets. The objection wasn't levelled at the Viennese Master, of course, but at having to listen to anything at all after the Shostakovich. Against this sort of reaction one has to weigh up an alternative consideration as to whether a listener wants to return to his home in a disturbed state of mind, or whether the performer has a moral responsibility to redress the emotional imbalance with a quite different musical experience. Clearly there is no single solution to the problem, because one cannot always cater for the many different individuals who go to make up an audience. Our usual compromise is to maintain our original design, so that at least the person who wants to hear no more has the choice of leaving the recital at the interval if he so desires.

For a long time I had thought the musical interpretation of this work to be clearly self-evident from the Composer's instructions in the score, and indeed we have never found ourselves confronted with any really problematical interpretative decisions. Yet I have still heard only one totally convincing and truthful performance, and on another occasion it was even made to sound thoroughly bland and undistinguished. Refer-

ring back to an earlier section of this essay, in which Shostakovich's handling of tempo in his own performances was discussed, it is probably not advisable to be absolutely literal in
following the Composer's concept of a single speed throughout
the entire piece. Ideally, one has to find a tempo which suits
both fast and slow music, so that the basic pulse remains fairly
constant (the metronome mark is a practical enough guide);
but whereas the central section relies heavily for its effect on a
rigidly metronomic beat the rest of the work requires rather
more flexibility – for instance, the first screaming outburst at
fig. 6 explodes out of nothing in the space of a single bar in the
first violin, and a natural inclination to press forward through
this bar should not be resisted; likewise the much more gradual
dissipation of the frenzy requires a carefully controlled and
barely perceptible winding down. Similarly, a very subtle
compressing of the entries between figs. 17 and 18 can help the
effect of the chords piling up.

The other crucially important consideration with this piece
(as with all the later quartets) is in the deployment of sound and
colour. It is not that the performer has to be expressively
inventive in this respect, because in fact so much of this music
seems to be very shrewdly orchestrated already: in other words,
if one studies and listens very carefully to what has been written
it is usually clear what type of sound is required; once this is
understood it is only necessary to be sure that one's ideas are
well projected, usually by means of careful underlining and
colouristic pointing. As it happens, I don't think I originally got
the opening quite right – it was too sinewy and severe, so now I
aim for something warmer and more human – a deep
reddish-brown, so to speak. But of the ensuing passage, when
all the parts have entered in softly expressive two-part counterpoint, there can be no doubt at all: the Beethoven Quartet
produced this sound so naturally and effortlessly, and could
hardly be nearer the ideal. A very gentle lilt in the $\frac{3}{4}$ bars is
implied, even at this slow tempo (not actually *that* slow at $\mathwithout =
84$), and indeed the imagination and definition of phrasing is
almost as important in Shostakovich as in eighteenth-century
music: for example, the shapes and chromaticisms in the
second violin part after fig. 5, and in their intensification in the
viola part at fig. 59, really do need to be exaggerated; lines like

these are unashamedly and overtly expressive, and it goes against Russian musical temperament to play down such things.

The extraordinary middle section of this quartet requires virtually no interpretation at all, so long as one follows exactly what is in the score – especially as regards the dynamic markings. The underlying effect is of a grey, monotonous landscape, and this cannot be achieved if the players are not disciplined in their observance of the *softer* dynamic markings in particular. It would not seem out of place to impart a faintly jazzy swing to that obsessively repetitive figure – ♪♩♪ ♪♩ – but again, this can easily be realised in the phrasing. The percussive taps on the belly of the instrument can be a problem in a number of respects. The obvious question 'Why are they there? What do they mean?' has already been posed by countless listeners, and the only certain reply is that, from experience in rehearsal, the music sounds far less effective without them. Balance can be difficult: it is not always easy to know exactly how hard to hit the instrument (after all, this is not exactly a technique one works on as part of the daily practice routine!). Also one has to be boringly practical, and consider the damage that can be caused to the instruments themselves – I remember we joked with Shostakovich about the implication that the original first violinist must have had a more expensive instrument than his colleagues (the first violin is not called upon to do any tapping). Our solution has been to suspend a cheap violin from a stand, so that this can be attacked with a clear conscience and a firm, confident swing of the arm! The effect of the return of these taps during the awful stillness of the viola solo at the end is often shattering, even when one knows they are coming, and the marking of *piano* might just be increased, depending on the resonance of the concert room. The same applies to the first violin's *pizzicati* at fig. 40 and fig. 46, where Shostakovich asked our leader to play these *forte* rather than *piano*. It is worth dwelling on the latter passage as I have always found this the most uncomfortable and sinister part of all, and the impression has not diminished. Nowhere is his obsession with semitone trills more manifest: three lines of them here, the upper part (second violin) creeping upwards, then back down, by steps of another semitone – all underneath that steely *pizzicato*. We aim to heighten the effect by exaggerating the 'surface noise' – the sound of the bow passing very lightly across the string, something like the faint sound of rushing wind. I had in mind a device used by Sibelius in his scena 'Höstkväll', and also in the central section of 'Lemminkäinen in Tuonela', where he emphasises the bow noise produced in a very soft string *tremolando* by adding an equally soft roll on the side drum. The effect here, as in the Shostakovich, is spine-chilling.

Passages such as this can create the most fantastic tension in an audience, and a similarly charged atmosphere is often produced by a passage in the second movement of the Twelfth Quartet, in which the main argument is sustained, mostly solo, by the first violin's *pizzicato* – I myself, being a silent viola player at this point, am particularly conscious of the extraordinary electricty given off by this music, and have learnt to appreciate the importance of remaining absolutely involved in the drama, both as performer and listener, in such passages as these: careless relaxation during bars of rest often dissipates tension to a marked and destructive degree.

The Twelfth Quartet is the ultimate examination of the performers' interpretative powers, in that it confronts them with a resourcefulness, a range of expression and imaginative colouring, unmatched elsewhere in the series. The evolutionary importance of this work has provoked detailed discussion and analysis from such eminent writers as Norman Kay and Hans Keller, and much excitement was engendered by that so-explicit twelve-note row on the cello which opens the piece. (Example 4) Further analysis is not relevant here, unless any performers happen to be unaware of the conflict between tonality and atonality which is one of the principal motivating

Example 4

forces behind the music – for it must be understood that this is not a serial composition in the Schoenberg tradition. In a way, that opening bar can be made to seem self-conscious by the immediate relaxation into pure D flat major, smoothly effected by the perfect cadence implied by the last two notes of the row (A flat to D flat). So the cellist has the option of playing these notes in a single unit – as a long anacrusis to the second bar – or alternatively, he can explore the expressive possibilities inherent in the chromatic intervals of the note row. Either way it makes considerable demands on his technique, as regards both the accuracy of his intonation and the flawlessness of his bowing, and the latter equally applies to those involved in the ensuing lines of sustained cantilena – the epitome of dark, noble, Russian string sound (especially when played by violinist Dmitry Tsyganov of the Beethoven String Quartet, the work's dedicatee). Indeed, the somewhat contrived chromaticism of those themes derived from the note row does make them rather awkward to play convincingly as melodies; this is not at all a characteristic one generally meets in Shostakovich's melodic style, but with familiarity one can quickly come to terms with his new angularity of line. (It should be remembered that Shostakovich wrote a vast number of songs and choral works, not forgetting the two completed operas, so the experience of composing for the voice invariably gave the lyrical side of his instrumental writing a kind of vocal ease and fluency.)

It can be fascinating (and not necessarily harmful) to draw parallels between the last quartets respectively of Shostakovich and Beethoven, and in the case of the present work the alternating between two unrelated tempi in the first movement does bring to mind a similar technique used by Beethoven (for example, the opening movements of the E flat and B flat quartets, Opp. 127 and 130 and the E major Piano Sonata, Op. 109; also the *Adagios* of the A minor quartet and the Ninth Symphony). Here, each of the two main subject groups is always associated with its own tempo, and effecting a convincing transition between the two is no more straightforward with Shostakovich than it is with his revered predecessor (the enormous bust which still sits in his study in Moscow bears genuine witness to this reverence, as does the finale of his Viola Sonata, his last completed work). The tempo change at fig. 4 is the first example of this: the new pulse is not really established until the appearance of the *pizzicato* accompaniment, yet the character of the new section needs to be imprinted right away by the first violin, even though he takes three bars of *Allegretto* to groggily come to life. (Example 5)

Example 5

It is in the second movement – in effect a metamorphosis of the traditional *scherzo*, slow movement and finale – that the players' range and versatility is really put to the test, and rising to this challenge of skill and intellect should always be uppermost in their minds. For example, the opening section of the movement culminates in a hair-raising assault on tonality and consonance, propelled forward by swirling sextuplets marked *sul ponticello*. This is one of the very few occasions in his chamber music where Shostakovich permits himself the expressive luxury of this effect, which clearly suggests that the players should exploit the opportunity to the full. There are two important decisions to be made in this movement, the first of which concerns the tempo of the outer *Allegretto* sections. At the suggested metronome mark those flaming hammer-swings which open the movement can sound too ponderous, and the exhilarating build-up of joyful energy at the end feels restrained and inhibited. So we follow the example of the Beethoven Quartet, whose slightly faster tempo in no way compromises the music's rigidly upright power. Likewise we were impressed by the pulsing vibrancy of their tone in the *Adagio*'s muted, triadic chant, but my colleague Christopher Rowland felt that a more disembodied, vibrato-less sound would be equally justifiable, particularly in the stark contrast it would provide for the cello's intensely yearning soliloquy. After much discussion, and having heard for myself from a recording that this version was no less eloquent, I finally agreed that for the Fitzwilliam it seemed to work well. In any case, the Beethoven Quartet sounds so individual here that it seemed pointless trying to emulate them.

It is very easy to underestimate the Fourteenth Quartet; but few people underestimate Mahler's Tenth, despite its incompleteness, and the two works say strikingly similar things to us (as well as being rooted in the same extreme key, F sharp major). At least, when all is finished, these two works leave us in similar emotional states – call it a recognition of a painful longing for life which is slipping away, a passionate love and desire to be alive. Did Mahler really believe in the Resurrection of the Second Symphony? In 1890 maybe, but in 1910/11? Shostakovich believed in no such thing, and the beauty and serenity at the end of the Fourteenth Quartet is no expectation of heaven. Here, more than anywhere else in Shostakovich, is that very special use of the major mode (as noted by the late Hugh Ottaway) which expresses at the same time radiance, sadness, joy, pain, in the way that perhaps Schubert of all composers knew best, and put into practice most eloquently in the Quintet (especially the *Adagio*); or Janáček, in the finale of 'Intimate Letters' – Joan Chissell found the Fourteenth 'as joyful as anything in Janáčk's Indian Summer'. Like all the major works of Shostakovich's final years this quartet is unique. They all share a privateness, a spareness of texture, and an obsession with death, but each views these common experiences through different eyes and feelings. No other work has this impassioned radiance: no other comes so close to Schubert or Janáček. Here perhaps lies one of the sources of the relative lack of attention it has so far attracted. The aura of death and personal despair which hangs over Shostakovich's last compositions seems to have created such a Romantic image for these works that it has become almost a yardstick for each piece to be judged by. One can end up trying to read too much into an individual work, over-influenced by what has gone before. This is not surprising when what has gone before was the Thirteenth Quartet. I well remember my first contact with the new Quartet, reading through the score on the train to Durham. I couldn't understand it; why such a trivial tune to start what was obviously going to be another depressing experience? And what nonsense at the opening of the Finale! There must surely be subversive elements lurking beneath these things. Our mistake was to interpret the opening too knowingly, to bring to it an awareness (or a suspicion) that all it not as it seems. We adopted a steady tempo, making the theme darker and heavier, more menacing; and the dissonant offshoot from the first violin's version became positively vicious and sarcastic. The *Adagio* was also too slow, again emphasising a dirge-like characteristic. But the Finale was too fast, possibly out of embarrassment. So the result was restless, breathless, neurotic. It was the comment, mentioned earlier, by Joan Chissell on the radio which prompted us to question this interpretation. In our most recent performances we have adopted a different approach; in reality, all this has meant is returning to the metronome marks, and to all of us the result has been a revelation – the work seems to have come alive in a tremendously exciting and exhilarating way, and in many respects it is now, for me personally, the finest of the last four Quartets. The shame is that it is certainly the least known of them, and also the least played. The Twelfth and Thirteenth Quartets have been performed occasionally by other ensembles, and the Fifteenth, because it is the last, and because it is such a controversial piece of music, has understandably attracted more attention than the Fourteenth, which is much less sensational than either of its bedfellows, and rather more traditional in lay-out – but that is not to suggest any slackening in formal integration.

The opening two bars may appear to be a somewhat barren 'till-ready' for the entry of the first subject on the cello, but in fact those repeated notes later prove increasingly significant as they undergo various transformations of character, reappearing at such precisely calculated moments as to be of structural importance as well. So all of these crucial factors must be behind their delivery at the outset; it is most unusual for a work of Shostakovich at this (or any) stage of his career to announce itself so strongly (the only other quartets to begin *forte* are the Second and Sixth), so the viola playing here really does need to be both arresting and purposeful. The two statements of the theme, by cello and first violin, are best presented in a genuinely jovial, carefree manner, and if there *is* any underlying menace it will come to the surface naturally, of its own accord. Characterisation of the material is essential, particularly with regard to all short notes, accents, glissandi and dynamics. By the time the first full climax is reached the cello has already established itself as the principal protagonist, and this somewhat unusual balance of power is maintained for quite lengthy spells during the subsequent course of the work. Naturally enough textural balance is also affected, as in the 'Prussian' quartets of Mozart, so that the viola in particular achieves a special independence, often originating in its responsibility for holding a strongly supporting bass line. Shostakovich takes this individual prominence a stage further by presenting each player with almost complete freedom of expression in recitative-like solo passages, and it goes without saying that the Composer is here depending a great deal on the interpretative authority and instrumental command of the quartet members – not to mention the subtlety required of each of them in the transitions from being ensemble player to soloist and back again, together with their attendant musical styles. The parallel with Mozart continues in that the work was dedicated to a cellist, in this case Sergey Shirinsky, of the Beethoven Quartet (the last of the four original members of this ensemble to receive the dedication of a Shostakovich Quartet – a touching example of this composer's specially close relationship with certain players).

These varying roles required of each instrumentalist in this work should not present too much of a problem as in his series of quartets, as well as in the other chamber works, Shostakovich as good as teaches us to be flexible and versatile – and having worked so closely with such celebrated virtuosi as Oistrakh and Rostropovich his frequent expectation of the chamber musician to have the power and projection of a soloist as well should not provoke undue surprise. There is one passage in this work where the dominance of the cello can cause difficulties, and it is crucial that these are solved because the passage in question constitutes the heart and soul of the entire quartet, appearing as an extended plateau of a climax in the *Adagio* (Example 6), so

Example 6

poignant and cumulative that it returns to form the closing section of the Finale. It is entirely appropriate that the cello should dominate here, but those ardently impassioned, Janáček-like sixths – made by the cello well up his A string with the first violin, in a particularly rich lower register, underneath him – are not entirely straightforward in terms of achieving a satisfactory balance and blend. This has to be worked at carefully if the effect of this unusual scoring is not to be weakened and made to sound incongruous. Furthermore, the other two players are faced with a problem of providing sufficient support for these intensely sustained lines with their march-like *pizzicati*. Were the cello at the bottom of the texture there would be no such problem, but of course he is at quite the opposite extreme of his register and the viola has to provide the resonance and depth underneath the rest of the ensemble; this does involve taking a certain risk with each note, but to hold back here would be very tame indeed (as in similar passages involving *pizzicato* in the Twelfth and Fifteenth Quartets). Shostakovich does in this work make unusual demands on the ability of the inner players to play *pizzicato* at a very high dynamic level, and the effectiveness of the final climax of the work is even more dependent on them than here, as the *pizzicato* accompaniment (muted now) is extended to produce its own drama.

Although Shostakovich himself sent us the score and parts of his last three quartets on none of these occasions did he presume to do so without first being asked. The existence of a Fourteenth Quartet was casually mentioned in a letter written to me from Copenhagen on 4 May 1973; naturally I replied with a request that he should send it straight away. As it happened we had to wait until the following March, when the music arrived with a covering letter apologising for the delay and explaining that he had been very ill and therefore unable to write it out. In much the same way we learnt that the Fifteenth Quartet had been completed, and this reached us towards the end of December 1974, together with greetings for Christmas – a wholly characteristic gesture this, especially when one remembers that no such festival is generally celebrated in the USSR. It was a chilling experience thumbing through that score for the first time; for over 20 pages nothing much seemed to happen at all – hardly even an accidental. Occasionally the staves would blacken with a brief eruption of activity, but then quickly settling back into the simplest quartet texture imaginable – and this often reduced to a single lonely line of notes meandering along, half-hoping to re-encounter its lost friends. And, of course, on reaching the end one had searched in vain for an *Allegro*, an *Allegretto*, or even an *Andante*. After the Fourteenth Quartet I think that we were half-expecting eccentricities: it was as if Shostakovich's creative mind had become so inwardly withdrawn that he was losing all sense of musical balance and artistic credibilty. Shostakovich was by no means the first composer to write an extended span of unrelieved slow music, but the first two movements looked so uneventful that one could barely contemplate an attempt at performance. And so it proved when we sat down to play it through: after about 130 bars the arms were beginning to ache, all sense of direction and structure had been lost, and after a few more bars we just had to stop. For over five minutes we had played little more than minims and crotchets at a very slow tempo, never louder than *piano*, and we were barely half-way through the movement, with five more to come, and no movement-breaks! It was baffling. Yet it is extraordinary what reserves of energy and perseverance one can draw upon when one has committed oneself – in this case to performances, to a commerical recording, but more important, to a man and his work. We were totally committed to Shostakovich, as we still are, and believed in him with faithful reverence. There *must* be something in this music, and we must keep trying! It is interesting to contemplate whether our attitude would have been the same in a different situation: imagine playing through a pile of music, looking for something new to add to one's repertoire, and coming across this piece, not knowing who wrote it. Would it have been immediately discarded? Probably not, in fact, because we had already been struck by the unearthly beauty of the opening *fugato*, and the central quasi-religious chant had an almost mesmeric effect on us . . . maybe that was it, the clue to the whole movement: we would somehow have to draw the listener into a kind of trance, so that his awareness of the passing of time was much deadened. Just as a hypnotist can send his subject into suspense by the swinging of a pocket watch, so we would have to aspire to that perfectly uniform motion of the chain by maintaining an absolutely regular rhythmic pulse throughout the movement. Normally one would recoil from such metronomic rigidity, but in this case the tempo is slow enough to alleviate any impression of being strait-jacketed – at least, it should be slow enough: initially we experienced the greatest difficulty in maintaining the very slow tempo indicated, partly because the themes are so drawn out, with no quaver motion to act as a steadying agent: indeed, in their Melodiya recording the Taneyev Quartet (who gave the first performance) fall into this same trap, so that by the end of the movement they are swinging along far too comfortably, and the feeling of *Adagio* is almost lost. The only entirely satisfactory way of avoiding this is to rehearse the movement with a metronome (a machine we use a great deal as a quartet, particulatly in eighteenth-century works, in which pulse is such a crucial aspect of the structure and vitality of the music). Sometimes we set the metronome a notch or two slower than the actual performing tempo – following the theory that by making something more difficult one ultimately makes the real thing easier. Mälzel's ingenious invention proved to us that the music really works this way, and so the composer was seen to be right yet again. Another approach to this movement would be to 'make something' of it; in other words, to try to keep the listener's attention by ultra-expressive means: lingering on this note, exaggerating the shape of that phrase, and so on. To do this suggests a lack of belief in the music; we did try it this way, but could not feel very sincere about what we were attempting to do; in any case, such over-interpretation seemed only to make the movement too episodic, resulting in an unwanted impression of even greater length. So we abandoned this experiment and set about working at it in the way we felt to be right; gradually the unnatural pace became more instinctively incorporated into the body vibrations. It is worth noting that after having performed the work a number of times we actually found that the Composer's metronome mark of ♩ = 80, which at first had seemed impractically slow, now suggested a more freely-flowing character than we intended, so thereafter we adopted a slightly slower tempo than that indicated; on hearing a recording by the Beethoven Quartet some time later we were pleased to discover that they had reached a similar conclusion. Bearing in mind that almost all Shostakovich's metronome marks for *Adagios* tend to be on the fast side it seems logical that the same should apply here. Certainly this tempo better expresses the underlying mood and tread of the movement.

However, this different concept regarding tempo now gave rise to misgivings as to the appropriateness of the sound we were producing for the opening fugal exposition. Originally we had imagined something very clear and pure, almost viol-like, which would then be contrasted by the utmost tenderness for the ensuing C major melody. The idea seemed logical enough but we gradually came to realise that it wasn't really working, mainly because the key of E flat minor has so many flats that the natural resonance of the instruments is considerably dampened (although it did sometimes prove effective if we happened to be playing in a resonant acoustic). In any case, it is most unlikely that Shostakovich himself would have had this sound in mind, so we elected to work at a more Russian-sounding tone, with a strongly-pulsed vibrato, in an effort to give the impression of old men rather than young theorists. The original sound for the C major made an equally effective contrast, so this was retained.

All these considerations apart, this section has continued to present problems: because of the key and the exposed nature of the part-writing near the beginning it is almost impossible for even the slightest technical blemish to pass undetected. These first few pages of the score demand absolutely accurate intonation with disciplined vibrato, flawless bow-strokes and finely controlled string crossings, a firm rhythmic pulse, and perfect internal balance – a not unreasonable approach to any piece of music, in fact! But here nothing less will suffice if the listener is to experience the full impact of Shostakovich's vision, so gravely beautiful that as each player prepares to play his heart is almost in his mouth for fear of destroying the spell – indeed, the fourth entry does momentarily disturb the tonality, but after this the polyphony ceases and E flat minor is unequivocally re-established with the most heart-rendingly noble simplicity. By the end of the main exposition (as opposed to the *fugal* exposition, which in a way constitutes the first subject-group) the time scale of the movement – indeed, of the whole quartet – should be fairly well established. The intentional monotony is now driven home in the next passage: no change of pulse, no escape from those hypnotic, plodding crochets. A kind of pagan-religious chant, in octaves between the second violin and the cello, begins; again, so very Russian in character, with its seventh degree of the scale unsharpened, recalling perhaps the *Andante Funebre* of Tchaikovsky's Third Quartet, or that dark, oppressive scene in Pimen's cell in *Boris Godunov*. The texture is clearly in two parts, and we emphasise the differentiation by having the first violin and viola play without vibrato (as in the Fifth Quartet, *Andante*), creating an extraordinarily hollow, deathly impression, while the others continue on their weary, mournful way; the A natural on to which the former players continually oscillate sounds particularly effective and yearning this way. Altogether, one of the truly great and original passages in Shostakovich. On the whole this movement is not quite so spare in texture as the others, but the next passage now splits down into lengthy solos and duos; it is the hardest part in which to sustain interest, and there is little the performers can do if the listener's attention does flag. They can play perfectly, accurately, with imagination in the sound and phrasing, and always with intense concentration, so that the atmosphere and tension is constantly maintained. As a whole this movement could almost be compared to the vast, monolithic landscapes of Siberia (which, even if one has never experienced them at first-hand, somehow come clearly to mind with the help of photographs and descriptive accounts, combined with a willing imagination). In a sense this music does not really belong to this era, in that nowadays we live our lives at such an unhealthily hectic pace (particularly in the Western World) that it is almost unnatural to have to adjust and accept a slower time-scale. Modern man needs instant, almost constant, speed and excitement, and one can see this trend through all spheres of life. Music like this Fifteenth Quartet of Shostakovich, or (more familiarly) the late *Adagios* of Beethoven and Bruckner, afford us the priceless opportunity of challenging the passing of time. One cannot stop time; one cannot even slow it or quicken it; but one can be less aware of it. Shostakovich helps us to achieve that here, just as in the central section of the Thirteenth Quartet he can, in a sinister way, do exactly the opposite by inexorably counting out every beat of Time.

After more than eleven minutes (which, on this scale, is a very long time) the first real 'event' occurs. In every performance we have given I am aware of a reaction spreading quickly through all those present – not only the listeners, but the four of us as well: I can even feel it happening to myself. It is a kind of release of tension, mingled with relief; yet even in the act of release Shostakovich is immediately imposing a new tension, of a neurotic, almost frightening kind. The countless times we have rehearsed the very end of the Thirteenth Quartet have served us well in this passage: in fact, it is almost like a nightmare, with that terrible ending being repeated over and over again. What Shostakovich asks for is really very straightforward: a single note starting imperceptibly and swelling to a fiercely accented cut-off, passed from one instrument to the next a dozen times. This need not be very difficult to do; yet the passage is so extraordinary, so new (in the quartet language at least) that to just play it literally would be a gross underappreciation of its significance. Our approach, in fact, was to prune it down even further – in other words, to use no vibrato at all; paradoxically to do 'literally' what is written. With the bow travelling so slowly, yet having to increase the pressure into the string in order to effect the *crescendo*, the danger is that the slightest inconsistency in the bow stoke can 'bend' the pitch of the note (something which vibrato would normally conceal); this can usually be averted with practice and care, but in any case it is worth the risk, because this is not 'quartet' music: our aim is to remove all sensation of characteristic *instrumental* colour, so that what the listener experiences is unidentifiable 'sound'.

In the next passage another general characteristic of late Shostakovich has to be tackled: the Composer entrusts his line of thought to a single player, and what is usually on trial is not his technique or virtuosity but his nerve, his intellect, his imagination, his powers of concentration and timing. Nowhere is the composer's vulnerability to interpretation, as outlined in the opening paragraph of this essay, more perilously pronounced as in such passages as this. But that was Shostakovich's decision; he must surely have been aware of the implications and dangers, yet was at the same time probably very pleased to 'hand over' to his players in this complimentary and complementary way. When we played to him he made very few specific comments or criticisms, yet he seemed pleased with what he heard, and I suspect that (possibly helped by his own experience as a performer) he was more concerned with the overall eloquence and interpretative conviction of the performance than with any small details which he might himself have imagined (or performed) differently. In other words, if he liked the whole he trusted his players' judgement on the details. But there are documented occasions when he *didn't* like the whole . . .

The Serenade is a kind of slow waltz with a limp; its melody seems to meander almost aimlessly, and of course this presents similar problems to those faced in the Elegy. Again, it is very hard to hold a steady tempo, but an increase in momentum destroys the character of the movement and, strangely enough, makes the music *less* gripping. It may seem perverse for some of these movements to be headed *Adagio*; at ♩ = 80 the Serenade is slow, but not really of an *Adagio* character; and the frantic activity of the Intermezzo and the opening of the Epilogue hardly sound like slow music; likewise the Nocturne flows along more like an *Andante* – the metronome mark here can seem uncomfortably fast. But in Shostakovich's output '*Adagio*' *can* incorporate all these things, and does so elsewhere, for example the Recitative in the Second Quartet. And in any case, we have seen that qualifying metronome marks give a clear indication of how '*Adagio*' should be interpreted: there are very few of the timeless 'slow as possible' Beethovenian *Adagios* in Shostakovich. All this apart, it is clear that there is some kind of poetic or philosophic motive behind the idea of giving all the movements of a fairly long span of music the same heading, with (for the most part) the same pulse as well.

Another 'event' occurs at the beginning of the next movement and that 'reaction from all involved' can again be sensed. This is the first of the eruptions which shouted from the page during initial thumb-through of the score. It must be very difficult for a violinist suddenly to have to launch himself into this violent torrent of notes after so much soporific inactivity, but the Composer's plan has been to surprise the player as well as the listener, making the effect that much more dramatic and real. The timing of this movement is perfect from all angles: for those who have really become ensnared in the pulsing inertia of this music the effect is startling – almost sadistic, precisely because it is unexpected; I have seen people jump with fright at this point. But if you are suffering from progressive boredom or impatience, the Composer has wickedly teased you by drawing out the inactivity almost *too* long, but not quite!

Hereafter the quartet moves in a slightly different direction, in that the Composer no longer feels the need to strip the music of all superficial interest. From this point the listener's attention is far less likely to wander, and in the Nocturne his nerves will be soothed by a melody of the utmost sweetness – *bitter*-sweet though, because its restlessness will never allow it to settle into one key. In terms of sheer beauty this has to be one of the high spots of the Fifteenth; the accompaniment even *looks* beautiful on the page (Example 7); in a programme note I fancifully described the second violin and cello parts as 'gently undulating shadows', and I felt rather proud of that because, as with the shrieks in the Serenade (but in a totally different way, of

Example 7

course), the listener must forget that he is listening to stringed instruments – the impression can be of a completely indefinable sound. The sheer bow-control demanded here is terrifying, and the passage as a whole presents an almost impossible challenge to the players to reproduce exactly the Composer's vision. Like the Elegy this movement exists on a generally low dynamic threshold – lower, in fact, because of the mutes – and the problems mount as the music dissipates into the most tenuous thread of sound. The effect of the *pizzicato* rhythm near the end should not be underestimated, as its significance is soon revealed. The players must aim to simulate muffled drumbeats, becoming more distinct as the mutes are removed, and finally arriving on stage with emphatic unanimity. Curiously, each melodic strain of the funeral march is played entirely solo, punctuated *tutti* by the march rhythm, and it is not easy to preserve the feeling of a march during these passages. One way is to imbue the melody with a clear and heavily articulated beat, even at the expense of denying it overall shape and refined phrasing. I find the cello's *pizzicato* version, under sustained three-part chords, absolutely rivetting, and I see no point in holding back here, even at the risk of breaking a string (it *has* happened!).

The Epilogue is not really a movement in its own right, but a painfully poignant recollection of previous experiences. It is important that these quotations are played as if genuinely recalling their original contexts, because the extraordinary thing is that they will still be highly coloured by all that has happened in the meantime. Shostakovich here exploits instrumental colour in a highly original way, giving the whole movement a truly eerie, almost supernatural, quality. Otherwise it is pointless making any other observations, as each player can only respond to the notes he sees and the emotions these generate, together with that uncanny awareness that each situation in which this piece is performed is more than usually unique, special – almost final; which is one reason why we don't play the Fifteenth Quartet all that often.

The aim of this essay has not been to provide a comprehensive instruction manual for would-be performers of Shostakovich's String Quartets; neither has any real attempt been made to cover every interpretative aspect of each of the fifteen quartets – which would in any case give rise to unnecessary duplication, since in music (as in most walks of life) one must always be capable of applying what one has learnt from a given situation to any applicable example later encountered. In relating our experience of studying, learning, and performing these works, together with ideas and feelings gained from an acquaintance with other music relevant to this topic (as well as a consideration of the reactions gleaned from perceptive listeners), we have attempted to show how a feasible concept of what the Composer desired to communicate can be proposed to receptive ears and hearts. It says much for the quality of these compositions that many of the points discussed can equally apply to the performance of music by other composers, although we have not denied ourselves the privilege of drawing on the love and understanding born out of personal involvement with Dmitry Dmitrievich – so if a disproportionate amount of space seems to have been devoted to the later quartets we would beg to claim justification in the right of the reader to benefit from the extra insight directly passed on to us by this great and humble man.

Robert Dearling

The First Twelve Symphonies: portrait of the artist as citizen-composer

It is the fate of many musical iconoclasts to be overtaken in the wildness of their excesses by those who become their spiritual or actual pupils: young men who, once they have been exposed to the fresh-thinking approach of their idols, take that as a springboard to new directions, the fruits of which tend to swamp the impact of the older composer's adventurousness. At the same time those early iconoclasts, as they grow more worldly-wise and less crusade-fixated, withdraw their far-reaching probes of experimentation and turn to feed on both the past and the best of a present they have helped to create.

Elements of these characteristics will be found in the music of C. P. E. Bach, of Stravinsky, and of the *Musique Concrète* experimentalists of the early 1950s. The 'prophetic utterances' of C. P. E. Bach, as Paul Henry Láng pointed out, were 'turned into reality only to be forgotten in the tumult they created'; those of Stravinsky (e.g.: the early ballets) will never be forgotten but were exceeded in adventurousness fairly quickly during the 'anything goes' atmosphere of the 1920s and '30s; and the acoustic-sonic researches of Pierre Henry, Michel Philippot, Pierre Schaeffer and others in the French *Musique Concrète* School were absorbed and sublimated in the richer and more pliable techniques of the Cologne electronic explorers and their followers.

Shostakovich's music fits fairly comfortably into this broad pattern, but the influence of outside pressures disrupted the natural process so that his symphonies show an unevenness and unpredictability that defeats categorisation. The young searcher, the iconoclast and the traditionalist are intermingled bewilderingly. A listener coming to Shostakovich's symphonies without the benefit of background information, opus numbers or dates, would be hard put to sort them into a logical chronology based upon musical style. No. 9, certainly, with its classical first movement (complete with exposition repeat), Musorgskian (or at least Ravellian) fourth movement, and irrepressible *joie de vivre*, is the earliest, with perhaps the immature layout of No. 6 coming next. Two flag-waving patriotic pieces, Nos. 2 and 3, follow, to be balanced by the less than patriotic No. 13 during a period of experimentation that included the use of voices in a symphonic context. The highly coloured orchestral palette exposed in No. 3 may have been extended in the voiceless No. 4; and could the technical gains thus made be used to true symphonic advantage in a series of patriotic but more maturely traditional works, Nos. 12, 7 and 8? Nos. 5 and 11 might then stand on their shoulders at the peak of that particular line. With its allusions to the past and its sheer confidence, No. 15 might follow as the composer reaches the height of his powers, but then a turn to ironic bitterness, in which the open-hearted gaiety of the first movement and most of the second is ruthlessly destroyed in a decisive and tragic disintegration in the last three movements, shows an ageing composer at last prepared, in No. 1, to come to terms with the savage uncertainties of life. Only with the greatest difficulty does he surmount this despair: No. 10 is a great, and almost the final, victory. It remains only for a defiant postscript, No. 14, to show the composer at last reconciled to the spectre of death.

Our chronologically innocent listener, then, would have placed the symphonies in the following order: 9, 6, 2, 3, 13, 4, 12, 7, 8, 5, 11, 15, 1, 10, 14. With such a vast divergency from reality possible in our conjecture, how can Shostakovich be fitted against the panorama of the twentieth century symphony with any logical conception of development or lines of influence? What, in short, moulded Shostakovich's symphonic nature? The iconoclasm of Nos. 2, 3, and 4 (1927–35) was not

generally known to the musical world until the 1960s, while the
deepening philosophical traditionalism of Nos. 5, 6, 7, and 8
(1938–43) postdates the experimentalism of the inter-war
years. By the 1950s, when Shostakovich should have been well
enough established to dictate his own direction, a succession of
works, each conceived in a style more unexpected than the last,
reveals a restless, if not a tortured, mind turning from
patriotism to bitterness, from joy to profound symphonic
commitment, in a disturbing display of unpredictability. The
pointers are to a strong outside influence that has nothing to do
with the overall direction or passing fashions of music. And so it
proves.

That influence is one that should never trouble an artist but
has done so in the case of Shostakovich and his compatriots,
and is doing so increasingly as it becomes more contentious:
politics. Christopher Norris has dealt with this subject elsewhere in this volume; I shall not trespass, therefore, except
where the shadow of political expediency violently tore Shostakovich from his chosen path of development.

Symphony No. 1 in F minor, Op. 10 (1925)

Written as an exercise for the composer's graduation from
Leningrad Conservatory, the Symphony No. 1 received its
première under Nikolai Malko on 12 May 1926, more than four
months before the composer's twentieth birthday. Shostakovich's technical mastery is already abundantly in evidence in
the irresponsible clowning of the first subject, embodying a
devil-may-care attitude that is relieved but not dispelled by the
enchanting waltz-like second subject on flute and other prominent woodwinds. Hints of stress invade the development as the
chamber-like sonorities give way to an angry percussive
outburst that is abruptly replaced by a return to the waltz in the
most innocuous F major. The full tumult of the orchestra is not
to be so easily thwarted, however, so the movement, unable to
find a solution to its problems, simply disassociates itself from
them and goes away. A similar mood of inoffensive fooling
informs the Scherzo at first, a piano entering for the first time to
marshal the material and confirm a direction. Brilliant flashes
of orchestration are suddenly swept aside by a chant-like Trio

section for woodwind over an ambiguous rhythm (four against three), but the Scherzo accelerates back and throws back its head in an exhilarating homeward dash that leaves the listener totally unprepared for what is to come. With the aural equivalent of seizing the movement, crumpling it into a ball and discarding it in disgust, the composer crushes the music with three shattering chords, *fff*, on solo piano. Stunned by the irrelevance, violas and cellos mutter a puzzled recollection of the main theme, only to be silenced by three further piano chords, the last, on a low A, one of the most decisive full stops in music:

Example 1

A frozen, featureless, moment of lingering life is terminated *pianissimo* by percussion and a single low string pizzicato note.

Our fun is over, the composer seems to say. Now let us deal with the real matters of life.

'Life', then, as now presented, is a tragic affair in D flat major, oboe and cello pleading for solace amid the brooding string harmonies. At the entry of trumpets and drums with a powerful military phrase, the music becomes disturbed, only to settle again for an even more soulful oboe solo. The military motif becomes ever more prominent but, having established its hold on the music, it withdraws in favour of melting clarinet and violin solos before taking charge once more even to the extent of invading the delicate 14-part string mist into which the movement disappears.

It is a mist which is abruptly torn aside by the Finale as it enters rudely, only to stand as if confused, awaiting an order. Indecisively, flutes, oboes and clarinets attempt to shape a melody but the order finally comes as two clarinets announce a running theme that is reinforced by piano. Eventually a viable melody emerges, and as it does so the clamour of the orchestra ceases so that the melody may be appreciated in its entirety on solo violin. The development exults in the strength of this melody and impels it towards a great and overpowering victory. At full speed the music turns a corner and there, standing stark and fearful, is the destructive rhythm of the slow movement, but now inverted and on solo timpani, *fff*. Behind it, like reinforcements, stand two other statements of it, effectively preventing progress. A solo cello offers the great melody as a kind of sacrifice, but without effect: having supervened so imperiously, the military motif dictates the rest of the movement.

It would have been easy for the nineteen-year-old composer to have courted immediate success with a 'happy ending' symphony, but his courage in presenting so disturbing a work is deeply to be admired and his skill in carrying it out justifies the success that the work received despite its introspective message.

Symphony No. 2 in C, Op. 14 (1927), 'October'

An early example of 'Socialist realism', this single-movement Symphony, written to commemorate the tenth anniversary of the October Revolution, includes in its scoring a factory hooter (in F sharp). This claim upon not particularly musical notoriety should not deafen us to the remarkable amount of skill that goes into the first part of the work. The opening paragraph of 36 *Largo* bars is maintained at the dynamic level of *ppp* but nevertheless achieves the effect of a *crescendo*. In addition, the writing for strings builds a static *accelerando* in which divided strings make successive entries in progressively diminishing note values, each group retaining its original pulse throughout. Over this dense pattern, solo brass and woodwind search for a theme, but it is a search that has to be abandoned in favour of an intense fugue. A succession of episodes, each one apparently designed to secure the attention more decisively than its predecessor, wastes no time on themes: all is dedicted to the enthronement of orchestral virtuosity. A clarinet solo reveals at one point a remarkable link with a later 'Revolutionary Symphony'; it is a tiny fragment of a revolutionary song that found a more prominent place in Symphony No. 12, 34 years later.

The factory hooter (the responsibility for which usually devolves onto orchestral brass) brings the entry of the chorus singing words by Alexander Bezymensky. They tell of the hopeless conditions faced by the proletariate and, inevitably, how Lenin rescued that class from their misery. The climax comes at the shouts of 'October!', 'Our banner!' 'Commun-ism!', and, loudest of all, 'Lenin!'. The second half of the work discards all thought of musical imagination: it is a straightfor-ward choral song that, if it had possessed greater melodic power, might have served as a revolutionary song and pre-vented the Symphony from falling into total neglect until it was rescued, along with Nos. 3 and 4, during the 1960s.

Symphony No. 3 in E flat, Op. 20 (1929), 'May Day'

In the late 1920s, as the Communist system in Russia moved into its second decade, those in charge were too involved in other things to think about the arts. Consequently, if poets, writers, artists, and composers wished to applaud the govern-ment and great communist leaders, so much to the good, but, in the corridors of politics, rules to guide them along approved lines had yet to be formulated. Left to proceed as his fancy took him, then, Shostakovich considered it right and proper that, if a new order had replaced the old, new musical sounds should replace traditional ones. He let his fancy take him where it would provided only that its discoveries did not approach too closely either the conservatism of the past or the hateful atonalism of the then current New Viennese School.

A detailed analysis of the myriad musical events that take place in the Symphony No. 3 would be pointless. At first glance the first three broad sections offer an orgy of optimism presented with a relentlessness rare in symphonic music. The orchestral colours are glaring simply because, with so much going on, what melodic interest there is has to be projected with maximum cutting force in order to be heard at all. Trumpets, clarinets, and woodwind *en bloc*, are allotted much of the musical responsibility. An orchestra has to work back-breakingly hard in order to produce effects that, often, barely justify the effort: extreme instrumental spans are exploited, the violins at times slithering around 'polishing their nails' at the top of their range, intricate passagework has to be negotiated at breakneck speed, there are severe problems of ensemble that only the most rigorous rehearsal will solve (and in which only the most sadistic conductor and critic will demand perfection), rhythm and tempo are subjected to frequent mutations, and above all, the brass players need leather lungs: the final trumpet solo, after a gruelling twenty minutes, is a searching test of any player's stamina. The result of all this may be superficially exhilarating but it will hardly satisfy those seeking organic symphonism. It seems on the face of it that Shostakovich is indulging his inventive flair and technical expertise with barely a breath of self-restraint, yet there is a design to it all, surely. As we chart the work's progress by reference to banners which, in a crowd of clamouring hues, mark important corners and landmarks, an illustrative design – a Socialist 'message' – emerges that is more subtle than Kirsanov's platitudinous poem that caps the work.

An *Allegretto* introduction for clarinets and stalking low pizzicato strings accelerates by two steps (a trumpet solo, then rising strings) to the main *Allegro*, in which fragmentary ideas proliferate in threatened chaos. A distinct second idea occurs on brass: a march that sets the strings tramping in crotchets, only to be caught up again in the excitement and driven at last to a heavy climax. Respite lasts, however, only an instant. Piccolo and clarinet now take up the chase and bring the music to a strenuous growling figure on low strings which is merely another episode of contrast before the main activity returns. A further climax occurs, but still the fury of the music is not quenched. Side drum announces a hectic march rhythm, *fff* (a dynamic level much in evidence in this Symphony), over which horn and trumpet join in a new parade. Piccolo, oboe and bassoon, with clarinet and brass interjections, seize this new opportunity to display their brilliance before the march reverts to trumpet and horn. Strangely, this device, so suited to the maintenance of impetus, is used here instead to lower the temperature in preparation for an *Andante* section that first searches for an identity and, with a sudden drum roll and a brass fanfare, seems to have found it in a cello and bass phrase strongly recalling the opening notes of Schubert's 'Unfinished Symphony'. The allusion is surely accidental, since no further reference is made to it during this quiet but restless section. At length a more serene melody enters on violins, *Lento*, but there is no real development.

Abruptly, lower strings announce a running Scherzo-like episode, *Allegro*, that quickly builds in strength and culminates in another resolute rhythm. This in turn crystallises into an almost noble section that strides confidently for 44 bars, only to terminate in a dizzying collapse. If Shostakovich built in a message, it is at this point that it declares itself. The exaggerated posturing of the music up to now may, one suggests, represent the old order in Russia: an artificial gaiety that ignores the real problems of the country. Such ostrich-like attitudes are doomed, and their collapse is vividly portrayed in a remarkably pictorial passage of writhing brass over a dense bed of percussion. The music attempts in monstrous unison to regain its lost vigour, only to fall back repeatedly onto a deadening bass drum stroke, *fff*. With sombre tones a solo tuba announces what may be meant as a lament for the passing of the old order.

Lower strings attempt to rise, only to be crushed by an imperious trombone oration, reinforced by trumpets. 'You went too far,' they seem to say. 'Now is the time for change.' And change there certainly is. With intense earnestness strings announce a muscular theme that prepares the way for the entry of the chorus. Now the orchestration is more restrained, more responsible, as the words of the overt (as opposed to any covert) message are hurled out with enormous force. There is little merit in the poem by S. Kirsanov, at least in that part of it selected by the composer for setting, to excite admiration. A certain wonder in the ability of the First of May to open new horizons and throw its light into the eyes of the future may have stirred the work's first audiences, but it now seems distinctly dated, if not naïve.

The Third Symphony received its first performance under Alexander Gauk on 21 January 1930 in Leningrad but it was received with only cautious enthusiasm. Its apparently diffuse form seemed uncomfortably close to 'formalism' while on the other hand this was not the work the authorities sought to lead the hoped-for Soviet-realism movement in the arts. Consequently, the work is not widely performed in Russia and was virtually unknown outside that country until the 1960s. Even today, some years after the blanket approval of the composer's music that came with his international acclaim, neither the Second nor the Third Symphony could be said to have even a tenuous place in the affections of concert-goers.

Symphony No. 4 in C minor, Op. 43 (1935/6)

If the Third Symphony displayed a strong Socialist message in its choral ending and perhaps a less obvious one in its formal layout and musical content (albeit one not acknowledged by the composer), the Fourth makes a virtue of being completely free of declared programmatic content. Such content is, however, strongly implicit, as we shall see. The composer was working on it at the time official forces were being ranged against him, and the work did not reach its promised first performance in December 1936. Nearly a year earlier an article, 'Confusion instead of Music', had appeared in *Pravda* in which the composer had been attacked for formalism and other 'crimes' against communistic sensitivities, and this article, together with resistance from the rehearsing orchestra as they struggled with their often unfairly demanding parts, contributed to Shostakovich's decision to withdraw the Symphony.

It was shelved for a quarter of a century, to be dusted off during a cultural thaw and given its first performance by a new generation of players to a new generation of listeners on 30 December 1961 in Moscow. Its Western première took place at the Edinburgh Festival the following year.

At that time, to Western listeners who were yet to get to know the Second and Third Symphonies, the Fourth was an engima. Unlike No. 1, the Fourth was considered strangely quirky and disjointed, and the odd references to the Fifth Symphony led some commentators to describe the latter as a 'reworking' of No. 4, a totally mistaken impression. With familarity has come the realisation that the Fourth relates to the Third as a natural extension of the earlier work's 'modernism', and to the Fifth as a watershed. After the Fourth Symphony and the trauma that came to the composer at the time of the Party attack of 1936, Shostakovich's music was never the same. Words have flowed, and will doubtless continue to flow, over and around this rock standing in the river of the composer's creativity: would his music have been better without its interference? No-one can say, of course, and there is, in any case, enough music of solid value in Shostakovich's existing symphonies; we need not concern ourselves with what might have been. It is worth suggesting, however, that, whatever the pain brought to the composer by the Party attack, it served to straighten a line of development that seemed in danger of cracking under its own volatility, and brought it squarely onto a path that was to lead to a series of unquestionable masterpieces.

In Symphony No. 4 Shostakovich acknowledges his debt to Mahler not only in the shape of some of the melodies but also in his ambitious instrumental requirements: two piccolos, two flutes, four oboes plus cor anglais, four clarinets plus a piccolo clarinet in E flat and a bass clarinet, three bassoons, two timpanists, triangle, castanets, woodblock, side drum, cymbals (two pairs), large drum, gong, xylophone, glockenspiel, celesta, two harps, and strings (20, 18, 16, 16, 14). It must be admitted that effects just as striking might have been made with greater self-restraint and more modest scoring – a fact that even the composer must have realised, for thereafter greater economy enters his composing.

As in the case of No. 3, the Fourth Symphony does not gain from too critical an analysis any more than does a ballet score. Between two enormously long, predominantly slow, movements, lies a moderately-paced Scherzo, not so long but still substantial. The first great fantasia howls its arrival in three piercing chords. A jagged, xylophone-bedecked descent lands it upon a tramping rhythm that acts as an accompaniment to the first theme on brass. Smoothed, tamed and trimmed, this theme was reincarnated in the finale of the Fifth Symphony, but here it serves as the launching point of a less cogent movement. The basic rhythm is maintained but is moderated for a suave melody shared between upper and lower strings, with interjections from other instruments. Peace is thrust aside boisterously as the first theme attempts to return. A mysterious link (woodwind triplets and pizzicato chords over the tramping rhythm) brings a completely new idea, emerging from darkness into a blaze of discordant light; then a solo bassoon introduces a predominantly quiet but disturbed section, disturbed, perhaps, by vague fragments of the first theme that seems to stand just out of earshot threatening. Eventually, the threat becomes reality: the orchestra flames in agony as the thing it fears can no longer be resisted. That awe-inspiring first theme returns, but its teeth are drawn: happy and inconsequential, it dances in on piccolo and piccolo clarinet. Its carefree state is developed in woodwind writing that plays with fugal concepts, but the strings, furious at temporarily having lost their initiative, enter with a real fugue: one of the most impetuous fugues in existence. This amazing episode increases even further in tension, to arrive ultimately at a point of stress which only percussion has the force to carry. Brass return to the first theme, are answered insolently by a distorted version on strings, who then drop inexplicably into a parody of a waltz that, without warning, literally dissolves. Angrily the orchestra makes a series of mighty efforts (the dynamic rising from *pp* to *fffff*) to wrench iself out of this apparent *impasse* and regain the comparative security of the first theme, but it achieves only another distorted version on trumpets and muted trombones. The theme, it seems, is paying dearly for losing its strength earlier, when its opportunity for recapitulation was thrown away in an unguarded moment of inconsequentiality on piccolo and piccolo clarinet. The *Coda* laments its passing in a bassoon solo, eerily relinquishing it to a cor anglais as the movement closes.

Less fantasia-like than its companions, the second movement, *Moderato con moto*, keeps fairly faithfully to the Beethoven scherzo layout of ABABA, in which A is the string theme that wears various guises as it progresses, and B, the 'Trio' section, is to serve in modified form as the first main theme of the Fifth Symphony. The final appearance of A on fluttering muted violins is accompanied by an intricate lace-work on percussion, pizzicato low strings and harp. So effective is this fascinating form of musical doodling that Shostakovich was to use it twice much later in his career: in the Cello Concerto No. 2 of 1966 and in his last Symphony of all, No. 15, of 1971.

Mahler gazes clearly, if in anguish, through the opening pages of the Finale, a grotesque funeral march, most imaginatively scored, that acts as an extended slow introduction to the *Allegro* part of the Finale. Once at the plateau of the faster tempo, Shostakovich's teeming brain disgorges ideas in dazzling profusion in an episode superficially resembling the first great fugue in the Finale of Nielsen's Fifth Symphony (1922), but here the intention and outcome are totally different. Nielsen's aim was to overcome disruptive forces in a violent display of academic writing which culminates in a titanic explosion; Shostakovich's is to build a homophonic structure of immense strength and energy, an intention that is thwarted by a curious collapse onto an innocuous ballet-like section that has apparently nothing whatever to do with the rest of the work. The waltz that emerges is almost pure Mahler; other ideas seem to be culled from the bright, playful, style that ran through Shostakovich's earlier ballets such as *The Age of Gold*, *The Bolt*, and *Hamlet*, and the opera *Lady Macbeth of Mtsensk*. The audience is lulled, charmed, ingratiated – and set for Shostakovich's most malicious trick. The sheer audacity of the idea leaves one breathless: after so much delightful, amusingly fantastic, harmless music, two timpanists burst in with an ugly canonic figure that is maintained while brass haul back the funeral march with elemental violence, shattering the listener's peace of mind and leaving audience and orchestra alike stunned and disbelieving. It was, after all, for the Symphony in which it appeared, that the funeral march has its *raison d'être*. Thereafter, deprived of unity and hope, the Symphony is left pulsating in a dense, sinister darkness. Its only solution is death.

Symphony No. 5 in D minor, Op. 47 (1937/8)

It is little wonder that the composer felt, after having killed his own Fourth Symphony with such savage decisiveness, that bold artistic tactics of this kind would not appeal to those who had so severely criticised him from their positions as self-appointed guardians of public enjoyment. Soviet realism should be equated with a positive outlook: negative attitudes should ruthlessly be crushed. One wonders what those officials would have made of the Fourth Symphony had they been given the opportunity to hear it at that time. Fortunately, perhaps, for Shostakovich's future, they did not; the effects of earlier works such as *Lady Macbeth* were enough to lead to the censure of

Shostakovich. One can only guess at the result had the Fourth Symphony got out.

'A Soviet Artist's Reply to Just Criticism', as Shostakovich called the Fifth Symphony, represents an entirely new direction in the composer's symphonic nature. Although taking some elements from the Fourth Symphony for use in the Fifth (presumably under the impression that the Fourth would never become generally known), he used them merely as starting points, the formal relation between the two works being non-existent. Since they have already been noted, we may now disregard them.

In comparison with the Fourth Symphony and, in fact, with the three earlier symphonies also, the Fifth has infinitely cleaner, less cluttered lines, a firmly traditional shape and formal plan, and above all an immensely healthy assurance and optimism. It was, furthermore, acclaimed by the authorities, and went virtually the whole way towards re-establishing Shostakovich as a leading Soviet composer. Ironically, the Socialist movement, representing radical political departure from traditionalism, wholeheartedly accepted this total capitulation to artistic traditionalism.

A brief flourish of strongly dotted canonic string leaps opens the first movement as a prelude to the main theme, sung quietly on violins. When at length the main second theme appears (violins over throbbing lower strings), it transpires that it is a new and infinitely more beautiful version of the dotted opening flourish, the taut sixths of the latter transformed into melodious octaves. The first entry of a piano announces the development section in which the stress of conflicting material is aggravated by the stern march rhythm, the intensity of which is heightened by a cutting side drum ostinato. A climax is approached inevitably, and the modified recapitulation follows just as inevitably in this example of the new, traditional, Shostakovich. The movement ends quietly in a mood of doubt, but the overall effect is more convincing, more comforting, than in any of his symphonic movements so far.

In second place comes a Scherzo in which, if the spirit of the younger Shostakovich is to be heard, so, too, is that of Mahler. Enticing rhythms and piquant melodies combine with generous use of *glissandi* to produce a contrasting episode that lies

ideally between the heroic grandeur of the first movement and
the introspective searching of the *Largo*.

Brass are omitted altogether in the slow movement, the
weight of the argument being thrown into the strings which are
divided into eight parts throughout (violins I, II, III; violas I,
II; cellos I, II, double basses). The crux of the movement is a
tiny phrase shown here as it appears on its first entrance and at
the height of the central climax, consisting of four crotchets, two
quavers and a final long note extended or contracted according
to context:

Comparative formal simplicity marks the first two movements of this Symphony, and if this simplicity recedes somewhat in the *Largo* it returns with intense dynamism in the
Finale. There are three distinct sections, as different from each
other as they could possibly be. The first hurtles towards the
listener, unleashing a *fortissimo* timpani pedal in forths. Three
trombones and tuba announce a belligerently optimistic theme
that catches other instruments in its impetus and drives
forward at an ever-increasing tempo and intensity. At the
height of the excitement a solo trumpet slices through the dense
texture with a new theme. Horns, then xylophone, signal their
approval and the music at length arrives at a stupendous
climax, *tutti*, *fff*, the brass at last marching off triumphantly as
the development section enters. This deals mainly with the
trumpet theme, now gravely introspective, on solo horn. In
contrast to that in the first movement, the development of the
finale is subdued, working out the implications of its material
with calm dignity in some alluring string writing. Just as
timpani had announced the exposition, so, too, do they herald
the recapitulation, but again there is a transformation. The

boisterous *crescendo* of the first bar of the movement and the hammering fourths that ensued are changed to a discreet rattle, *pp*, supported by side drum. Sleeping brass and woodwind stir into life, the latter soon setting up a chatter as the music traverses a long *crescendo*, gathering its forces for the recapitulation-coda complex, firmly in D major. Nothing could be more assertive of the composer's faith in his own ability, although one cannot help wondering, as he builds the Symphony towards its mighty climax, whether his tongue was in his cheek.

Wherever it was, however, Shostakovich's tongue gave us few clues to his thoughts as he conceived the Fifth Symphony. Platitudes about 'stabilising my personality' and 'the making of a man' seem designed to placate the authorities rather than enlighten the listener. In any case, the positive nature of the Symphony, even if it is a somewhat reserved positivism until the affirmative final section of the last movement, scored heavily in Shostakovich's favour when the work made its triumphantly successful première under Yevgeny Mravinsky in Leningrad in November 1937, and it achieved popularity quickly in the West once conductors such as Rodzinsky and Stokowski showed an interest in it. Since then it has not left the standard repertoire, sharing with Nos. 1 and 10 the distinction of being among Shostakovich's most popular symphonies.

Symphony No. 6 in B minor, Op. 54 (1939)

When the Sixth Symphony received its first performance on 3 December, 1939 at the Moscow Festival of Soviet Music it was welcomed with muted applause, and the authorities were clearly puzzled by its oddly uncommunicative nature. Word had got out that the composer had been planning a huge symphonic tribute to Lenin but had postponed its composition due to a feeling that, psychologically, he was not yet ready for such a vast challenge. Not only, therefore, was the new symphony not the hoped-for Lenin commemoration; neither was it a particularly satisfying piece in its own right. The greatest hurdle the listener had to conquer was its distinctly lop-sided shape: a long, profound slow movement followed by a short fast Scherzo and a shorter, faster Finale. The composer left no explanation for this plan; we are therefore thrown back upon conjecture since this layout is unusual enough to call for an explanation. Did the composer feel that it was necessary to produce a new symphony as a quick follow-up to the applauded No. 5 but, due to the immense amount of time he had wasted on the Lenin Project, he was reduced to issuing three unconnected movements? If so, perhaps the slow first movement is the only survival of his Lenin labours. On the other hand – a more likely alternative – did he have a symphony ready but for some reason did not wish to release the second of its two slow movements, which would have taken third place in the design? If this were the case, what became of that second slow movement, and why, in any case, did he not withhold the Symphony until he had completed it with *another* slow movement?

As it stands, the work has taken a respected place in the cycle of symphonies but it is neither so popular nor so well known as most of its companions. The first movement, *Largo*, uses a musical language more traditional than any so far heard in the symphonies: by being restrained and undemonstrative, it takes a definite backward step even from the arch-conventionalism of No. 5. The composer's 'modernism' is not in evidence here, a fact that inescapably must be attributed to outside influences. The first idea appears in dark unison on cor anglais, two clarinets, two bassoons, violas and cellos. It is expressive but resolute in nature. When flutes, oboes, the E flat clarinet and violins enter in bar five it is not to bring light but rather to inject tension – perhaps even pain – into the music, a decisive upward figure soon adding further stress. With symphonic economy these elements are developed, the mood of sombre brooding being maintained until a trumpet brings a moment of hope that fades again as the cor anglais sings a tragic second subject over a trembling, disjointed accompaniment. The development avoids the kind of confrontation between themes that might lead to a climax, being more concerned with fragmentation of its material and a kind of mysterious, exploratory pensiveness that seems to resolve the music's problems in a remote region inaccessible to the listener. When the recapitulation at last arrives, heralded by a repeated G sharp on solo horn, a greater confidence has entered the music, but uncertainty lingers as the *Largo* withdraws finally into shadow.

The composer dismisses the philosophical problems he set

himself in the *Largo* by throwing a party. He announces his
Scherzo on the little E flat clarinet over the lightest of muted
pizzicato violin accompaniments. Flute, piccolo, and other
instruments quickly join the fun, and a new idea, rising slowly
on violins as if teasingly peering round a curtain, is greeted with
three joyful squeals of delight. All, it seems, are welcome, even
the rumbustious brass and percussion. As at most good
parties, however, there is an over-indulgent guest who attracts
too much attention and embarrasses the others. Here, he is
characterised by bass clarinet and three bassoons, his raucous,
slurred statements met at first by sharp admonitory slaps from
xylophone and pizzicato violins, *ff*, but his coarse behaviour
encourages others to exceed good taste and in no time the whole
party dissolves into a free-for-all. The wine, or vodka, had
flowed too freely. The central Trio section which brought this
crass disruption at last gives way, via a solo timpani link, *fff*, to
a reprise of the Scherzo, flute and bass clarinet proceeding
comically in reverse motion, but the new, gracefully ascending
guest who was so heartily welcomed on his first appearance
now merits hardly a flicker of an eyebrow. There is nothing one
can do to redeem the occasion. That Trio section has spoilt the
party: the guests are subdued now and apart from some
artificially gay chatter and a few weak quips, it is clearly time to
disperse.

It really is necessary in performance to allow a generous
pause between the Scherzo and the Presto finale. Too prompt
an entry of the latter weakens the effect of both movements. A
tripping violin theme, interrupted by woodwind flourishes,
brings allied ideas that build a high-spirited web that at length
gives way to a staid, awkward alternative on bassoons, clarinets
and violins, *marcartissimo*. This idea, modified, is to carry the
weight of excitement in the *Coda*, but a certain disruption of
both melody and time signature has to be overcome before the
clear light of the recapitulation may carry the music inevitably
to this conclusion.

With its world of varied, apparently disassociated, moods,
Symphony No. 6 is probably the least satisfying of all
Shostakovich's symphonies, but if we care to leave aside our
preconceptions of what a symphony should or should not be we
may yet enjoy each movement for what it is: a tone poem to be

appreciated without reference to the other two tone poems that happen to accompany it.

Symphony No. 7 in C, Op. 60, (1941), 'Leningrad'

Many compositions commemorate episodes in the Second World War. One thinks immediately of Martinu's moving orchestral essay recalling the tragedy of Lidice, and Georgij Firtich composed a cantata dealing with the siege of Leningrad, but never has a more intimate connection existed between a war subject and a composer's setting of it than that between the battle for Leningrad and Shostakovich's Symphony No. 7. The composer was actually in that city during the German bombardment, and the first three movements were composed as the shells fell. A parallel might be drawn between this case and the War poet Wilfred Owen, who died in action just one week before the end of the First World War. So immediate was the danger to the composer that the Soviet government finally insisted upon his evacuation to Kuibyshev, at which retreat he at last completed the 'Leningrad' Symphony. It is important – even vital – that these facts be borne in mind.

So intense was the interest in this great patriotic Symphony that concert promoters in both Russia and America were most anxious to secure copies for performance while the popular acknowledgement of Russia's resistance to the Nazi invasion endured. In Russia, the work's first performance under Mravinsky took on the atmosphere of a quasi-religious celebration even though the final victory was still to be attained, and frequent wartime performances of the work raised the composer's name to the level of war hero in the minds of the public. Meanwhile a microfilm copy of the whole score had been sent by air in a small tin box to Tehran, whence it had been sent by car to Cairo and had then been transferred to another aircraft for despatch to America. There, both Leopold Stokowski and Arturo Toscanini impatiently awaited its arrival, their respective sponsors striving to secure rights for the first Western performance. In the event, NBC won the day for Toscanini, who gave the first American performance of the work in a broadcast on 19 July 1942, just about twelve months after the composer, in war-wrecked Leningrad, began its composition.

Fortunately, Toscanini's performance on that day has been preserved on gramophone records for the interest of posterity.

As we have seen, Russian audiences had no reservations about the Symphony, but one Western critic was not slow to seize the opportunity the work offered him to turn a clever phrase. The critic Ernest Newman, seeing beyond the patriotic purpose of the work and viewing with a disdainful eye its 70-minute length and somewhat exaggerated solemnity, commented that 'to find its place on the musical map one should look along the seventieth degree of longitude and the last degree of platitude'. As the longest symphony Shostakovich wrote, it is true to say that there is less invention than needed to support its vast scale: one encounters huge plains of time during which nothing moves but a slowly unfolding solo woodwind soliloquy, and the notorious development section of the first movement may be appreciated only as an exercise standing on the dark side of Ravel's *Bolero*: an immensely protracted design in which the same long melody is repeated twelve times in gradually thickening orchestral colours over a side drum (and later other percussion) *crescendo* of unchanging rhythm. This depicts the inhuman German Army approaching relentlessly, like a marching horde of military robots.

The composer himself left a commentary for this work, the first of his frankly descriptive symphonies:

The Seventh Symphony is a programme composition inspired by the grim events of 1941. It consists of four movements. The first tells how our pleasant and peaceful life was disrupted by the ominous force of war. I did not intend to describe the war in a naturalistic manner (the drone of aircraft, the rumble of tanks, artillery salvos, etc.). I wrote no so-called battle-music. I was trying to present the spirit and essence of those harsh events.

The exposition of the first movement tells of the happy life led by the people . . . such as the Leningrad volunteer fighters before the war . . . the entire city . . . the entire country. The theme of war governs the middle passages.

The second movement is a lyrical Scherzo recalling times and events that were happy, It is tinged by melancholy.

The third movement a pathetic *Adagio*, expressing ecstatic love of life and the beauties of nature, passes uninterrupted into the fourth which, like the rest, is a fundamental movement of the

Symphony. The first movement is expressive of struggle, the fourth of approaching victory.

The second, third, and fourth movements are merely an appendage, albeit a formidable one, to the first. The last, of course, depicts final victory, a victory proclaimed in terms of decisively Russian character. From the point of view of his Kuibishev refuge in December 1941 Shostakovich could regard the battle of Leningrad with a perspective that involved him less personally and he felt freer to portray an ultimate Russian victory over Nazism. The ambiguous (self-preserving?) nature of the first movement has no place in his Finale.

The middle two movements exist more for formal reasons than for pictorial ones. It should be pointed out, however, while we are questioning Shostakovich's programme, that the *Scherzo* goes about depicting 'times and events that were happy' in a distinctly unconvincing manner, and the C sharp minor Trio section, far from being 'tinged by melancholy', is full of the most appallingly harrowing devices. As the complex and profound *Adagio* unfolds, can the listener really visualise in the music 'love of life and the beauties of nature'? The sensitive listener may be forgiven for receiving instead the impression of a desolate Siberian winter landscape set with vast frozen mountains.

Symphony No. 8 in C minor, Op. 65 (1943)

By 1943 Shostakovich had at last struggled by a tortuous route to a plateau of intense artistic fulfilment that he was to occupy for a decade. At each end of this decade stands a Symphony of immense strength and import; between them the giant rests. The sequence of the 8th, 9th and 10th Symphonies has an elegant symmetry that cannot be paralleled precisely elsewhere in symphonic literature. Nearest, perhaps, comes Beethoven's group of Symphonies Nos. 3, 4, and 5, where the strength evident in No. 3 is distilled and made concise in No. 5, the milder No. 4 dividing these two essays with sublimely contrasting levity. Yet Beethoven's Fourth does not occupy the same plane of jocularity as that upon which Shostakovich's 9th rests. The latter might be described as a divertimento; the former never. Similarly, although Vaughan William's Fifth Symphony offers a wonderful period of contrast between its two hard-hitting companions, it is a totally different kind of contrast: furthermore, Vaughan Williams's Fourth is no less concise than No. 6, and the latter's Finale, quite unlike the Finale of Shostakovich's Tenth, is a study in pessimism. The symphonic utterances of Shostakovich during the years 1943–1953, then, offer a unique experience in which we see, more clearly than 'the making of a man' in No. 5, the man wholly made.

Yet it is to the first movement of No. 5 that the composer turns for the opening mood of No. 8. The powerfully dotted phrase on lower strings, intensified in this case by the early addition of violas and second violins, diminishes in intensity to allow the appearance of a long, posed violin melody. It barely whispers its presence: Shostakovich directs that all the strings should bow *sul tasto* (ie: across the fingerboard), thus drastically reducing their tone. The effect is of a veiled, timorous theme, fearful of what it may precipitate. Having tested the temperature, so to speak, it becomes bolder and soon reaches an ecstatic height. Eventually, the music moves onto dark woodwind to clear the way for the second main theme. Over a pulsating string rhythm, violins sing of beauty and wellbeing, cor anglais and violas affirming the mood in fifths.

When flutes return with the opening dotted motif it is a signal for the music to dispense with ecstasy: there are important symphonic problems to solve. The first entry of percussion in the symphony (timpani, then side drum) marks a tragic increase in tension and an aural *accelerando* despite the maintenance of the *Adagio* pulse. A tumultous climax marked *ffff* at last releases the tension and a new tempo (*Allegro non troppo*) heralds the start of open conflict – a state that the beginning of the work seemed so concerned to avert. In a basic common time, oboes, cor anglais and clarinets wail out in quaver triplets, but even more telling are the ominous crotchet triplets of the four horns and cellos that lead to a ruthless, percussive march, trumpets and xylophone crushing all opposition. Inevitably a climax arrives in a series of terrifying, roaring convulsions interspersed with imperious statements on three trumpets and two trombones. A cor anglais solo laments lost peace over a trembling string foundation. At length the second main subject returns, but the tranquillity so earnestly sought at the start of the work is never attained.

The second movement is a stern *Allegretto* in D flat basically in common time but with disruptive changes of pulse. Emotionally the music is curiously negative, the scoring, which explores the extreme upper and lower limits of the woodwind group, reverting somewhat to the self-indulgent style of the Third Symphony. In form, the movement is a Scherzo and Trio, the exploratory woodwind colouring taking place largely in the central Trio section, but the matters dealt with in the first movement have been too profound to allow the Scherzo to contain any of the expected playfulness. The overall impression is, instead, one of indignant energy.

In Symphonies Nos. 3 and 4 we have seen how Shostakovich, in order to make his intended effects, was obliged to overwork not only his own fertile inventiveness but also the endurance of his listeners as they were forced to accept ever more diverse devices. The march in the first movement of the Seventh Symphony swings too far in the opposite direction in that it puts one single idea exhaustively to work to make the composer's point. At last, in the third movement of Symphony No. 8, the right balance is found. An obsessive, ever-present, fast crotchet rhythm, denoting perhaps the mindless drive of war, and hysterical wind shrieks are the sole ingredients of the outer sections of a movement that makes a vivid impression upon the listener on first hearing and is likely to increase and intensify that impression subsequently. The shrieks, each terminated with a sharp, violent *sf* staccato crotchet, may represent the whine and crash of falling shells; isolated staccato crotchets (ranging in dynamic between *sf* and *sffff*) may depict cannon-fire while the trumpet solo and fierce side drum of the central section may show the rallying calls and small-arms fire of infantry conflict. The composer left no specific instructions upon how to listen to this movement, but it is unthinkable that any other than a war scenario was in his mind. The effect is devastating as the movement builds in a gradual and unquenchable *stretto* climax on tearing dissonances over the crotchet rhythm of timpani, *ff*, only to shatter and mutate as the fourth movement, *Largo*, enters. This is the crux of the

Symphony. Thereafter, a lowering of tension is vital if the neurotic nature of the work is to be balanced. The composer chooses a time-honoured strategy to dissipate the tension: that of variations. By simple slow embellishment over a ground bass, the composer by degrees restores solidarity in a passacaglia, the successive segments of which laboriously lift the music from despair to guarded optimism. At the start of the Finale, *Allegretto*, a solo bassoon, tentatively at first, proposes a new theme that is to form the basis of another set of variations. In all there are 19 variations during the course of which occur two fugues and, at a moment of dread, a return to the climax of the third movement. For a space the music is paralysed, but with the remaining five variations and *coda*, hope and optimism at last return.

At home, Shostakovich's Symphony No. 8 stood beside No. 7 in popularity almost from its première under Yevgeny Mravinsky (to whom it was dedicated) in Moscow on 4th November 1943, but abroad it fared less well. While the 'Leningrad' Symphony was dismissed for its banality, the 8th was regarded as too philosophical, a viewpoint encouraged by the quiet and protracted ending. More recently it has taken a firmer hold on Western audiences, but its close symphonic argument remains under-appreciated.

Symphony No. 9 in E flat, Op. 70 (1945)

The fact that there are five movements, the last three of which are contiguous, is the only point in common between the Eighth and Ninth Symphonies. Audiences expecting a noble paean to mark the great victory over Nazism were bitterly disappointed and directed their criticisms at the new Symphony, refusing to accept it on its own terms and blaming the composer for not writing what they had expected him to write. In addition, had not Beethoven's Ninth been the greatest of all, and therefore should not *any* composer's Ninth strive towards that end? To do otherwise suggests the blackest blasphemy.

The first movement's layout is reactionary in the extreme. In frank, uncomplicated sonata form with an exposition repeat, it uses, moreover, a musical language traditional in style with mild modern flavouring. The first subject appears immediately on violins alternating with flute and oboe. Punctually, and correctly in the dominant, the second subject enters: a trombone (over a brash side drum rhythm) providing a pedal to a whimsical piccolo melody that seems, adventurously, to prefer C major:

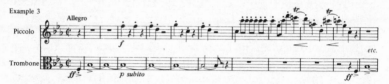

Good-natured working-out takes place in the development, the recapitulation arriving at last with reinforcing timpani strokes. Too early, the trombone attempts to recapitulate the second subject, only to be jeered at for its clumsiness by two muted trumpets, *ff*. Nevertheless, the trombone makes five further efforts, each one totally ignored by the rest of the orchestra, before it gains success, only to find that its partner the piccolo is off daydreaming somewhere. Its whimsical part has to be taken, at short notice it seems, by a solo violin. Only at the very end of the subject, a moment or so before a solo flute announces the arrival of the *coda*, does the piccolo pull itself together.

With graceful restraint a clarinet, to be joined soon by another and by the rest of the woodwind, unfolds the melody of the *Moderato* second movement. A contrasting section for strings precipitates a moment of anxiety, but a solo flute reclaims the limelight and re-establishes a mood of grace that even the return of the strings cannot dislodge. The movement ends tranquilly on a long-held piccolo F sharp over hesitant pizzicato strings.

To the clarinet once again falls the responsibility of opening the third movement, a Scherzo in 6/8 time, but on this occasion it is not so much grace as good humour that this instrument conveys. As before, the clarinet rapidly draws support from the rest of the woodwind before strings counter with a different idea. Brass and percussion soon make telling contributions, and indeed, as in the 'shellfire' movement of the 8th Symphony a solo trumpet leads the way in the central Trio section. With chilling effect, three trombones and tuba, *ff*, interrupt the joy of the Scherzo with the sombre tones of the fourth movement,

Largo. A solo bassoon orates lamentingly, another grim statement by heavy brass confirming its tone of tragedy. Upon its second appearance, however, in the midst of its grim statement, the bassoon slips unexpectedly into the mischievous theme of the Finale. It is as if a great statesman were announcing a national catastrophe only to break into a smile: 'I'm only joking, after all!'

A somewhat colder wind blows through the music at times, threatening the jollity of the whole, but the various strands are eventually gathered into a triumphal march of joy that abruptly changes into a gallop. Shostakovich's celebration of victory ends, after all that has happened to disturb its programme, in breakneck hilarity.

Symphony No. 10 in E minor, Op. 93 (1953)

The Party attack of January 1936 had the effect of realigning Shostakovich's creative direction. On 10 February 1948 came another and even more hurtful attack in a resolution issued by the Communist Party Central Committee headed by Zhdanov. Shostakovich, Prokofiev and other leading composers were severely censured for failing to write what the party thought communist audiences ought to hear. Prokofiev was openly hostile to his tormentors while Shostakovich responded once again by withholding his music from the public. Having reached a peak of surpassing technical and philosophical strength, the composer's sensibilities must have been severely injured by this new attack. It is possible, however, that it had a positive effect. In 1953, after the death of Stalin, the music at last released by the composer contained a new element: an affirmation of personality expressed in the musical monogram DSCH (*D*mitri *SCH*ostakowitsch, in the German transliteration, becoming the notes D–E flat–C–B):

Example 4

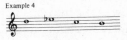

Fortuitously, this phrase in isolation holds a dark threat in its tragic tonal ambivalence. It is a sequence that seems to embody the nature of much of the composer's music up to that time. Thenceforth, it was to appear in many works, including the Violin Concerto No. 1, the String Quartet No. 8, and, as a self-affirming statement of defiance and warning, in Symphony No. 10. It does not appear immediately, however; its power is held in reserve until the crucial third movement.

With effort, cellos and basses claw upwards out of the darkness that precedes the first movement. The string band searches vainly for an identity, pausing ever and again in blind confusion. At last a solo clarinet announces a definite melody that is accepted tentatively by the strings and then built into a strong statement of determination, only to subside as the clarinet again carries the weight of the theme. A second subject now appears: timid, uncertain, on solo flute over pizzicato accompaniment. Quietly growing in confidence, this theme experiences a moment of shrill woodwind anguish before itself calming as it devolves on to violins.

Two bassoons and double bassoon over an ominous timpani roll announce the start of the development section with a reference to the opening theme. A complex web of woodwind tone is constructed in time to support horns and strings in a great climax, in which all the material of the movement is thrown into a tense battle, trumpets and percussion answering imperious horn calls as the music twists in tortured string quavers. The climactic peak is maintained with some miraculous feats of scoring over nearly a hundred bars of moderate tempo. It illustrates yet again the composer's ability to think and write in terms of immense, cogently organised paragraphs over vast time scales. As the movement descends from its turbulent peak it finds yet more value in its established subjects, bringing through them, at last, a tranquil close.

The tentative piccolo tones at the end of the first movement linger like a regretful leave-taking in the memory. With savage violence they are shattered by the entry of the second movement, *Allegro*, a study in concentrated fury rarely equalled in music. A dynamic of *ff* is sustained for most of the movement, and the hectic pace relaxes for never an instant. As in all the other movements, strings open with three rising notes; here, the effect is of an irresistible *moto perpetuo* that drives along under wailing woodwind, clattering side drum and, in the central section, an emphatic brass march. With almost unbearable intensity the movement hurtles towards the final *sfff tutti* semiquaver, bringing a silence as pregnant as the foregoing clamour. Into this tense silence comes a movement of deceptive simplicity that brings with it a statement as personal as any uttered by a modern composer.

This third movement is marked *Allegretto*: material in it had been used previously in the Scherzo of the Violin Concerto No. 1, where it had rather less significance. First violins announce an innocuous theme, soon to be answered in close canon by second violins. A new, toy-like melody enters on piccolo, flute and oboe and is transferred to strings, before flute and two cor anglais forge a link back to the opening theme. Bassoon with delicate percussion accompaniment carries the melody for a time, but, towards the end of its solo, pizzicato cellos and basses, quickly changing to *arco*, draw a phrase from the toy-like melody and project it urgently into a crescendo:

Example 5

At the *ff* termination of the lower strings' phrase, which, it will be seen, is heralded by Shostakovich's personal signature, a solo horn enters with a gripping phrase, *f*, *espressivo*, repeated immediately, *piano*. This is one of the most moving and vitally important moments in symphonic music: the composer, unmistakably identified by the DSCH motif, utters a stern warning. It is answered by a most unexpected reprise: the opening phrase of the first movement. Each time the horn call occurs it is acknowledged, once by piccolo and flute unison, and once by a solitary tam-tam stroke; and the fifth, sixth, and seventh statements are accompanied by pizzicato strings that suggest the first theme of the present movement. This is then taken up by cor anglais. Woodwind canons lead to a full restatement, both carefree and uncaring, of the toy-like theme that generates greater and greater tension and precipitates a tortured climax. The earlier warnings had gone unheeded; it is time for a severer lesson. With titanic effect the noble horn call, forgotten for a moment in the melée, enters on four horns in unison, *ff*, and the movement is at last chastened. It ends with one final distant horn call and the DSCH motif etched out lightly by high woodwind.

The composer at first had doubts about the length of the *Andante* with which the Finale begins, but eventually felt that he had constructed an interlude between the philosophical third movement and the high-spirited Finale that provided exactly what was required. Most sensitive listeners would probably agree. Again choosing three rising notes with which to open the movement, cellos and basses climb to audibility. An oboe pronounces a plangent melody that at two points rises in protest. Other solo woodwind continue the sombre mood of complaint, and oboe repeats its protest. Clarinet, having gradually insinuated itself, abruptly unlocks the door and releases the *Allegro*. Once under way, there seems to be no stopping the optimism and momentum of this movement, but imperceptibly a threatening element closes in and at last stands revealed: the evil second movement takes complete charge, but the Symphony, at this point, is not strong enough to resist its influence, and it marshals a monstrous unison *tutti* statement of DSCH with which to repel the intruder. For a moment the music is stunned, its momentum only slowly recovering, and then only with the assistance of the DSCH phrase standing on guard nearby on *piano* trombones. The oboe's protest returns, now on three oboes and three clarinets, extending into a wailing unison. Incongruously, a garrulous solo bassoon restates the first subject of the *Allegro*, and festivities resume despite warning horn statements of DSCH. Now, it seems, optimism under the aegis of DSCH, may be not only allowed but encouraged, and the movement is given its head as timpani, *ff*, repeatedly assert DSCH in the final bars.

Thus Shostakovich's great decade of genius terminated with an undoubted masterpiece in which his personal musical motto was exposed, if not over-exposed, and finally secured a victory for the composer's ego. At once greeted in both Eastern and

Western hemispheres as a superb work, the Tenth elegantly balances Symphony No. 8 standing at the beginning of that decade, a symphony that was criticised by the communist authorities and neglected by the rest of the world until the general approval of the composer's music brought about by the Tenth Symphony and other works of the period finally brought it into perspective. We may now regard Shostakovich's 8th–9th–10th tryptich as among the most satisfying in symphonic literature.

Symphony No. 11 in G minor, Op. 103 (1957) 'The Year 1905'

While the Tenth Symphony might be said to be a personal triumph by the composer over adversity, the Eleventh possesses an explicit external programme that completely controls its form and content. Not since the Second and Third Symphonies had Shostakovich composed a continuous symphony, although, as we have seen in Nos. 8 and 9, he tended to link some groups of movements in order to present a continuous argument.

The argument chosen for the Eleventh Symphony is the abortive Revolution of 1905, and Shostakovich's handling of it is clear-cut and highly emotional. He employs a vastly expanded scale of time in which to paint this picture. Even so, at a playing time of about an hour, it is shorter than Symphony No. 7 and only a few minutes longer than Nos. 4 and 8. The huge expanses of almost static music seem unnecessarily protracted at first, but when seen in conjunction with the all-important programme, they will be found to contribute positively to the effect of the whole. It is for this reason that the work has to be considered alongside the events of 1905: without them, some sections of the work cannot be supported from either an artistic or a symphonic viewpoint. Either by fortune or good judgement, the order of events Shostakovich selected for portrayal in the Eleventh Symphony fits ideally with the slow-fast-slow-fast plan he had established in earlier works.

The first movement, *Adagio*, is entitled 'Palace Square'. After many years of subjugation under the Tsars' iron rule the Russian people were driven by despair to approach their oppressors and ask for mercy and consideration. In this first movement the people are depicted standing mutely pleading in the square before the Palace. The icy weather is conveyed in the music alongside the hopelessness of the people and the unmistakable but unspoken threat of revenge: the first by hollow, frozen chords, the second by sombre, static melodies and harmonies, and the third by a muttering timpani triplet figure first heard in bar 14. A muted trumpet solo, later echoed by muted horn, petitions for compassion but is ignored. Taking up the triplet rhythm of the timpani, a solo flute sings the people's song 'Listen', and this is repeated by muted trumpet over a quasi-military side drum figure. Other folk songs occur, each one telling of the plight of the ordinary people, but the significance of each is disregarded by those within the Palace.

At the start of the second movement, 'Ninth of January', a running theme on lower strings acts as a bass to itself in augmentation on clarinets and bassoons, thus typifying the close symphonic relationship in this work between motifs, rhythms and melodies. The 9th of January 1905 (known elsewhere according to the Gregorian calendar as 22 January) is known as 'Bloody Sunday' in Russia. Singing hymns and carrying icons, a crowd of workers approached the Winter Palace in unarmed protest, hoping to make representations to the Tsar for clemency. Shostakovich skilfully depicts the gathering crowd, at first earnest and orderly but gradually giving way to indignation. When peasants and workers are at last assembled, their mute message plain and their expectant faces turned to the windows of the Palace, a return to the music of the Palace Square movement renews their supplication to their Tsar, but, tragically, he was absent from the Palace. Cossacks from the Romanov bodyguard, taking the hymns for revolutionary songs and icons for weapons, and lacking direct orders from the Czar, moved amongst the crowd with guns and swords. In a passage of searing realism, the composer portrays the ensuing scene of agony and death with a truly remarkable display of endurance and vivid writing. Page after page of harrowing unisons alternate with savage percussion rhythms as massacred peasants fall into the snow, the inhumanity of the scene taking on a nightmare machine-like aspect. With shocking abruptness the battle is over, the square is silent and lifeless, and the freezing air trembles. Temporarily vanquished, the trumpet call drifts from a distance over the dead bodies, the flute melody 'Listen' now droops in grief, and the muttering timpani triplets endure to the end of the movement.

'Eternal Memory', the third movement, *Adagio*, commemorates the victims of that too-passive revolution. Its main burden is the song 'You fell as victims', heard on muted violas after an introductory pizzicato figure that continues as an accompaniment. The song grows impassioned as other strings join in. A funeral scene slowly unfolds, recalling in its anguish that terrible day before subsiding to allow a repeat of the tragically lovely viola melody.

The Finale, 'Tocsin', warns that the people will triumph just as certainly as the guilty will be punished. Once again we may marvel at Shostakovich's economy of invention and his sheer stamina. A savage fanfare commands immediate attention, and the peasants are again on the march, gathering overwhelming support and crushing every obstacle. It is a ruthless display of violent resolve, no less than 102 pages of score culminating in a mighty affirmation of the fanfare and a shattering *fff* stroke on cymbals and bass drum. We find ourselves once again in the Palace Square. With infinite regret the cor anglais chants a lament taken from the second movement. With tight-lipped determination and amid insistent percussion strokes, a bass clarinet hurls out the opening theme of that movement with utmost malevolence. Once again the music gathers power at a breathtaking rate, and in an unstoppable galloping *coda* the true tocsin sounds out: a warning bell that yet again recalls the massacre of the second movement.

Symphony No. 12 in D minor, Op. 112 (1961), 'The Year 1917'

Shostakovich had planned to write a symphony to the memory of Lenin but those plans came to nothing and the war presented more immediate subjects for musical treatment. The opportunity arose again in 1961 when, having dealt with the tragic events of 1905 in the Eleventh Symphony, he came to treat the successful revolution of 1917 in No. 12. A dedication 'To the Memory of Vladimir Ilyich Lenin' appears on the title page, and the title 'The Year 1917' stands at the head of the score.

For non-musical but entirely understandable reasons neither

the Eleventh nor the Twelfth Symphonies have received much sympathy in the West. The subject of revolution is not so close to the heart of an American or a West European as it is to a Russian and it is therefore difficult to feel one's way inside not only the music but also Shostakovich's motives for writing it. The effort is worth making in the case of No. 11; less so, it must be admitted, in No. 12, which, in an exaggerated performance, will lose a great deal of its symphonic effect and sound merely empty and bombastic.

Like No. 11, it is in four connected movements that lead one through the events of the Revolution, in this case the successful one of 1917. The first two movements depict different aspects of the days leading up to that event: the first, 'Revolutionary Petrograd', is a general picture of the angry mood of the people who, without a firm plan, tend to consider that the thought stands for the deed. An attitude of disorganised exultation has to be curbed so that the energy thus wasted might be converted into action. The movement is in abbreviated sonata form with an introduction that reverts in mood to the opening of the Seventh Symphony, a stretch of music which also represented the mood of the people before a momentous event. In the second movement, 'Razliv', which is the name of Lenin's den not far from St Petersburg, that revolutionary leader is pictured in isolation planning the event in all its detail. There seems to be in this slow movement feelings of both fear and resolve.

'Aurora', the name of the third movement, commemorates the battle cruiser whose first shots upon the Winter Palace signalled the start of the Revolution. It is a movement that leads inevitably to the Finale, 'Dawn of Humanity', a piece that lays itself open to charges of the most blatant pretentiousness.

It is evident that the composer was thinking along grandiose lines in his 'Lenin' Symphony for, in addition to a fairly large *batterie* (timpani, triangle, side drum, cymbals, bass drum, and tam-tam), the recommended string contingent numbers between 64 and 84. It is to be regretted in a way that the work had to be shackled to a programme that dictated the nature of the Finale since there are many remarkable things in the work together with a close-knit symphonism that will send the seeker of thematic evolution and cross-references furiously scanning the pages of the score. Of more obvious interest are the following features, noted at random.

The main *Allegro* of the first movement seems to pick up from the point at which the Eleventh Symphony ceases. It has a similar drive, is impelled just as firmly by percussive elements, and continues the same air of earnest intent. It will be noted that parts of the movement, too, quote from the second movement of that Symphony. There is, in addition, an unmistakable 'Russianness' and an openly emotional content about it that strongly recalls Tchaikovsky. An important feature of the work is the use Shostakovich makes of percussion. The common uses are ever-present, of course, but an interesting colouristic effect is the ostinato timpani pedal in quavers or semi-quavers, both loud and soft, a device borrowed by Moisey Vainberg and other Russian composers to telling effect. When used at low dynamic level, as in the link between the first and second movements and in 'Aurora', the effect is unbelievably sinister. Another effective invention is the recurring three-note pizzicato interjection in the second movement that seems to signal the passing of time as complicated plans are laid and the circled date on the calendar draws near. A solo tenor trombone speaks in grave tones at the end of 'Razliv'. Could this be a portrayal of Lenin himself giving final orders and bestowing earnest good wishes upon his lieutenants? In the Finale there is some winning string writing as the 'New Age' flowers and prospers, but one must not overlook the deft woodwind writing in a movement that tends to be swamped with the message carried over-forcefully by brass and percussion as the final *sffff* quaver approaches.

The Twelfth may not be among the greatest of Shostakovich's symphonies, but it does have moments of atmospheric power and occasional strokes of imaginative daring. It represents a kind of *rapprochement* between Shostakovich's brooding private idiom and the Soviet ideals of epic directness and clear-cut programmatic content. After this, from the Thirteenth Symphony onward, the private and public dimensions of his music were to draw increasingly apart.

Ronald Stevenson

The Piano Music

The antipodes of Shostakovich's music are his Symphonies and Quartets: his public music and his private music. Between them lies his piano music, which belongs to both the private world of the studio and the public world of the concert platform. More than any other instrument, the piano is an orchestra; yet it can be accommodated to a chamber music style. Shostakovich's *oeuvre* includes both styles of piano music: the 'orchestral' and the *da camera*.

What makes Shostakovich an essentially symphonic composer is his duality, for the creative friction of dualities is the very stuff of symphony. Shostakovich is both tragedian and satirist – King Lear and Till Eulenspiegel in one. In conversation with him in Edinburgh in 1962 (he spoke a little English and had studied it in preparation for his visit) I asked him if he could give some pointers as to his aesthetic. He replied that his aesthetic included both Bach and Offenbach. Those few words tell much: they embrace his penchant for profundity and levity. I observed the same dichotomy in his person. During a concert at the 1962 Edinburgh Festival, I sat just a few seats away from him and observed him with as much avidity as was compatible with discretion. Listening to music by other composers, he sat self-contained. Listening to his own music, he physically betrayed his total involvement: he crossed and uncrossed his legs, leaned forward then back, and adjusted his spectacles with a gauche movement of the back of his hand, like a child brushing away a tear. He was a human lightning conductor, carrying the electrical discharges of his music to the soles of his feet. His face was a tragic mask. A martyr to music. Later, at the Fourth Congress of the Union of Soviet Composers, held in Moscow in December 1968, I met him again and once more had opportunity to have a little conversation. Here I saw his other persona, the Till Eulenspiegel. I engaged his interest in football (an old love of his). We enthused about the respective merits of Glasgow Rangers and the Moscow Dynamos. His complexion had a pallor and the plaster mask of the secular saint cracked in the grin of a gargoyle. At a Kremlin banquet, Madame Furtseva, the Minister of Culture, announced that Dmitry Dmitrievich would make a speech. This 'speech' consisted of a few jerky phrases: 'I have attended the first, second, third and fourth Congresses of the Union of Soviet Composers. I hope to attend the fifth, sixth, seventh, eighth. . . .' That was all. It was delivered *staccato*. The voice was high-pitched, piping. The manner was 'briosy'. The human lightning-conductor was sparking. To me, lightning is the symbol of Shostakovich's music: it has the power to strike tragedy and the ability to etch a gothic grotesquerie across the heavens in its witty, zig-zag calligraphy.

Now more than any other solo instrument, the piano can thunder in its bass and give tragic expression by the most powerful and sustained resonance; while, at its other extreme, its treble is capable only of a skeletal dance with the dry sonority of rattling bones. So here is an ideal instrument for the expression of Shostakovich's dual creative persona.

There is, of course, a balancing factor between these extremes of gravity and levity, and this balancing factor is lyrical melody and dialectic polyphony (another duality). Shostakovich confides these elements, as do all composers, to the medium register of the piano, where they sound most clearly. Many composers, from Liszt onwards, have exploited the full expressive gamut of the piano. But no composer, other than Shostakovich, has found in the piano an instrument whose extreme resonances (from the most sustained to the most brittle) constitute the repository of his elected affinities of

tragedy and satire. Other piano composers have manifested
dual creative character: Liszt was both Abbé and Mephisto;
Busoni, both Faust and Arlecchino. But there are worlds of
difference between Liszt's polarisation of religious aspiration
and diablerie, Busoni's philosophy and elegant irony, and
Shostakovich's tragedy and satire. Liszt's and Busoni's dualism was the outcome of national and cultural cross-currents: in
Liszt's case, Hungarian and cosmopolitan; in Busoni's, Italian
and German. Shostakovich manifested no such cross-currents;
his dualism was rather the result of his coalescing of twin
Russian souls. In one creative character he combined a
Dostoevskian capacity for tragedy and a Gogolian capacity for
satire. Dostoevsky's genius no more embraced satire than
Gogol's encompassed tragedy. Shostakovich's genius fused
both. That is part of his unique achievement. It was only
natural that his wide-ranging style should find expression in the
symphony; but it was also hammered out on the anvil of the
piano – the hammer-blows of tragedy emitting the very sparks
of satire.

Another Russian master of the *Hammerklavier* – one of its most
Promethean figures – is basic to all Russian pianism from the
Romantic age onwards: Anton Rubinstein (1829–1894). He
was Director of the St Petersburg Conservatoire from 1887 to
1890. (Remember: Shostakovich was born in Petersburg and
attended its Conservatoire.) Rubinstein established a tradition
as surely as the Imperial Russian Ballet engendered
Diaghilev's *Ballets Russes*. Rubinstein's combination of the
highest ideals of pianism, plus a wild, untamed, heroic
performance-style, both determined his policy of setting very
high standards and stringent diploma requirements for students at the St Petersburg Conservatoire. He demanded big
repertoires and accuracy from his students. His own notorious
inaccuracy (which was swept away in the tidal wave of his
inspiration) predetermined that he was the sternest task-
master for accuracy in student performance. His Seven Historical Recitals – colossal programmes, each twice as long as
today's usual recital, spanning the entire range of keyboard
music from the Elizabethan to the late Romantics – were given
in Russia, Germany and Austria; and were extended to 32
Lecture-Recitals for the Petrograd Conservatoire students.

They were heard by many of the great pianists who lived into the twentieth century: such virtuosi as Busoni, Paderewski, Rachmaninov, Hambourg, Gabrilowitsch and Lhevinne, who all remembered Anton Rubinstein as the Master. His Historical Recitals reverberated for many years after their last chord had been played. They created in Russia – and particularly in St Petersburg – an atmosphere in pianistic circles almost like that of touting at great steeplechase courses. If this comparison seems exaggerated, it will not appear so if contemporary accounts are read about the series of recitals given in Petersburg in 1912 by Ferruccio Busoni and Anton Rubinstein's pupil, Joseph Hofmann. Each of these pianists commanded a large and vociferous following in that city and in Moscow. (Busoni occupied the post of Professor of Piano at the Moscow Conservatoire in 1890–91.) Those recitals in 1912 became occasions for demonstrations by the music public, with campfollowers clambering on to seats in the concert halls and shouting their approbation as if for a general on a battlefield. Such frenzy was aroused that when Busoni's Dutch pupil Egon Petri played in the Soviet Union in 1927 (the first Western pianist to play there after the October Revolution), Russian pianophiles still spoke to Petri of his master's recitals of 1912, as though they had been given only a season before, instead of fifteen years before. And as late as 1964, the veteran Soviet pianist and piano pedagogue Maria Nikolayevna Barinova published a book (Musyka Press, Moscow) specifically devoted to a comparative study of the respective piano styles of Busoni and Hofmann.

Nikolai Rubinstein founded the Russian Musical Society in 1859 and the Moscow Conservatoire in 1864. Like his elder brother Anton, he too was a virtuoso pianist and composer. Among his pupils were Sauer, Siloti and Taneyev. Nikolai Medtner was also a student at the Moscow Conservatoire under Safonov. Medtner left the USSR in 1921 but returned to give recitals in 1927, when Shostakovich heard him. Medtner's music, even though he was an ex-patriot Russian, has much in common with the aesthetic of Shostakovich's later music.

Other outstanding Muscovite piano teachers were Nikolai Zverev (his class in the mid-1880s included Rachmaninov and Scriabin) and Elena Gnesina, who founded her own School of

Piano Pedagogy in Moscow – an even larger establishment than the Moscow Conservatoire and still functioning – she was a Busoni pupil in Moscow in 1890 and lived till the 1960s, numbering Gilels and Khachaturian among her pupils.

Such was the historical background against which Shostakovich's pianism and piano-writing developed. This is not to imply that Shostakovich was directly influenced by such figures as Anton Rubinstein, Busoni or Hofmann, but he was assuredly influenced by the cult of the piano which they generated.

The phenomenon of the composer/pianist, which was the rule, the almost unvaried pattern, for creative musicians from at least Clementi to Medtner (with the obvious exceptions of Berlioz, Verdi and Wagner), was longer-lived in exemplars from Russia – and from Russian Poland – than anywhere else; including in its historical progress such examples as Felix Blumenfeld (the teacher of Horowitz), Scriabin, Rachmaninov, Prokofiev, Medtner, Paderewski, de Pachmann, Godowsky, Hofmann and Wanda Landowska – not to mention a minor galaxy of lesser luminaries.

Shostakovich's mother, Sofia Vasilyevna, had studied piano at St Petersburg Conservatoire and was a piano teacher. (The father, Dmitry Boleslavovich, by profession a chemist, was also a music-lover and an amateur singer.) Shostakovich's older sister Maria taught piano at the Leningrad Ballet School and 'second study' piano at the Leningrad Conservatoire. His younger sister Zoya also studied piano, though later opted for a career as a veterinary surgeon. The mother was the first piano teacher of all three children. Dmitry Dmitrievich might have his father's name, but he had his mother's features and her shape of hands. Shostakovich's hands were fine-fingered and only of medium size and stretch. (A composer/pianist's hands nearly always predetermine the way his music 'lies' on the keyboard. For instance, César Franck's piano music, and Busoni's and Rachmaninov's, is obviously conceived by large hands. Godowsky's, on the contrary, is moulded by a small hand which could negotiate the subtlest intricacy of figuration.)

So Shostakovich began piano lessons at the age of nine. Most virtuosi have begun earlier. The gifted child who begins piano study at four or five has a flying start on the later learner, because his reflexes are much more adapted to rapidity and ease of co-ordination. Paderewsky began piano lessons at seven: one of the latest beginners among the great virtuosi. His *meccanique* was generally not as facile as that of his confrères who had been prodigies; he concentrated on eloquence, making a virtue out of necessity. From Shostakovich's piano recordings made in later years, particularly of some of his Preludes and Fugues, it is apparent that he, too, had something less than a flawless technique; interesting as it is to hear a composer play his own work.

After receiving a general education at Shidlovskaya's Commercial School in Petrograd, Shostakovich studied music at Glyaser's Music School from 1916 to 1918. About ten years of age – only a year after beginning piano lessons with his mother – he composed a long programmatic piano piece entitled *Soldier*: his first 'war music', an embryonic premonition of his 'Leningrad' Symphony. He destroyed the manuscript of *Soldier* and other pieces, including a Pushkin opera *The Gypsies*. In 1919 he entered the Petrograd Conservatoire for four years, where his professor was Leonid Nikolayev, head of the piano department. In 1923 – still only seventeen – Shostakovich gave a graduation recital in Leningrad, including the Bach-Liszt A minor Prelude and Fugue, Beethoven's *Appassionata* and some of his own compositions: a typical Anton Rubinstein 'grand manner' programme. The journal *Zhizn' Iskusstva* (*Art Activities*) wrote that he made 'a tremendous impression'.

Shostakovich's professor of composition at the Petrograd Conservatoire was Maximilian Steinberg. He exercised no predominant influence on Shostakovich's piano style, because Steinberg's instrument was the violin. His influence on Shostakovich was directed towards the orchestra: Steinberg was a pupil (and son-in-law) of Rimsky-Korsakov. Another of Rimsky-Korsakov's pupils, Alexander Glazunov, exercised a more lasting influence on Shostakovich, because Glazunov took a never-forgotten paternal interest in him. Initially under Balakirev's stimulus, Glazunov wrote a considerable body of work for the piano, including large-scale piano sonatas, as well as a wealth of music for most other media, excluding opera. Glazunov must have been reminded of his own first Symphony, composed at sixteen (and re-orchestrated five times), when Shostakovich produced *his* first Symphony at nineteen years of age. In 1882, when Glazunov was seventeen, his first String

Quartet was premièred in public. Anton Rubinstein took his hand and led him to the stage, as Mendelssohn had taken the twelve-year-old Rubinstein's hand at the boy's first London concert in Hanover Square, London in 1842. Glazunov, of all Russian composers, excepting Medtner, was most concerned with form in music. For a time – significantly when Glazunov was abroad, away from Russia in the later Twenties and Thirties – Shostakovich temporarily forsook form for experiment. But Glazunov's precepts, along with Maxim Gorky's formulation of socialist realism ('nationalist in form, socialist in content'), ultimately prevailed in Shostakovich's music. For instance, Shostakovich's later fugal writing owes allegiance to the very powerful and architectonic fugue in Glazunov's 2nd Piano Sonata.

There's some confusion about Shostakovich's opus 1. His *Three Fantastic Dances* originally bore that opus number, but this enumeration was later changed to opus 5; the orchestral Scherzo in F sharp minor eventually bearing the first opus number. Opus 2 was a set of 8 piano Preludes (1919–20) based on an unusual tonality-scheme:

1 – G major. 2 – G minor. 5 – A minor. 6 – F minor.
3 – E flat minor. 4 – B major. 7 and 8 – D flat major.

This scheme is Lisztian in its progression of tonalities which form two augmented triads, bounded by a tritone. Liszt had encouraged the young Glazunov and Liszt's influence on Russian musicians, after his Russian tour of 1842, may be ascertained from Vladimir Stasov's essays (Barrie and Rockliff, London, 1968). These preludes were followed by a further group of five preludes (without opus number), contributed to a set of twenty-four composed by G. Clements, P. Feldt and Shostakovich, who were all fellow-students, each composer writing a group of pieces. The tonality-scheme here followed that of the Chopin preludes. Shostakovich contributed pieces in A minor, G major, E minor, D flat major and F minor. All these early Preludes are written in an economic, rather 'French' piano style, demanding neat finger-work and a slender lyricism. There is occasional quirkishness, as in the D flat major Prelude which doesn't come to a close but perversely stops dead – and 'dead-pan' – in the middle of a phrase. In a lyrical context this is a bit of self-conscious cheek.

The *3 Fantastic Dances, op. 5* (1922) contain a subtler irony within a more refined lyricism. Two *allegrettos* frame an *andantino*. They are all exercises in the elision of tonality. The first is a *humoresque* (its opening rhythm is identical to Dvořák's celebrated *Humoresque*) which begins as though it were in B flat minor, then begins to sound like F minor. Only in the 8th bar is the home key of a simple C major established. It's rather like the musical equivalent of sleight-of-hand. The second dance, a waltz of the mixed lineage of Tchaikovsky and Prokofiev – exquisite ballet music – is in G major: we know that because its dominant recurs so often (proving Tovey's point: reiterate a chord sufficiently and it sounds like a dominant); yet the tonic chord of G only appears in the last bar of two pages. (One thinks here of such tonality-elisions as the opening of Beethoven's Fifth: what key is it in? And of the *Tristan Prelude*, which is indisputably in A minor yet contains not one chord of A minor.) The last of Shostakovich's three dances is a little polka. It is like a sketch for his later polka from the *Golden Age* ballet, but not as openly impudent. In his Shostakovich catalogue (Boosey, London, 1977) Malcolm MacDonald lists this *Fantastic Dance No. 3* as being in C major. But there is only one chord of C major in the whole piece – the last chord. It begins in A flat major, to which key it returns often. When it veers to C it is to C *minor*, not C major (until the very end). Perhaps it might be heard as a Nielsenesque example of 'progressive tonality': that is, it begins in one tonality and progresses through others to end in a different key from the opening. Until the very last chord it sounds as though it's going to end in A flat: there's a bar-and-a-half of the dominant of A flat until the sudden switch to C major at the end. Again, it's a kind of conjurer's trick in musical terms – or a game of hide-and-seek set to music. These are three delightful pieces, easy enough to give pleasure to young people and amateurs.

The Dances of 1922 were followed by orchestral and chamber music over the next three years. In 1926 Shostakovich returned to writing piano music in his Sonata no. 1, op. 12. It is a one-movement form cast in three sections (not in two, as erroneously stated in the MacDonald catalogue): *allegro* (containing a brief parenthetical *meno mosso* and *adagio*); *lento*; *allegro* (with a slight broadening in the coda). This Sonata declares itself like a series of slogans, like fists on a revolutionary poster.

It is Constructivism-in-music. Alexander Vassilevich Moso-
lov's symphonic poem *The Iron Foundry* (1928) is probably the
most characteristic example of Constructivist music, though
Honegger's *Pacific 231* (1924) may have influenced it.

The first declaration of Constructivism was found in Tarabu-
kin's booklet of that name published in 1922. A more succinct
definition was published in the magazine *LEF* in 1923:

> Constructivism is the organisation of the given material on the
> principles of tectonics, structure and construction, the form
> becoming defined in the process of creation, by the utilitarian aim
> of the object.

Translated into Shostakovich's Sonata, this concept would
read something like this: the piano is a music-machine made by
carpenters and engineers; let us celebrate it as a machine. It is
the *Hammerklavier*. A proto-revolutionary composer, Beethoven, so designated his Sonata op. 106. Let us make it the
'hammer and sickle' music-machine! Let us glory in pounding
chords and slashing *glissandi*!

Admirable enthusiasm. A young man's zeal for a young
revolution. But in retrospect its main interest is that it so
typifies its time and place. Besides, these 'shock tactics' were
nothing new. Another Russian, Leo Ornstein (born near
Odessa in 1895, and another student of the St Petersburg
Conservatoire and also another protégé of Glazunov) had
shocked his teacher Leschetitzky – and many others – by
playing his (Ornstein's) *Wild Men's Dance*. James Huneker
wrote of Ornstein's performance: 'I bewail the murderous
means of expression with which Leo Ornstein patrolled the
piano. He stormed its keys, scooping chunks of slag and
spouting scoriae like a vicious volcano. I was stunned, especially after *glissandi* that ripped up the keyboard and fizzed and
foamed over the stage.' The *Wild Men's Dance* was perhaps the
first twentieth-century piece to use chord-clusters aggressively.
Shostakovich's first Sonata also uses tone-clusters:

Example 1

The Ornstein *Dance* was published in 1915, though composed a few years earlier, and copies certainly circulated in the USSR. After 1906, the eleven-year-old Ornstein had moved with his family to America.

The American composer Henry Cowell (often considered the originator of chord-cluster technique) did not publish his first employment of it till 1922 (*The Tides of Manaunaun*) though this, too, was written a few years earlier. Cowell was the first American composer to visit the Soviet Union and to give piano recitals of his own work there. That visit took place *after* Shostakovich composed his first Piano Sonata, but Cowell's music certainly circulated in the USSR in the mid-twenties, a period when there was much American aid to Russia and much cultural intertraffic between the two countries. Cowell''s *Tiger* (after Blake), a ferocious piano piece using the palms and forearms, was actually published in the USSR in 1929. The Russo-American Nicolas Slonimsky in *American Composers on American Music* (Ungar, N.Y. 1962, reprint of 1933) tells us that Cowell went to Russia in 1929. He was 'received as a personification of industrial America, with machines governing the tide of life: "And I saw clearly the electric floodlights of Broadway filling the room, and the New York skyline hovering above the mist," wrote a Russian intellectal.'

This was the ethos of Soviet Constructivism, whose concepts were developed in theatre by Meyerhold, in architecture by the Vesnin brothers, in cinema by Vertov, in industrial and typographical design by Rodchenko and in poster design by Klutsis, Lissitzky and the Stenberg brothers. Their ideal was the artist-as-engineer. Perhaps the logical conclusion was that the Shostakovich Sonata should have attained its mechanical perfection in a piano-roll recording!

The *genres* included in the Shostakovich Sonata are: a tarantella, a nocturne, and a *moto perpetuo*; but if the tarantella originated in a Neapolitan frenzied dance after being bitten by the tarantula-spider, here it is a grotesque marionette-dance with mechanical mosquitos. The nocturne is as if Vertov's *Manifesto on the disarmament of cinematography* had been set to music, with its cry of 'Away from the sweet hugs of Romance!' And the *moto perpetuo*, as music's most mechanical form, is the goal of the whole work. The opening of the Sonata is an example of a quasi-Schoenbergian note-row.

Example 2

The pianistic lay-out of the *lento* (what I have characterised as
the nocturne) – on three staves, with Lisztian notation of stems
down for the left hand and up for the right – is very rare in
Shostakovich. Generally, he doesn't give much thought to
detail of editing his piano music: indeed, it has generally been
edited by others. He belongs to those composers who write
spontaneously (Britten was the same) and seldom revise.
Neither is he interested in detailed piano lay-out – the
distribution of texture between the hands. Professor Grigory
Kogan has devoted a volume to this subject (*On Pianoforte
Facture* or *Scoring for Keyboard*: Soviet Composer Publishing
House, Moscow, 1961) in which the very few Shostakovich
examples have little interest in comparison with the examples
quoted from Busoni, Godowsky and other masters of the piano.
Professor Kogan has since produced a *School of Piano Transcription* in six volumes (Muzyka, Moscow, 1970–78) which repro-
duces as many as four transcriptions together with the original
in an unique comparative study of piano-writing: something
that probably would not have interested Shostakovich at all! At
least, there is no evidence from his piano music that he would
have applied the knowledge gleaned from such a work. He just
wasn't that type of composer.

Henry Cowell was by no means the only Western composer
to visit Russia in the Twenties. Hindemith and Berg had been
there, so young Shostakovich had heard *Gebrauchsmusik* and
Expressionismus. In 1929 Bartók gave four recitals in Moscow,
Kharkov, Odessa and Leningrad. So Shostakovich had heard
Bartók's dry, percussive piano-style, both in composition and
performance. Earlier, in 1926, Milhaud had visited the USSR.
So Shostakovich had heard Milhaud's polytonality. In his
memoirs, *Notes Without Music* (Dobson, London, 1952),
Milhaud recounts their meeting: '. . . a young man with
dreamy eyes hidden behind enormous spectacles, came to show
me a symphony, which, in spite of its rather conventional form
and construction, betrayed genuine gifts, and even had a
certain quality of greatness, if it is remembered that its

composer Shostakovich was only eighteen at the time. . .'

In 1927 Shostakovich was awarded a Certificate of Merit in the First International Chopin Piano Competition in Warsaw. (He was said to have some Polish blood on his father's side. Certainly a Slav melancholy and a certain hypersensitive, febrile nervousness link Shostakovich to Chopin.) But he quickly abandoned any plans of pursuing a career as virtuoso, though he often performed his own works in public and recorded some of his Preludes and Fugues as late as his fifties – though not very well. And it wasn't only the question of his being out of practice: his nervous, strung-up character was such that he was inclined to take fast tempi – tempi which his fingers couldn't negotiate. This febrile nervousness made him often demand rapid tempi, even when advising conductors in preparing his orchestral works: I observed this in rehearsal at the 1962 Edinburgh Festival: he was for ever saying 'Faster! Faster!' So his metronome-markings should be taken with even more than a grain of salt – unless, of course, the purist wishes to include Shostakovich's own pianistic inaccuracies as part of a spurious 'authenticity'! He was also emotionally shy as a public performer: listen to his recording of the slow movement of his 2nd Piano Concerto. On paper, the music is beautiful: in his performance it is dry and dull – and again, too hurried.

However much he might have deserved his Certificate of Merit as a Chopin-player in Warsaw in 1927, one would scarcely credit it to hear Shostakovich's next piano *opus*, the *Aphorisms op. 13*, written in the same year. There are ten of them, not nine as D. Rabinovich wrongly states in his Shostakovich Biography (Lawrence and Wishart, London, 1954). The first *Aphorism* is a *Recitative*. The only thing recitative-like about it is its Bartókian reiterated monotones. Like most of the set it has an abrupt, inconsequential ending. *Aphorism no. 2* is a *Serenade*. And a very dry anti-Romantic serenade it is. Its monody is punctuated by guitar-like chords. The second section has some haphazard two-part counterpoint, note-against-note, still with the occasional guitar-like chord. The time-signatures go through the motions of constant inconsistency: almost never two consecutive bars the same. Again an abrupt ending, which seems to say 'take it or leave it.'

The title of the *3rd Aphorism – Nocturne* is perverse. It's an *anti*-nocturne. It sounds like a sketch for the sexual onomato-

poeia of Shostakovich's opera *Lady Macbeth of Mtsensk*. Percy
Grainger claimed that all the world knew that the *Tristan Prelude*
began with an erection: well here in this 'Nocturne' we have
that, but we also have what Robert Burns crudely called 'a
thuddering escalade'.

Example 3

An orgasm.

Example 4

And finally – what else? – exhaustion.

Example 5

This kind of music – with such a title as 'Nocturne' – forces me
to reflect that Shostakovich was probably also shy of expressing
the tenderness of physical love: at least when I ponder it, I can
think of very little in his music that might be described as gently
voluptuous.

Aphorism 4 is subtitled *Elegy*. It's very slow and it's marked
mesto(sad), but it doesn't grieve for long. It lasts precisely eight
bars. An elegy might be expected to follow a funeral, but expect
the reverse in this world of pranks and cranks! Now we have
Aphorism 5: a *Marche Funèbre*. Its tempo is – yes, you've guessed –
quick. In fact a quick march. It is full of imitation-trumpet-calls
that sound more like 'Come to the Cookhouse door, boys!' than

any cortège. Perhaps it's a funeral march to a crematorium. Such black humour is in the same vein as this music. And what after the 'funeral march'? An *Étude* which is a more futile five-finger exercise than any by Czerny. Whilst one hand doodles, the other gets stuck on Bartókian monotones.

If the 'funeral march' uses a quick march, *Aphorism 7* is a vertiginous waltz based on the *Dies Irae* with some Milhaud-like bitonality.

Example 6

Aphorism 8 is supposed to be a canon, is written on three staves but doesn't *need* to be, especially as there are so few notes. It's composed with as many rests as notes (shades of Webern!) The three-part writing is of that twentieth-century kind: written without any thought of how the contrapuntal parts may or may not combine. The motto seems: if it won't fit, never mind: pull the thing along by the scruff of the neck.

Legend is the subtitle of *Aphorism 9*. It's quick and very quiet throughout; full of *ostinati*; bitonal; starting with two parts, then adding a 'voice' until in ends in four parts. It is a species of *moto perpetuo*: one or other part is kept in quavers all the time. The last *Aphorism* (no. 10) is subtitled *Lullaby*. It is vaguely 'Spanish' in its intonation (had the young Dmitry been hearing De Falla?): slow and in the Phrygian mode (very Spanish) until it ends in a chord of A major with an extra note B added. There's a softly padding octave bass, underpinning a 'Moorish' type of tune, full of *melismatas*. This is the only nearly normal piece in the lot! What an unpleasant set of pieces! *Graffiti* would be a more apt title than *Aphorisms*!

After composing the *Aphorisms*, Shostakovich spent the next four years writing orchestral, film, theatre, ballet, vocal and operatic music; including Symphonies 2 and 3 and the three-act satirical opera after Gogol, *The Nose*, and the four-act tragic opera *Lady Macbeth of Mtsenk*. In 1932 and 1933 he composed a set of 24 *Preludes* for piano, op. 34 and premièred them in Moscow on 24 May 1933. The only other outstanding compos-ers who have essayed 24 Preludes for piano after Chopin's incomparable set are Busoni, Scriabin, York Bowen and Alan

Bush. Like the Busoni and Scriabin sets, and unlike those of
Debussy, Rachmaninov, York Bowen and Alan Bush, Shostakovich's op. 34 follows Chopin's tonality plan of basing the
series of preludes on the coupling of relative major and minor
keys which explore the cycle of fifths from C major to D minor.

The impudence of the *Aphorisms* has not entirely disappeared,
though here in the Preludes it does not preclude spontaneous
and serious music-making but most often co-exists with it, as a
kind of grotesque sting-in-the-tail. In this connection, it is
worth mentioning the impression of Shostakovich gleaned by
the great Polish composer-pianist Leopold Godowsky, when
they met in the USSR in 1935. On the suggestion of Godowsky's former pupil Heinrich Neuhaus (the teacher of Sviatoslav
Richter), Godowsky gave masterclasses in Russia and met
many Soviet musicians, including Shostakovich. In a letter to
Paul Howard of Australia dated 'about September 1936',
Godowsky wrote:

> I found Shostakovich as insipid as his music – though seemingly
> modest and timid, his music is incredibly impudent.

(Incidentally, Godowsky considered the USSR 'the social,
economic and political laboratory of the world', so his view of
Shostakovich was not that of a man biased against the Soviet
Union and Soviet composers.) And another great Polish
musician, the harpsichordist, pianist, composer and writer on
music, Wanda Landowska (In *Landowska on Music*, Secker and
Warburg, London, 1965) wrote:

> Shostakovich certainly has the sense of rhythm. But why these
> unsuccessful attempts at being grotesque, at humour?

The first prelude of op. 34 presents a memory of Rimsky
Korsakov's *Scheherezade* above an Alberti bass. Incidentally, the
texture is clarified in bars 3 and 14 if the middle pedal is
employed.

Example 7
Moderato ♩ = 69

Prelude 2 is a Fantastic Dance, reminiscent of op. 5. Bars 5, 4 and 8 before the end can again be clarified by employment of the middle and damper pedals and by redistribution between the hands.

Example 8

Prelude 3 begins as a *Song without Words* and ends quasi orchestrally with a dramatic bass octave tremolo.

Prelude 4 is a three-part Fugue.

Prelude 5, a *moto perpetuo*, may be made more brilliant by employing Busoni's principle of using consecutive five-finger groups, where practicable. No. 6 is a mordant polka, like a caricature of Georg Grosz made audible. It also shows some Viennese Mahlerish influence. Towards the end it changes from a polka to a bitter, goose-stepping march. It's very near to Kurt Weill. No. 7 is another Song without Words. No. 8 is a kind of updated Schubertian *moment musical*. No. 9 is a tarantella, not far removed from Walton's *Façade*. No. 10 is a Nocturne more like updated John Field (the Irish and 'Russian' Field) than like Chopin; and its chaste melody is spurned by a grotesque interruption towards the close. No. 11 is a neo-Bachian jig, suddenly marked *amoroso* at its coda. No. 12 is an arpeggio-study; No. 13 a march with an *ostinato* chordal bass like timpani.

Prelude 14 in E flat minor is really something! It is really a symphonic *adagio* (Stokowski made a superb transcription of it for orchestra.) A mighty miniature. For the first time we hear Shostakovich the tragedian in his piano music. Significantly, it plumbs the lowest regions of the piano. What occasioned this cataclysm? It certainly was created out of a profound awareness of evil. At its climax it fairly shrieks out. And it subsides only reluctantly – spent with its impassioned pleading.

Prelude No. 15 is a *scène de ballet*. No. 16 is a spectral march, a night watch, the *chiaroscuro* shifting of its tonalities like a Rembrandt painting made audible. No. 17 is a slow bittersweet waltz. No. 18 is a spiky two-part invention with dance-like episodes. Prelude No. 19 is a lyrical *barcarolle*, its sweetness occasionally turning sour. No. 20 is a furious military two-step; no. 21 a piquant Russian dance in $\frac{5}{4}$ time; no. 22 a lyrical *adagio*. Prelude 23 is a sombre *pastorale*, with a trombone-like theme in octaves. The middle pedal may here be employed to advantage again. The final Prelude (no. 24) is a witty gavotte which manages to avert a threat of drama and to cock a snook as it exits, Eulenspiegelish. A remarkable set of pieces, it marks a considerable advance over Shostakovich's earlier piano music.

In the same year that saw the completion of the Preludes – 1933 – his first Piano Concerto appeared. Scored for string orchestra and trumpet, it is not an imposing work but, rather, a celebration of the Russian circus. The next decade brought to fruition some of Shostakovich's greatest works: notably four more symphonies (no. 5 being probably the most outstanding); his first String Quartet and his Piano Quintet, which contains a fine fugue.

In 1942 he composed his Piano Sonata no. 2, op. 61, the second of his two works so designated. It is dedicated to the memory of his old piano professor, Leonid Nikolaev. It is cast in three movements: the first in sonata form (one of the very few examples of the true *sonata allegro* in Shostakovich's work – he curiously avoided the form in his symphonies); a *largo* in ternary song-form; and a *con moto finale* in variation-form (with an *adagio* variation before the coda). Though this Sonata transcends the Constructivism and quirkiness of his previous piano music, it nevertheless exhibits a conflict of aesthetic principles. Its outer movements identify with Boris Asafiev's theory adumbrated in his book *Music Form as Process* (Soviet State Publishers, Moscow, 1930) and developed in his *Elements of Musical Intonation* (Moscow, 1942). Asafiev (1884–1950) was the leading Soviet musicologist of his generation and was also a composer. He applied to music Engel's 'Theory of Reflection', an epistemological concept developed by Lenin in *Materialism and Empirio-criticism*, which postulates that the material world is reflected by human beings. Asafiev deduced his concept of intonation from that idea – alleging that the rhythms and inflexions of a composer's native speech determine his feeling for rhythm and melody. A nationalist composer will create

motives with national intonations: just as the seed determines
the growth of the flower, so national intonations will create
national form. This form could be filled with socialist content
by engaging in struggle, by plunging into the thick of life; not by
making music a private confessional or a refusal to act
positively in relation to society. As I say, that is the aesthetic
which lies behind the outer movements of Shostakovich's
second Piano Sonata; and a little later I'll demonstrate how it
operates.

But a different aesthetic motivates the slow movement. This
is a private document: pages from an expressionistic diary,
almost like the diaries of Kafka. The influence here was that of
Shostakovich's close friend the music and art critic Ivan
Sollertinsky (1902–44), who wrote a study of Schoenberg in
1934. This movement contains much quasi-12 note music and
is characterised by chords (or broken chords) built on 4ths and
7ths. Its recapitulation also employs a rather Schoenbergian
use of canon. Although tonality is not completely abandoned,
its anchorage is only tenuously maintained. Just as Shostakovich came under heavy critical fire from Zhdanov in 1936 over
the *Lady Macbeth of Mtsenk* affair, so were the ideas of his friend
Sollertinsky violently attacked. Perhaps the second Piano
Sonata, more than any other of Shostakovich's works, embodies his attempts to come to terms with the Marxist-Engelsian
aesthetic; and yet this intensely personal slow movement seems
to be saying that there must be room in life for secrets. (Pascal:
'The heart has its reasons whereof reason takes no account'.)

But such a Greek-trained scholar as St Paul in Corinthians I,
verses 7–9 declares: '. . . except ye utter by the tongue words
easy to be understood, how shall it be known what is spoken, for
ye shall speak into the air?'. This reminds me of Busoni's
essayette *Simplicity of Music in the Future* (1922). He mentions
that his library contained many editions of Edgar Alan Poe
with portraits, but Manet's portrait of him 'etched with a few
strokes', summed up all of them. Busoni then asks: 'Shouldn't
music also seek to express essentiality in few notes, set down
with mastery?' The main theme of Shostakovich's 2nd Piano
Sonata, in recapturing the simplicity of a wise child, is
reminiscent of the Polonaise from Busoni's *Sonatina ad usum
infantis* (1916).

Example 9

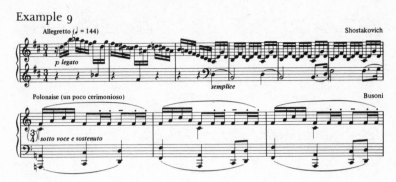

The second subject of Shostakovich's first movement certainly reflects, in its musical image of an onward mass march, the socialist principle of plunging joyfully into the thick of life.

Such is the onrush that the two subjects are recapitulated simultaneously in a brilliant use of bimodality contained enharmonically in one basic tonality (the E flat in context sounding like a D sharp.)

Example 10

In the *finale* the B minor – E flat major axis, which operated harmonically in the first movement, now operates melodically: the vertical structure has been converted into the horizontal; the warp and woof has been unwound into a single strand.

Example 11

The first 30 bars of the *finale* consist of nothing but monody –
unharmonised melody, folk-song-like: a very rare thing in
piano music and one demanding eloquence of the performer.
This melody is built on an unusual scale:

> B – C – C sharp – D – E flat –
> E – F sharp – G – A – A sharp (B flat) – B

– another feature which is reminiscent of Busoni's idea of more
than a hundred new scales in his *New Aesthetic* (1906). That long
melody of Shostakovich's is very like a late piano piece of
Musorgky, *In the Village*:

Example 11a

Which brings us back to Asafiev's aesthetic and his conception
of intonation. Glinka, in his memoirs, characterises the minor
plagal cadence (which we hear in the first phrase of the song *The
Volga Boatmen*) as the essence of Russian folksong. Notice how
the first two bars of Example 11 contain this minor plagal
cadence. Now what Shostakovich does is not merely to
harmonise the cadence (in many inventive different ways) but
also to vary the cadence E minor/B minor to E flat minor/B
minor, so that the onmarch of the E flat tonality from the first
movement has eventually produced a deeper significance in the
final cadence of the whole work.

Example 12

Between 1944 and 1945 Shostakovich composed a *Children's Notebook op. 69* for piano (the British edition is entitled *Six Children's Pieces*). This *Notebook* was written for the composer's daughter Galya. It comprises six miniatures: March, Waltz, The Bear, Funny Story, Sad Story, Clockwork Doll. From 1952–62 he added another children's piano album to the *Notebook*, a set of six slightly longer pieces, *Dances of the Dolls*: Lyric-Waltz, Gavotte, Romance, Polka, Waltz-Joke, Hurdy-gurdy and Dance. Both these albums belong to the fine Soviet tradition of celebrated composers writing original piano music for children. Prokofiev, Khachaturian and Sviridov have contributed admirable examples, though Kabalevsky is the most voluminous Soviet composer of children's music; having especially identified himself with the 'music for youth' movement in the USSR. (A further Shostakovich album for amateur pianists was published by the Soviet Composer Publishing House, Moscow in 1967, consisting of arrangements of excerpts from the symphonies, the chamber music and the stage and film works.)

In 1953 Shostakovich wrote another work in which he further identified himself with the educational work of Kabalevsky: this was the Concertino for two pianos, op. 94. It belongs to the genre of 'youth concerto' associated with Kabalevsky: that is, a short concerto work of somewhat less-than-virtuoso difficulty and not posing too profound problems of interpretation, such as only maturity can solve; in short, a work which gives fairly advanced students material adapted to their abilities and mirroring the relish for life that should be natural to young people. The Shostakovich Concertino was written for the composer's son Maxim the well-known young conductor, whose instrument was the piano. The form of the piece is interesting, as it is what might be termed a double rondo. The introductory chorale-like *adagio* (which in type is reminiscent of the dialogue in the slow movement of Beethoven's 4th Piano Concerto) is one rondo theme, which makes three appearances: at the beginning, in the middle and just before the brief *allegro* coda. But between these three statements, another structure, an *allegretto* is developed in rondo-sonata form, with a dance-like subject contrasted with a march-like theme and some episodic passage-work *en route*. Shostakovich's *2nd Piano Concerto op. 102* (originally published as op. 101) is also really a Concertino. It too was written for his son Maxim, and continues Busoni's idea of a new classicality. Another smaller work in a similar vein is Shostakovich's *Tarantella* for two pianos, arranged from the music he wrote for the film *The Gadfly* (1955). This *Tarantella* is a neo-Rossinian *jeu d'esprit* that winks at the spirit of Offenbach. Absolutely nothing for musicological analysis! – Simply music for enjoyment. (Both the *Concertino* and *Tarantella* are published in the West in the 'Sowjetische Musik' series, Edition Sikorski, Hamburg.)

I have left till last Shostakovich's 24 *Preludes and Fugues* op. 87 (1951). Rabinovich's conjecture – that 'Shostakovich is probably the only composer since Bach who has dared attempt a repetition of that composer's great feat' – is incorrect. Bach's contemporary Bernhardt Christian Weber (organist at Tennstedt, Thuringia, in the early eighteenth century) also wrote a set of preludes and fuges in all major and minor keys, actually bearing the same title as Bach's – *Das Wohltemperierte Klavier*; a manuscript copy of which, held in the library of the Brussels Conservatoire, is dated 1689 (four years after Bach's birth!) – though this is probably an error and it almost certainly post-dates Bach's first volume. Another work descending from the 'Forty-Eight' is the set of *36 Fugues* by the Czech-born composer Antonín Rejcha, published in Vienna in 1805 and dedicated to Haydn: works of astonishing invention and daring, exploring all manner of rhythmic, melodic, harmonic and contrapuntal irregularities, some derived from folk-music and anticipatory of Bartók.

There are two other twentieth-century works to which Shostakovich's op. 87 relates: Hindemith's *Ludus Tonalis* (1942) for piano, which contains twelve fugues in as many keys, joined by interludes and framed by a prelude and postlude; and the

other work is Busoni's *Fantasia Contrappuntistica* (1910) which
embodies a visionary completion of the unfinished fugue in
Bach's *Art of Fugue*.

Shostakovich, like Rejcha and Hindemith, allows his fugal
answers to be at any interval from the subject. Where
Shostakovich models himself too closely on Bach, as in the C
sharp minor Prelude, his work suffers from comparison; but
where he is himself, as in, for instance, the G sharp minor
Prelude (in passacaglia form) and Fugue, he has writtten some
of his noblest music. It is certainly fugal writing which far
outsoars the fine piano fugues written by other Soviet composers such as Belorusets, Bunin, Dovchenko, Osokin and Sviridov. Irwin Freundlich, who has edited the op. 87, comments
pertinently in his preface to the collection (Boosey/Leeds/
Sikorski – London, New York, Hamburg) about no. 15 in D flat
major. To paraphrase and abridge his comments: the Prelude
(a symphonic scherzo) ends in a 'tussle to reaffirm the tonality'.
The Fugue picks up this idea: its subject comprises eleven
different notes. The missing twelfth of the note-row only
appears at the end, when there is another argument between a
straight-forward perfect cadence and the note-row; decisive
tonality putting the entire 12-note row to rout with a resounding dominant-to-tonic. Tonality triumphs!

In the preface to his edition of the second part of Bach's
Well-tempered Clavier (Breitkopf), Busoni indicates some ways in
which fugue form may evolve. One way would be for it to
become absorbed imperceptibly into other forms, 'dissolving
instead of consolidating'. That is an accurate prophecy of what
happens in Shostakovich's A major Prelude and Fugue, in
which the traditional roles are reversed: that is, the Prelude's
subject belongs to the traditional fugal type and is even
answered fugally, yet the Fugue is made entirely out of
arpeggios, which are traditionally preludial.

Busoni sums up the symbolism of fugal law in the axiom:
'harmony in combat – equal rights accorded to all voices united
in a fundamental idea.' That last phrase about music might
stand, word for word, as a *credo* of socialism. It is fitting that the
greatest composer so far produced by the Soviet Union should
have written his most considerable body of piano works in this
polyphonic form.

Geoffrey Norris

The Operas

It is a striking paradox that during the 1920s, when the Soviet theatre was reaping benefits from the richly inventive talents of such directors as Tairov, Vakhtangov and, above all, Meyerhold, so few new works of enduring importance should have been written for it. Just as the straight theatre continued to draw its repertory from Gogol, Chekhov, Turgenev and other Russian and Western classics, so the music theatre relied, in the main, on the works of Glinka, Rimsky-Korsakov, Tchaikovsky and Musorgsky and the staple operas of Western composers. These were exciting years of artistic experiment in the young Soviet state; yet this very striving for new modes of expression raised problems, particularly in the opera theatre, that for years were to prove virtually insoluble. Suitable subjects for libretti questions of musical style, the very conventions of opera – all aroused such doubt and discussion in Russian musical circles that few composers felt inclined (or able) to embark on such a large-scale, risky undertaking as a new opera that might be compatible with the prevailing revolutionary mood.

Nevertheless, around the mid-1920s there were some attempts at original creative work in the Russian music theatre. The fact that the results were largely ephemeral should not discourage us from examining them briefly, for they are revealing signs of the times and provide a useful background against which to study Shostakovich's operas. As in other areas of early Soviet music, opera falls into two principal categories: the fiercely 'proletarian', stylistically traditional kind favoured by the Russian Association of Proletarian Musicians [RAPM], and the more forward-looking works promoted by the Association for Contemporary Music [ASM]. To the former can be attributed such musical 'spectacles' as *Dvadtsat' pyatoye* [*The 25th*], a dramatization of Mayakovsky's epic poem about the Civil War, *Khorosho: oktyabr'skaya poema* [*Fine: an October Poem*] (1927). Staged in 1927 at the Maly Theatre, Leningrad, *The 25th* called for actors to recite the lines of Kerensky, Kuskova, Milyukov and other figures in the Provisional Government, and combined elements of pantomime with episodes of choral singing and speaking; the musical score, subordinate to the verse and the action, was by the now totally forgotten Strassenburg. In the same year the former Mariinsky Theatre celebrated the tenth anniversary of the October Revolution with another Civil War spectacle entitled *Shturma Perekopa* [*The Storming of Perekop*], this time with incidental music by a composer who did stand the test of time, Shaporin; and in Moscow, at the Bolshoi, the anniversary was marked by an allegorical entertainment with music by Nebolsin, *Geroicheskoye deistvo* [*Heroic Act*], in which Capitalism was personified as

a monstrous blood-sucking creature. Repulsive, vast and bloated, Capitalism holds mankind enslaved in its gigantic, blood-stained, sharp-clawed clutches. . . The workers cast off their fetters. The victorious red banners furl upwards. A colossal hammer descends from above. . . A few mighty blows, and the head of the vile creature is split open, the claws relax, the creature crashes down into the abyss. A tremendous victory hymn to mankind is heard . . . a group of leaders stands above the remains of the conquered monster.[1]

Revolutionary zeal can also be blamed for the extraordinary notion that 19th-century classical operas could be rendered more significant to the masses if they were furnished with new librettos and titles. *Tosca* was remodelled (and performed in 1924) as *V bor'be za Kommunu* [*The Struggle for the Commune*], with a libretto by Spassky and Vinogradov that shifted the action from Rome to the Paris of 1871. All the names of the characters were changed, as were certain elements which did not conform with Soviet ideology: for example, the Madonna being painted by Angelotti (here called Arlain) became in this new version a fresco glorifying the Commune and the international Red Army. Happily, though, this essay in mutilation failed to endear itself even to the proletarian audiences for which it was intended; and Lunacharsky summed up his own reactions to it in a pun, remarking that *Tosca* had been transformed into *toská*, the Russian word for boredom.

Similarly naïve attempts at topicality were inflicted on Glinka's *Ivan Susanin*, which became *Serp i molot* [*Hammer and Sickle*], and on Meyerbeer's *Les Huguenots* (*Dekabristy* [*The Decembrists*]). But of much greater significance to the development of Soviet opera, at least in the short term, were the performances, sponsored by the ASM, of works by contemporary Western composers. Berg's *Wozzeck*, first performed in Berlin in 1925, was given in Leningrad less than two years later; Křenek's *Der Sprung über den Schatten* (Frankfurt 1924) was staged in Leningrad in 1927 and his *Johnny spielt auf* (Leipzig 1927) was given in Leningrad in 1928 and Moscow in 1929. And the 1920s also saw the Russian premières of Schreker's *Der ferne Klang* (1925) and Prokofiev's *Lyubov' k tryom apel'sinam* [*The Love for Three Oranges*] (1926). Boris Asafiev, the leading spokesman of the ASM, never doubted the value of such performances:

> Acquaintance with the best examples of contemporary Western music will help the development of Soviet music, will free it from amateurishness and profiteering on 'revolutionism', and will lead to the invention of new forms and means of artistic musical expression; by showing the masses the musical art of the West we will provide criteria for the evaluation of the works of Soviet musical creativity.[2]

The implications of this statement are clear. Asafiev saw no future in the narrow application of socialist ideals to opera, the self-conscious effort to appeal to the lowest common denominator of society. He was urging Russian composers to widen their stylistic horizons, to free themselves from the dull conservatism that had dogged so much early Soviet music for the stage; and he was encouraging them to look further afield for libretti than in those tales of war and revolution that had constituted operas like Pashchenko's *Orlinyi bunt* [*The Eagles' Revolt*, 1925], based on the Pugachov uprising of the 1770s, Zolotaryov's *Dekabristy* [*The Decembrists*, 1925], dealing with the 1825 rebellion, and Gladkovsky's and Prussak's *Za krasnyi Petrograd* [*For Red Petrograd*, 1925], the first opera on a specifically Soviet theme (the defence of Petrograd against the White Guard in 1919). In 1930 Asafiev's hopes for something genuinely new on the Russian opera stage were realized in three works: Deshevov's *Lyod i stal'* [*Ice and Steel*], Knipper's *Severnyi veter* [*The North Wind*] and Shostakovich's *Nos* [*The Nose*]. All three took bold steps forward in musical language; and, although both *Ice and Steel* and *The North Wind* were still based on revolutionary, patriotic subjects, the libretto of *The Nose* broke with tradition entirely.

The Nose could well have shared the fate of obscurity that overtook both *Ice and Steel* and *The North Wind* had not the score contained so many manifestations of an extraordinarily potent creative gift that immediately put it on a higher plane than anything else being composed in Russia at the time, and rendered it ultimately resilient to the fluctuations in Soviet attitudes to music. The early reactions, however, were not wholly promising. Just as *Ice and Steel* was described as 'dramaturgically meagre and grey'[3] and *The North Wind* has been scorned[4] for its failure to match in the music the heroic theme of the libretto (the execution of commissars in Baku during the Civil War), so *The Nose* prompted the journal *Proletarskii muzykant* [*The Proletarian Musician*] to show Shostakovich, even before the opera's première, 'the error of his ways' and to warn him that his work was progressing 'up a blind alley'.[5] After the première Semyon Kukurichkin, writing under his pseudonym A. Gres, described *The Nose* – in an article entitled 'Ruchnaya bomba anarkhista' [An anarchist's hand-grenade] – as a 'destructive phenomenon', a 'talented row', and accused the opera of 'spreading panic across the whole front of the music theatre establishment'.[6] But Ivan Sollertinsky, the critic and a close friend of Shostakovich, expressed a more positive point of view. Shostakovich, he wrote,

has finished with the old form of opera . . . he has shown opera composers the need for creating a new musical language, instead of drawing on the clichés of those imitators of Tchaikovsky and Korsakov . . . he has offered the most interesting musical experiments, based on rhythm and timbre alone . . . he is perhaps the first among Russian opera composers to make his heroes speak not in conventional arias and cantilenas but in living language, setting everyday speech to music. . . The opera theatre is at the crossroads. The birth of Soviet opera is not far off. . .[7]

Sollertinsky was quite right that Soviet opera was at the crossroads, but even he, astute observer though he was, could not have foreseen the turn it was to take with the onset of socialist realism a few years later. Russia would never again see anything like *The Nose*. Nor was it to to see *The Nose* for very much longer: after the première on 18 January 1930 at the Maly Theatre, Leningrad, it survived thirteen more performances that season and two more in 1931. It then dropped from the repertory, and remained neglected, as 'an example of extreme "leftist" formalistic experimentalism',[8] for some forty years, until its revival in 1974 at the Moscow Chamber Music Theatre.

One of the factors contributing to the early demise of *The Nose* was its caustic satire, a trait that permeates much Russian art of the 1920s but which came to be frowned upon as stricter ideological control was applied to the arts in the early 1930s. It was this satirical element, in fact, that drew Shostakovich to the story in the first place:

Since I believed that at the time [1927] an opera on a classical subject would be most topical if that subject had a satirical character, I began to look for a subject among the three 'whales' of Russian satire – Gogol, Saltykov-Shchedrin and Chekhov. In the end I settled on Gogol's *The Nose*.[9]

Shostakovich went on to explain why he had chosen *The Nose* rather than any other of Gogol's works:

One has only to read this story to see that *The Nose*, as a satire on the reign of Nicholas I, is more powerful than any of Gogol's other stories. Secondly, it seemed to me that, not being a professional literary man myself, I could recast the story as an opera more easily than *Dead Souls*. Thirdly, the colourful language of the text of *The Nose*, more expressive than Gogol's other 'St Petersburg Tales', presented more interesting problems of 'musicalizing' the text. Fourthly, it offers many interesting theatrical possibilities.[10]

In preparing the libretto Shostakovich enlisted the help of
Georgy Ionin and A[lexander] Preys; he also approached
Yevgeny Zamyatin, one of the best known satirists of the day
and author of the influential novel *My* [*We*] (1920), but it seems
that he acted primarily in an advisory capacity. The libretto
was devised 'on the principle of a literary montage'.[11] Although
it follows the general sequence of events in the Gogol and
preserves much of Gogol's dialogue, Shostakovich found that
there was occasionally not enough text and that scenes were too
short. 'But I decided', he said, 'not to rework his text. Wherever
words were required that were not in the story, I took text from
other works.'[12] Thus, the opera also contains phrases from
Starosvetskiye pomeshchiki [*Old World Landowners*], *Maiskaya noch'*
[*May Night*], *Taras Bul'ba* and *Povest' o tom, kak possorilsya Ivan
Ivanovich s Ivanom Nikiforovichem* [*The Tale of How Ivan Ivanovich
Quarrelled with Ivan Nikiforovich*], as well as Smerdyakov's song
from Dostoyevsky's *Brat'ya Karamazovy* [*The Brothers Karamazov*]
(book 1, part 5, chapter 2), which occurs at the beginning of
scene 6 of the opera.

Shostakovich has also noted two particular deviations from
the Gogol story. First, he added a scene (scene 7) about the
pursuit of the Nose on the outskirts of St Petersburg and its
attempts to board a stage coach. In the Gogol this episode is
merely reported by the policeman who finally apprehends the
Nose: 'We caught it just as it was about to drive off in the Riga
stage coach'. Secondly, Shostakovich moved Gogol's scene in
the Gostinyi Dvor, the St Petersburg shopping arcade (scene 4
in the opera), to the Kazan Cathedral, a couple of hundred
yards further down the Nevsky Prospekt. Gogol's scene, too,
had originally been set in the Cathedral; but when he submitted
the story to the editorial board of the *Moskovskii nablyudatel'*
[The Moscow Observer] in 1835, the censors objected to the
blasphemy of having a comic scene in a cathedral, and Gogol
was obliged to move it to a secular venue.

On one level, of course, the story can be seen simply as a
scintillating piece of whimsy: a minor civil official, Platon
Kovalyov, loses his nose, which turns up in a breakfast roll
being eaten by the barber Ivan Yakovlevich, and thereafter
takes on a life of its own. The newspapers refuse to carry
Kovalyov's advertisement for the Nose's return ('A paper can

get a bad name. If everyone started announcing his nose had run away, I don't know how it would all end. And enough false reports and rumours get past editorial already. . .'). Sightings of the Nose are reported all over St Petersburg, and people come from far and wide to catch a glimpse of it. But eventually it is caught and restored to its owner, who can then appear, without fear of ridicule, on his habitual walks down the Nevsky Prospekt. The fantasy of the story, however, barely conceals the elements of sharp satire that lie just below the surface: the press, the medical profession, the police, the Church, the civil service, the pomposity of petty officials – none of them comes out of it unscathed. (The additional sexual implications of Gogol's story need not concern us unduly here, though they are plain enough to see.) Drawing on those reserves of wry wit with which to a lesser (rarely to a greater) degree he endowed other works, Shostakovich brilliantly translated Gogol's ideas into musical terms, producing an opera that is compact in its design, sharp-edged in its humour, and bubbling with irrepressible energy. And although the story is set in the time of Nicholas I, the opera, in turn, was a no less pungent comment on the Russia of the 1920s.

The comedy is not overstated in the music. Indeed, Shostakovich found it unnecessary 'to reinforce Gogol's satirical story with tinges of "irony" or "parody" in the the music'.[13] Rather, he allowed the pace and character of the text to dictate the pace and character of the vocal line, adapting to his own modernist, experimental idiom of the moment those principles of musical realism, of recitative closely allied to verbal inflection, that had been a familiar facet of Russian opera (particularly Musorgsky's) ever since Dargomyzhsky had first mooted the idea in the 1860s with his *Kamennyi gost'* [*The Stone Guest*]. Shostakovich's recitative in *The Nose*, animated, nervy and 'brilliantly eccentric', as the composer Sergey Slonimsky has described it,[14] is backed by harsh dissonant harmony and spiky rhythms of unerring drive and vitality, and is matched by a no less eccentric use of the orchestra, with a notable predilection for weird instrumental combinations, the juxtaposition of isolated solo sounds at the extremes of instrumental registers (as in the Introduction) and a complexity of orchestral timbre (at its most exposed in the elaborate percussion interlude that separates scenes 2 and 3). Occasionally, too, the orchestra is used to deliberate pictorial effect to underline the grotesquerie of the story, as for example in the giant sneeze that opens the opera and in the rude orchestral gruntings that accompany Koval-yov's Bedroom Scene (scene 3).

If we compare *The Nose* with, say, the First Symphony (1924–5), it seems astonishing that in so short a time Shostako-vich's style should have moved on to so unconventional a plane; yet he had begun exploring the possibilities of original orchestral sonorities in the Second Symphony (1927), and both the First Piano Sonata (1926) and the *Aphorisms* (1927) reveal his interest in music based not on melody but on rhythm and close motivic argument. But his treatment of the voice in *The Nose* has no precedent in his earlier music. The vocal lines throughout *The Nose* are uncompromisingly difficult in their rhythmic instabil-ity, the wide spacing of (often) awkward intervals, and in the extremely complex manner in which parts are combined. Shostakovich's intention, however, was that the music should complement the text, not dominate it; and where he does allow the music to obscure the words – as in the roles of Praskovya Osipovna and the Policeman – it is generally for some theatrical effect. These two roles, short though they are, are good examples of Shostakovich's fine etching of character: Pras-kovya Osipovna the irritable and irritating wife, conveyed in just a few pages of the virtuoso nagging; the Policeman (significantly a *kvartal'nyi* – a non-commissioned officer) the absurdly officious official, vividly brought to life in his high-lying, screeching tenor line (up to E flat above top C) and resolute, arrogant music. The eponymous Nose itself, another tenor role, remains largely aloof from the drama, detached in every sense, and, aside from displaying a certain slyness and a gift for disguise, acts chiefly as a catalyst in the events surrounding Kovalyov, who is the central character. In the opera he has all the ridiculous pomposity of the Gogol original, coupled with a tongue-in-cheek sympathy for his plight, as in Example 1 where the recitative relaxes momentarily for Kovalyov's expression of regret that, without a nose, he can no longer visit his smart friends Madame Chekhtaryova and Madame Podtochina (and the latter's pretty daughter).

These neat and witty character studies are enhanced by being set in a taut operatic framework, in which Shostakovich

Example 1

KOVALYOV: On Thursdays I visit Madame Chekhtaryova, the wife of a
state councillor; and then there's Madame Podtochina,
Pelageya Grigoryevna, the general's wife—she has a
very pretty daughter.

preserves a skilful balance between scenes of comparative inactivity and few characters (the slow-moving scene in Kazan Cathedral; the letter-reading portion of scene 8) and busy crowd scenes, like the one in the newspaper office and the scene outside St Petersburg, with its masterly sense of cumulative chaos. The complexities of scenes like these clearly presented problems that the 1930s performances could not readily overcome: as one of the singers at the première records, 'It was difficult to present [the opera] in such a way that something useful and interesting might come out of our efforts'.[15] Yet subsequent performances – notably the 1974 Moscow revival and, more recently, performances in London (1979) conducted by Maxim Shostakovich – have shown that the opera can work to brilliant effect on stage, and that Shostakovich has a sure feel for the theatre that marked him for prominence as an opera composer. It is scarcely surprising, therefore, that within a few months of the première of *The Nose* he was having thoughts on a new opera project, *Ledi Makbet Mtsenskogo uyezda* [*Lady Macbeth of the Mtsensk District*].

But it is convenient at this stage to pause briefly to consider one of Shostakovich's uncompleted operas, *Igroki* [*The Gamblers*], because it has points of contact both with *The Nose* and with *Lady Macbeth*. He worked on *The Gamblers* in 1942, deciding to set Gogol's play (1836–42) word-for-word rather than devise a fresh libretto. Other Russian composers had had similar ideas in the past: Pushkin's 'little tragedies' had been set by Dargomyzhsky (*Kamennyi gost'* [*The Stone Guest*]), Rimsky-Korsakov (*Mozart and Salieri*), Cui (*Pir vo vremya chumy* [*A Feast in Time of Plague*]) and Rakhmaninov (*Skupoi rytsar'* [*The Miserly Knight*]); and Gogol's *Zhenit'ba* [*The Marriage*] had been attempted by Musorgsky. But just as Musorgsky left *The Marriage* incomplete, so did Shostakovich *The Gamblers*. There are two possible reasons. First, he had completed eight scenes and had written about one hour's music; but there were still another seventeen scenes to go, and the opera could clearly have grown to unwieldy proportions. Secondly there was the question of subject matter. Russia was in the midst of the Second World War, and was looking to its composers for heroic, uplifting music of the kind that Shostakovich had already offered in his Seventh Symphony, that Miaskovsky had provided in his series of war symphonies and that Prokofiev, later, was to write in his Fifth Symphony. Gogol's story of Ikharyov and the machinations of his fellow card-sharpers could have held little relevance for battle-scarred Russia, and the opera could barely have hoped for a performance in such difficult times. Whatever the reasons, Shostakovich abandoned *The Gamblers* at the end of scene 8. He seems to have played through a few extracts in private,[16] but the extant music was not heard in full until Gennady Rozhdestvensky gave a concert performance of it in Leningrad on 18 September 1978, with the Leningrad Philharmonic Orchestra and artists from the Moscow Chamber Music Theatre.

The Gamblers is related to *The Nose* both in its comic (or tragi-comic) subject and in the recitative-style of the vocal writing. But in the latter there are essential differences as well, for, in contrast to the often phrenetic, breathless recitative of *The Nose*, that in *The Gamblers* is more relaxed, more broadly conceived in almost melodic lines, more in the manner of Musorgsky's 'melodic recitative'. In *The Gamblers* there are more concessions to lyricism than in *The Nose*, more pauses for reflection on the subtle nuances of Gogol's text. And, although due weight is given to the comic episodes (notably in the delightful parody of *recitativo accompagnato* as the gamblers drool over their food in scene 8), the generally sombre mood contrasts sharply with the persistent high spirits of *The Nose*. This is due in part to the smoother, less fragmented musical material, in part to the orchestration, richer and more euphoniously combined than in the more sparsely textured, more soloistic scoring of *The Nose*.

These darker strains also run through *Lady Macbeth of the Mtsensk District*, the four-act opera that occupied Shostakovich from October 1930 to December 1932. He planned it as the first part of a trilogy of operas 'dealing with the position of women at different times in Russia',[17] and took as his theme the tragic demise of a woman desperate to find true love and happiness but stifled by the corrupt life of the 19th-century Russian provinces. Collaborating once more with A. Preys, he took as the source for the libretto a highly coloured novella (1865) by Nikolai Leskov. The reference to Shakespeare's heroine in the story's title is explained in the very first paragraph:

> Occasionally in our area you come across characters, some of whom you can never recall without a mental shudder, even though many years may have passed since you met them. Among these characters is the merchant's wife Katerina Lvovna Izmailova, who once played a part in such a terrible drama that the men in our area began to call her the Lady Macbeth of the Mtsensk District.

In Leskov's story, Katerina is seen as the prime culprit in this 'terrible drama'; she rarely engages sympathy for the crimes she commits. But Shostakovich's view of his heroine was rather different:

> [Leskov] finds no grounds either for moral or for psychological justification. I interpreted Katerina Izmailova as a vigorous, talented, beautiful woman, who perishes in the dismal, cruel domestic environment of the Russia of merchants and serfs. In the Leskov this woman is a murderer who destroys her husband, her father-in-law and her husband's young nephew. Moreover, the last murder appears especially malicious and unjustified, since it is dictated exclusively by self-interest, the desire to get rid of the chief claimant to her husband's inheritance. . . I interpret Katerina Izmailova as having a complex, integral, tragic nature. She is an affectionate woman, a deeply sensitive woman, by no means lacking in feeling.[18]

With these fundamental discrepancies between Leskov's view

of Katerina and Shostakovich's, there were clearly a number of changes to be made in the fashioning of the libretto. Although the opera follows the story quite closely, and there are substantial passages in the opera that were lifted straight from Leskov, there are significant differences, which are most easily explained by looking at the opera plot and then considering certain aspects of it in detail.

The opera is set in the Mtsensk district, in provincial Russia. Katerina Izmailova, married to a wealthy but ineffectual merchant, is bored with her stultifying life, and while her husband is away on business she takes up with a strong, handsome young worker on the estate, Sergey. In Act 2 Katerina's father-in-law Boris (himself planning to seduce her) discovers she is having an affair with Sergey and has him flogged. Worn out by this strenuous activity, Boris becomes hungry and demands that Katerina prepare supper; this she does, sprinkling rat-poison on to some mushrooms, which Boris eats. He dies. Later, while Sergey and Katerina are in her bedroom, her husband returns; Sergey kills him, and they hide the body in the cellar. In Act 3 the body is discovered by a drunken peasant during the celebrations of Sergey's and Katerina's wedding; the police are called and the couple are arrested. The final act is set on the road to prison in Siberia. Sergey, ever the opportunist, turns his attentions from Katerina to Sonetka, a young and alluring convict. Katerina, realizing that Sergey had been using her merely to gain power and wealth for himself, drowns herself, dragging Sonetka with her.

It is in the murder of the father-in-law, Boris, that we notice the first deviation from Leskov. In the story the motive for his murder is Katerina's disgust at his cruelty, particularly in having Sergey so savagely beaten. In the opera the murder is further justified because the audience (though not Katerina) is made aware of his lecherous intentions; in the original Leskov there is not a hint of his plan to seduce her. There are one or two other shifts of emphasis and blame. In the story it is Katerina who murders her husband by strangling him and then hitting him over the head with a cast-iron candlestick; in the opera the murder is committed by Sergey, and under provocation from the husband. Also in the story Katerina commits a further murder, that of her nephew, the co-heir of her husband's estate, by suffocating him with a pillow; the local villagers see her do it, and report the crime to the police. This murder has no place in the opera, and Shostakovich invents the scene of the discovery of the body in the cellar to bring about her arrest and downfall.

Having established by means of these twists to Leskov's story his more sympathetic view of Katerina's nature and a justification for the one murder she herself commits in the opera (that of the father-in-law), Shostakovich proceeds to underline it in her music. Of all the characters in the opera, Katerina is the only one to display genuine human emotions – emotions of exasperation, affection, passion, anguish and, at the end, abject despair – as opposed to the false or grotesquely caricatured emotions of the other characters. There is in her music alone a sincerity, a nobility, which Shostakovich achieves through the intense lyricism of her vocal line, whether in the cry of exasperation in the opening pages of the opera, her passionate entreaties to Sergey in scene 5, her dreams of happiness and her yearnings for sexual fulfilment in scene 3, or the pathetic, falling lines of her lament in the final scene, heightened by the simplicity of the accompaniment on the cor anglais (Example 2). One Soviet commentator has singled out the aria in scene 3 as 'one of the finest pages of the opera [because] it subtly resurrects the Russian popular song of the 19th century'.[19] Yet it seems to me that the impact of such passages lies not in the fact that they evoke the 19th-century *romans* but in that their very substance, their highly charged lyricism, contrast so sharply with the other music in the opera. When lyrical music is allotted

Example 2

KATERINA: It is hard, after such honour and respect, to stand before a judge.
It is hard, after endearments and caresses, to feel the lash on your back.

to other characters, it is tinged with insincerity. Take, for example, the scene where Katerina's husband – a 'weak-willed degenerate', as Shostakovich has described him[20] – is leaving the estate for his business trip. His farewell aria is couched in a sumptuous, extravagantly melodious vein and underpinned with rich, romantic harmonies that could well have found place in a Tchaikovsky opera; but the flow of the melody is crudely interrupted by strident phrases on the trombones and tubas (Example 3). Comparably, Sergey's declarations of love for

Example 3

ZINOVY: Farewell, Katerina! (to his father) Tell her to remain obedient.
BORIS: Swear it!

Katerina in scene 5, ardent enough in melodic outline, are accompanied – and negated, as it were – by brash janglings on the orchestra to suggest the emptiness, the cheapness of his gestures. The music for Boris, on the other hand, never has any pretensions to finer feelings, and throughout he is shown as the 'power-loving despot' whose basic character is one of 'inhuman brutality',[21] and whose terse, plodding vocal line rarely lapses into melody (Example 4).

[Shostakovich described *Lady Macbeth* as a tragic-satirical

Example 4
Largo ♩ = 58

BORIS:
Pri-go-tov ot-ra-vu dlya krys   Op-yat   mu- ku vsyu po-e - li.

bn.

bass cl., bn., contra bn., drum, vcs., db.

p pizz.   etc.

BORIS: Prepare some poison for the rats.
They've eaten all the flour again.

opera, and although he did not intend to imply that the work set
out deliberately to mock or to ridicule there are certain
elements of humour to relieve the darkness of the drama: the
jovial priest in scene 4, for example, or the (rather laboured)
scene in the police station (scene 7), redolent, as Olin Downes
remarked in his review of the New York première,[22] of the
Keystone Kops. Shostakovich's chief aim, however, was to
write an opera that was a 'revealing satire, a stripping away of
masks'.[23] He sought to portray on stage, in a manner not seen
either before or since in the Soviet opera theatre, the depths of
misery that can be inflicted on a human being by the evil and
putridity of society around her. Such a subject, embodying as it
does themes of lust, cruelty, infidelity, betrayal and death,
invites comparison with Berg's *Wozzeck*, which Shostakovich
heard and admired at its Leningrad performances; but the
analogy should not be taken too far. Shostakovich himself
denied that either *Lady Macbeth* or *The Nose* owed anything to
Wozzeck, and the compositional principles of each composer,
and their modes of expression, are patently disparate.

It is, however, instructive to compare *Lady Macbeth* with
Shostakovich's own orchestral music of the period; for, just as
The Nose is very much a stylistic companion piece to the Second
and Third Symphonies, and *The Gamblers* to the Seventh
Symphony, so *Lady Macbeth* is closely related to the Fourth
Symphony in its bold, rhetorical gestures, its powerful blend of
lyricism and dissonance, its close working out of thematic
material, and its mastery of orchestral resources. Indeed, the
orchestra is integral to the opera. No longer is it subordinate to
the text; rather is it on an equal footing, a formidable expressive
force. It is used not only to expose elements of hypocrisy (as in
Sergey's music mentioned above) or to stress, in its sombre
colouring, the weight of the drama, but it also has a decisive role

to play in binding the opera together and driving it inexorably towards the ultimate tragedy. The orchestral entr'actes, far from being mere functional interludes, are inextricably linked, emotionally and thematically, with the scenes they separate; and the magnificent passacaglia entr'acte between scenes 4 and 5, as the full horror of the story starts to unfold, is amongst Shostakovich's finest music of the period, equal in power to anything in the Fourth Symphony.

The tremendous impact of *Lady Macbeth* makes its subsequent history all the more regrettable. It had its première in Leningrad at the Maly Theatre, on 22 January 1934; it was then given in Moscow two days later at the Nemirovich-Danchenko Music Theatre. Abroad it was first given at Cleveland on 31 January 1935 and then in London (in a concert performance at the Queen's Hall) on 18 March 1936. And it was a success. The conductor of the Leningrad première, Samuil Samosud, remarked:

> I declare *Lady Macbeth* a work of genius, and I am convinced that posterity will confirm this estimate. One cannot help feeling proud that, in a Soviet musical theatre, an opera has been created that overshadows all that can possibly be accomplished in the operatic art of the capitalist world. Here, too, our culture has indeed not only overtaken, but surpassed, the most advanced capitalist countries.[24]

Alexander Ostretsov, writing in the official organ of the Composers' Union, *Sovetskaya muzyka*, commented that the opera

> could have been written only by a Soviet composer brought up in the best traditions of Soviet culture and actively fighting by means of his art for the victory of the new social *Weltanschauung*. In its serious artistic worth and high level of musical mastery . . . the opera is the result of the general success of socialist construction, of the correct policy of the Party towards all sections of the country's cultural life, and of the deep significance of that new upwelling of creative strength evoked on the musical front by the historic decree of the Central Committee of the All-Union Communist Party of 23 April 1932.[25]

The decree mentioned by Ostretsov was the one that in 1932 drew together the diverse strands of the RAPM and ASM and

brought all Soviet music under the control of the Composers'
Union and so, in effect, of the Communist Party. As Sir Isaiah
Berlin has said, this signified that there was to be 'no more
argument; no more disturbance of men's minds. A dead level of
state-controlled orthodoxy followed'.[26] Soviet composers were
now directed towards that elusive goal of socialist realism; and
the Soviet critical acclaim of *Lady Macbeth* in 1934 indicated
that, for the time being at any rate, the opera had scored a
resounding success.

But things were soon to change. In January 1936 Stalin
attended a performance of the opera, and was offended by its
explicit subject and by the modernism of its musical language.
Almost immediately the opera was condemned, in a now
notorious editorial, 'Sumbur vmesto muzyki' [Chaos instead of
Music], in the Party newspaper *Pravda*:

> From the first minute the listener is shocked by a deliberately
> discordant, confused stream of sounds. Fragments of melody,
> embryonic phrases appear, only to disappear again in the din, the
> grinding and the screaming. To follow this 'music' is difficult, to
> remember it impossible. So it goes on almost throughout the opera.
> Cries take the place of song. If by chance the composer lapses into
> simple, comprehensible melody, he is scared at such a misfortune
> and quickly plunges into confusion again... All this is coarse,
> primitive and vulgar. The music quacks, grunts and growls, and
> suffocates itself in order to express the amatory scenes as naturalis-
> tically as possible. And 'love' is smeared all over the opera in this
> vulgar manner. The merchant's double bed occupies the central
> position on the stage. On it all problems are solved.[27]

And in the penultimate paragraph the unnamed critic muses:

> *Lady Macbeth* enjoys great success with audiences abroad. Is it not
> because the opera is absolutely unpolitical and confusing that they
> praise it? Is it not explained by the fact that it tickles the perverted
> tastes of the bourgeoisie with its fidgety, screaming, neurotic
> music?

That we can disregard this entirely politically inspired drivel as
a piece of serious musical criticism is plain. Nevertheless, the
article was to have immediate and far-reaching consequences
for Soviet Russian music. One immediate effect, of course, was
that the opera was withdrawn from the repertory. The

sentiments voiced in *Pravda* were endorsed by discussions between the leading musicians and musicologists in the Moscow and Leningrad branches of the Composers' Union, and their findings were published in *Sovetskaya muzyka* (the issues for March and May 1936).

The effects of the *Lady Macbeth* crisis on Shostakovich himself can best be judged from other chapters in this book, for he never again contemplated an opera on the scale or of the emotional complexity of *Lady Macbeth*. Although he looked to subjects like Chekhov's *Chornyi monakh* [*The Black Monk*] for inspiration, and actually completed, as we have seen, eight scenes of *The Gamblers*, all his future ideas for operas remained unfulfilled, save for the little operetta *Moscow-Cheryomushki* that he wrote in 1958.

To Soviet opera in general, *Pravda* gave a clear indication that *Lady Macbeth* was decidedly not now a work that should be imitated. Rather, the key to socialist realism lay in another opera which, simultaneously with the condemnation of *Lady Macbeth*, was being officially acclaimed: Ivan Dzerzhinsky's *Tikhii Don* [*The Quiet Don*], based on Sholokhov's epic novel. And this undemanding piece, combining cloying sentimentality, a strain of heroism and a simple, direct musical idiom, was for many years to be the model for the new, preferred genre of Soviet 'song' opera.

Throughout Stalin's lifetime *Lady Macbeth* remained a proscribed work. However, with the death of Stalin in 1953 and the consequent thawing of the cultural climate, a revival became more possible; and the opera was given a second première at the Stanislavsky-Nemirovich-Danchenko Music Theatre, Moscow, on 26 December 1962 (the official date is given as 8 January 1963), under its original sub-title *Katerina Izmailova*. It is appropriate to call this a second première, for Shostakovich had made a great many changes to the opera, sufficient at least for him to give the revision a new opus number establishing it firmly as a work of the 1950s. Musically the second version differs little from the first. In some places Shostakovich rewrote Katerina's lines, primarily to reduce the range. He also rewrote and lengthened the entr'actes between the first and second and seventh and eighth scenes, and cut the suggestive trombone glissandi at the climax of Sergey's seduction of Katerina.

The chief alterations, however, affected the text, which Shostakovich toned down in places to give less cause for offence (for although the artistic climate was less cool than in Stalin's day, there was still a Victorian coyness about what could and could not be portrayed on stage). Thus, Katerina's sexual yearnings in scene 3 are reduced to wistful reflections on the birds and bees. The language of the Bedroom Scene is similarly diluted: whereas Katerina originally murmured to Sergey 'Kiss me so that my lips may smart from your kiss, that the blood may rush to my head, that the ikons may fall from the ikon case', she now sings 'Ah my love, as you lay there with [Boris] taunting you [after the flogging], all the blood rushed to my head and I nearly died at the sight of your suffering'. Similarly, at the beginning of scene 2, where workmen are abusing the maid Axinya, 'breasts' (or rather the more colloquial expression implicit in the Russian word *vymya*) becomes 'shoulders', 'Come on, feel her' becomes 'Good old Axinya', and so on. None of these changes strikes at the roots of the opera, but they do have the effect of draining some of its sap. The original *Lady Macbeth*, by contrast, is an opera of raw emotions, and earns its place in any discussion of Shostakovich's music not simply because of the scandal that surrounded it in 1936 but also because it is a powerful psychological drama, a potent example of Shostakovich's rare dramatic skill, and a towering monument of the Soviet music theatre.

Notes

1. *Komsomol'skaya pravda* (28 October 1927) and *Rabochaya Moskva* (30 October 1927); quoted in A. Gozenpud: *Russkii sovetskii opernyi teatr 1917–1941* (Leningrad, 1963), p. 148.
2. I. Glebov [B. Asafiev]: 'Muzykal'nyi zapad i my', *Zhizn'iskusstva* (1927), no. 43, p. 1.
3. I. Sollertinsky, in *Rabochii i teatr* (1930), no. 52, p. 8.
4. A. Gozenpud, op. cit., p. 147.
5. '*Nos*: opera D. Shostakovicha', *Proletariskii muzykant* (1929), nos. 7–8, p. 39.
6. A. Gres: 'Ruchnaya bomba anarkhista', *Rabochii i teatr* (1930), no. 10, p. 7.
7. I. Sollertinsky: '*Nos*: orudiye dal'noboinoye', *Rabochii i teatr* (1930), no. 7, p. 7.
8. M. Sabinina: 'Dolgozhdannaya prem'era', *Muzykal'naya zhizn'* (1975), no. 1, p. 4.

9. D. Shostakovich: 'Pered prem'eroi', *Rabochii i teatr* (1930), no. 3, p. 11.

10. ibid.

11. ibid.

12. from a discussion on *The Nose* in Leningrad (14 January 1930); quoted in S. Khentova: *Molodye gody Shostakovicha*, i (Leningrad and Moscow, 1975), p. 215.

13. D. Shostakovich, in *Novyi zritel'* (1928), no. 35; quoted in G. Pribegina, ed.: *D. Shostakovich o vremeni i o sebe 1926–1975* (Moscow, 1980), p. 18.

14. S. Slonimsky: 'Prem'era *Igrokov* D. Shostakovicha', *Sovetskaya muzyka* (1979), no. 1, p. 76.

15. B. Geft: 'Kak ya pel v opere *Nos*', *Smena* (25 September 1966); quoted in S. Khentova: op. cit., p. 219.

16. see S. Khentova: *D. D. Shostakovich v gody Velikoi Otechestvennoi voiny* (Leningrad, 1979), p. 166.

17. D. Shostakovich, in *Sovetskoye iskusstvo* (16 October 1932); quoted in G. Pribegina, ed.: op. cit., p. 31.

18. D. Shostakovich, in *Sovetskoye iskusstvo* (14 December 1933); quoted in G. Pribegina, ed.: op. cit., pp. 35–36.

19. I. Martynov: *Dmitrii Shostakovich* (Moscow and Leningrad, 1946), p. 29.

20. D. Shostakovich, in *Sovetskoye iskusstvo* (14 December 1933); quoted in G. Pribegina, ed.: op. cit., p. 36.

21. ibid.

22. *The New York Times* (6 February 1935).

23. D. Shostakovich, in *Sovetskoye iskusstvo* (16 October 1932); quoted in G. Pribegina, ed.: op. cit., p. 31.

24. quoted by Nicolas Slonimsky, *The Musical Quarterly*, xxviii (1942), and in B. Schwarz: *Music and Musical Life in Soviet Russia 1917–1970* (London, 1972), p. 120.

25. quoted in G. Abraham: *Eight Soviet Composers* (London, 1943), p. 25.

26. I. Berlin: *Personal Impressions* (London, 1980), p. 159.

27. 'Sumbur vmesto muzyki: ob opere *Ledi Makbet Mtsenskogo uyezda*', *Pravda* (28 January 1936), p. 3.

Malcolm MacDonald

Words and Music in Late Shostakovich

> In recent years, I've become convinced
> that the word is more effective than
> music. Unfortunately, it is so. When I
> combine music with words, it becomes
> harder to misinterpret my intent.

Thus Shostakovich (if it is Shostakovich) in the much-disputed
Memoirs.[1] Authentic or not, these words are worth noticing, for
they do point up what feels like an expressive shift in his later
music, where texts – and what music may do in relation to those
texts – become much more important than hitherto. Before
1962, say, he had written a fair amount of vocal music, both for
solo voice and chorus, including several song-cycles that have
remained almost unknown in the West. But almost all these
works lay at the periphery of a creative career that was centred
in the symphonies and major chamber and instrumental works.
(The notable exception was the cycle *From Jewish Folk-Poetry*,
whose large scale and wide-ranging choice of subject-matter in
a sensitive area of the Soviet polity, at a sensitive time – 1948 –
provides a significant pointer to later developments.) After
1962, vocal music came much more to the forefront of
Shostakovich's concerns, with two wholly vocal symphonies
and several major cycles, both with piano and with orchestra.

The change can be precisely located between the Twelfth
Symphony, completed in 1961 and the Thirteenth, begun in the

latter half of 1962. The Twelfth, subtitled *1917*, an evocation of the October Revolution and intended originally as a 'portrait' of Lenin, is for me (and, I believe, many others) the most disappointing of Shostakovich's symphonies. Despite some fine things in the opening Allegro and the very atmospheric little 'Aurora' movement, there is a hollowness about it, especially in the finale, surely one of the most emptily bombastic pieces he ever wrote. 'I wasn't able to realize my ideas, the material put up resistance', says the Memoirs,[2] perhaps significantly. The Thirteenth, on the other hand, for solo bass, male-voice chorus and orchestra, to texts by Yevgeny Yevtushenko, seems to me to be one of his finest and most satisfying works, an original structural conception in music of consistent psychological depth. If the Thirteenth was already taking shape in the composer's mind while he was writing the Twelfth, that might itself have been a contributory factor in the earlier symphony's failure, for No. 13 is the obverse of all that No. 12 claims to stand for. But what had happened between the two symphonies? A glance at the list of Shostakovich's works reveals that the main thing he had done in that intervening period, just before beginning the Thirteenth Symphony, was to orchestrate Musorgsky's *Songs and Dances of Death*.

That is surely suggestive. Even without the chapter devoted to Musorgsky in the Memoirs – a chapter which rings wholly true, and which there could be no obvious reason to fabricate – we can hardly doubt that Shostakovich felt a deep identification with the earlier composer. He had already made his own orchestrations of *Boris Godunov* (in 1939–40) and *Khovanshchina* (in 1959), while Musorgsky's influence can clearly be felt on *Lady Macbeth of Mtsensk* and several of the more 'epic' symphonies, particularly Nos. 7, 8, 10, and 11.[3] Though *Songs and Dances of Death* is in no sense a 'model' for the Thirteenth Symphony – as it surely is, to some extent, for the Fourteenth – the symphony is, in a general sense, an intensely 'Musorgskian' conception, using the combination of words and music to express certain aspects of (recent) Russian history as well as delineating an individual response to them.

It is perhaps no longer necessary – as it was in the first years of the Symphony's existence, when it was known in the West largely through a murky 'pirated' recording – to defend the work from the charge of being 'unsymphonic'. As an organic musico-dramatic design it is far more convincing than the Twelfth, and its tonal structure, which turns on the relations of thirds, both major and minor (B flat minor with a 'secondary' tonality of G minor in the first movement; a move to C in the second, the C becoming subsumed as a degree of the E minor of the central movement, the remotest tonal pole from B flat; the fourth movement underpinned by a pedal G sharp; the finale in B flat major with G major as 'secondary' tonality) is both rich and satisfying. But the true sense of organic life and self-consistency in the work is motivic and colouristic: cross-connections abound, some obvious, some not, and one continues to discover more of them even after knowing the score for years.[4] However, it is not so much the symphonism, but the relationship and dual functions of music and text that I want to touch on, in this and in subsequent vocal works by Shostakovich.

Shostakovich's word-setting, both here and later, rejects mere lyrical appeal: it is austere, usually syllabic, responding to the natural speech-inflexions with repeated notes or conjunct motion – at most slightly widening its range and broadening into *cantabile* phrases for emotional heightening. Certainly it gains thereby a noble simplicity that sometimes brings it close to folksong. But it also limits the role of the vocal lines, enhancing their importance purely as carriers of information, as transmitters of the text: throughout these late vocal works, Shostakovich is at pains to make every word clearly audible, so that the contrast between the restraint of the voice parts and (at first) the prodigality of instrumental invention often clearly implies a counterpoint of ideas. The listener becomes aware of both correspondences and discrepancies.

This is perhaps least true of the starkly impressive first movement, the setting of Yevtushenko's 'Babi Yar'. Maybe the most striking thing here is simply that Shostakovich is, for the first time, using words as an integral part of a weighty symphonic statement (the brief hortatory final choruses of the Second and Third Symphonies are clearly lightweight stuff by comparison); and that they are not comfortable words for any audience. The Babi Yar massacre was a Nazi atrocity, but Yevtushenko's text is even-handed in adducing further

examples of anti-Semitism: in ancient Egypt, in the Cruci-
fixion, Anne Frank, the Dreyfus Case, and a Byelostok pogrom
– this last a specifically Russian instance, which draws from
Shostakovich some of the most brilliantly sinister music in the
score, music whose grotesquely twisted 'folk' idiom is significant, and which leads to a passionate apostrophe to the
Russian people against anti-Semites in their midst. The subsequent revisions to the text of the Symphony have not affected
these important passages.

The second movement, the scherzo, celebrates Humour –
specifically as a political force – in a rumbustious C major.
Yevtushenko's poem incarnates Humour as a subversive
satirist, a 'brave little man' only too likely to find himself under
arrest or even executed 'for political crimes'. Interestingly
enough, Shostakovich bases parts of the movement on music
from a little-known and much earlier song-cycle of his, the *Six
Romances to Verses by English Poets* for voice and piano, op. 62, of
1942. Specifically, the movement draws upon his setting of
Robert Burn's 'Macpherson's Farewell' (in Marshak's Russian
translation, more explicitly titled 'Macpherson before his
execution'):

> Sae rantingly, sae wantonly,
> Sae gauntingly gae'd he;
> He played a spring, an danced it roun'
> Below the gallows-tree.

The combination of jesting and execution must have recommended this song to Shostakovich as worthy of revival when he
came to set Yevtushenko's 'Humour'; he may also have been
reminded of the final lines of Burn's poem, where Macpherson
gives vent to scornful pity for those too afraid to risk death.
There are black and bitter undertones to this movement, then:
but it impresses chiefly by its exuberant invention – the icy
parody of the Eleventh Symphony's 'Palace Square' sonorities
between figures 47 and 50 in the score, the tongue-in-cheek
death-march with its tritone drum-beat as Humour is led off
'for political crimes' – and its defiant optimism, which bursts
into a full-throated 'revolutionary song' at figure 65 when
Humour storms the Winter Palace. There is no devaluation of
the spirit of 1917 here, whatever shadows hindsight may cast on
it.

'At the Store' is in its way a counterpart to 'Babi Yar', for the text again identifies a particular group – in this case, Women – as an exploited section of the community; while the music returns, though in highly metamorphosed and perhaps subliminal forms, to much of the first movement's basic material. The static E tonality, furthest from the scheme of the other movements, seems to reinforce the impression that the women in the store, being short-changed by the shopkeeper, are somehow imprisoned in their dreary existence, which through war and history has been one of endurance and unremitting toil – proof of their 'strength to do anything', and yet they are powerless to avoid being cheated out of their hard-earned money. The return of the grey opening music at the end apparently mirrors the composer's doubt that this state of affairs can ever be changed.

Another link with 'Babi Yar' is the grim little folklike tune which arises as a refrain, three times, to a skeletal accompaniment of pizzicato strings and *secco* piano chords. It is instantly reminiscent – though different in contour – of the motif of the Jew-baiting thugs in Byelostok (cf. Exx. 1*a* and *b*). The text, on 1*b*'s first appearance, says: 'They smell of onions, cucumbers, and "Kabul" sauce' – and we recall the 'stink of vodka and onions' from the Byelostok episode. This is a perplexing

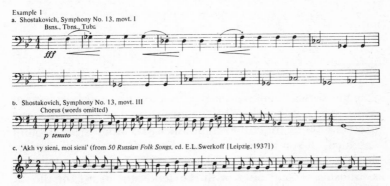

Example 1
a. Shostakovich, Symphony No. 13, movt. I
Bsns., Tbns., Tuba

b. Shostakovich, Symphony No. 13, movt. III
Chorus (words omitted)
p tenuto

c. 'Akh vy sieni, moi sieni' (from *50 Russian Folk Songs*, ed. E.L. Swerkoff [Leipzig, 1937])

parallelism which Shostakovich has created here (for it is his doing, not Yevtushenko's): he can hardly be identifying the downtrodden women with the drunken anti-Semites. But he may be hinting at something that in its way, and to some views of the universe, is equally unpalatable: their common humanity, or at least their common Russian-ness. The women, without ever thinking it, are the backbone of the Russian people; the anti-Semites think that of themselves. Even the possession of a national identity is an area in which human beings can be corrupted: thus the 'vernacular' aspect of both tunes, which belong to a common Russian folksong 'type' – for instance '*Akh vy seni, moi seni*' (Example 1c), used in the fourth Tableau of Stravinsky's *Petrushka*.

'Fears', as we are told, is the only poem which Yevtushenko wrote especially for inclusion in the Symphony: a fact which only increases the question-marks surrounding its uncomfortable resonances. How much, if at all, did Shostakovich indicate to Yevtushenko what kind of text he desired here? – because 'Fears' is in some ways the most subversive poem of the lot, and Shostakovich would surely have been within his rights in declining to set it if he felt it went too far. The opening line, 'Fears are fading in Russia', explicitly confirms their former existence and their lingering power; when the second stanza says 'Today this is passed', the inconsistency is obvious, and Shostakovich points it up with the creepiest music in the entire Symphony, the would-be reassuring vocal line enveloped first by hollow, ghostly fanfares, and then by convulsive, shivering, string tremolos.

Example 2

The memories of the war, when 'we didn't fear to march off in snowstorms, under fire', brings no heroic marching song (the presence of one in 'Humour' points up its absence here) but a subdued, down-at-heel, ironic, Kurt-Weillish tune whose accompaniment – *col legno* strings and *secco* piano chords – establishes a connection with the 'folk' tune in 'At the Store', though the melody itself has little relation, apart from its vernacular directness, with either of the tunes in Example 1. Again, it seems to stand for an aspect – not an ignoble one in this instance – of Russian nationalism; but the fist-clenching declaration which emerges from it (about Russia having conquered her own fears and now striking fears into her enemies) seems unlikely, barely motivated. And then of course there is the ending, in which the poet speaks of his own fear that even now he is not really writing 'with full force': how much is this a personal confession of Yevtushenko's, how much an admonition to the composer? But the sounding-board against which the poem plays its shifts of attitude to the fears of the past, and whether or not they still persist, is the leaden G-sharp pedal which remains immovably throughout much of the movement, even underpinning the war-march section: an oppressive force that shows no inclination to do anything other than go on sitting there.

Yet it does move, eventually, onto B flat; and the little waltz-tune that begins the final movement, 'A Career' – free of all cloying sentiment yet too studiedly sinuous to be merely carefree – constitutes an unexpected, and quite complex, emotional response. It is a *knowing* tune, as revealed by its little chromatic curl of the lip, which harks back to the very opening gesture of 'Babi Yar' (Example 3), yet there seems to be a hint of forgiveness

Example 3
a. 'A Career', opening

b. 'Babi Yar', opening

in its knowledge, an emotional accommodation at least with things as they are. The movement's second main theme, a chortling bassoon refrain (quoted later as part of Example 5, below) seems to be another member of the 'folksy' family of tunes we have identified. It launches the soloist aptly enough on his satirical account – which, especially after the closing line of 'Fears', can hardly lack contemporary significance – of the astronomer of Galileo's time who *also* knew that the Earth revolved round the Sun, but had more sense than to say so – to the great benefit of his career.

One might wonder, at first, whether these two themes are sufficient to bear the weight of a symphonic finale; but Shostakovich has no conventionally triumphant ending in view, and he knows the kinds of greatness his tunes will be able to bear having thrust upon them. The waltz-tune Example 3 turns stealthy and stalking in an episode for pizzicato strings alone, and the movement gains nobility as the chorus sings admiringly of the true 'careers', those of great and unafraid men – Shakespeare, Pasteur, Newton, or Tolstoy. Especially Tolstoy, it seems, as they reiterate the name ('*i Tolstogo*') to a heroic, sweeping phrase. And here Shostakovich does a strange thing. Yevtushenko's text, as originally published,[5] reads at this point *i Tolstogo . . . L'va!'* ('and [of] Tolstoy . . . Lev!'), a necessary qualification in view of the many Tolstoys in Russian literature, but not much more than that. Shostakovich sets '*L'va*' twice – first interrogatively, as a query from the soloist, then as a thunderous affirmative from the chorus; and in this way he introduces, or at least makes an explicit, a shade of meaning not open on the surface of the poem (Lev Tolstoy? – You bet your life Lev Tolstoy, and no other Tolstoy).[6]

At this point, and with the message that 'Genius will conquer regardless of the charges made against it', the trotting, folksy tune that first appeared on bassoon transforms itself into a powerful, determined fugato, precipitating the main climax of the movement and leading the way (restored now to its original faintly comical bassoon – which somehow no longer sounds so comical) to the soloist's Adagio apostrophe of the conquerors of the air and the conquerors of disease. Marked *espressivo, maestoso molto*, it is calm spacious music, moving in its warmth and quiet confidence. The final line ('Therefore, I shall work at my career by endeavouring *not* to work at it') is hardly one to set Red Square ablaze – but it *is* an optimistic sentiment, as the nobility of the setting makes clear; and the coda which ensues is one of Shostakovich's most ravishing inspirations. Solo violin and viola let us hear Example 3 one last time, with great tenderness, harmonized with heart-easing simplicity; the celesta tinkles away with a reminiscence of the fugato; and the Symphony ends with the B-flat bell on which it began. There is no brassy triumph, yet it is one of Shostakovich's most profoundly optimistic endings, profound because it paints no idealized picture, but accepts the life portrayed in Yevtushenko's texts as the way things really are – and realistic acceptance is the necessary preliminary to change.

The year after he composed Symphony No. 13, Shostakovich made an orchestral version of *From Jewish Folk Poetry*, thus bringing it before a wider audience, and perhaps pointing up its significance – with its songs of privation and misery as well as the happier ones about love and life on the collective farms – as a pendant to 'Babi Yar'. Then in the following year, 1964, there appeared his second collaboration with Yevtushenko – *The Execution of Stepan Razin*, a 'poem' (so designated on the title-page) for bass soloist, mixed chorus, and orchestra, op. 119. In comparison to Symphony No. 13, this has received scant critical attention, but it seems to me scarcely less impressive an achievement: his most sheerly dramatic vocal-orchestral conception. If the Memoirs are to be believed, it was originally planned as the first movement of a new symphony, presumably on an even vaster scale than the Thirteenth, but the opposite happened to the genesis of the earlier work: Shostakovich 'came to a halt' at the end of it.[7] One can easily see how this could be so: the mixture of seething fury and contemptuous triumph in which the work ends needs no further development or commentary.

In some ways *Stepan Razin* comes closest of all Shostakovich's music to the Musorgsky of the operas: it is his personal contribution to that tradition of Russian epic theatre – violent, colourful, yet brooding – of which *Boris Godunov* and *Khovanshchina* are the classic examples. A scene from Russian history is brought vividly to life before our ears – the death of the 17th century Cossack who led a rebellion of unpropertied peasants against the Tsar. But the music encompasses and articulates the composer's thoughts about the individual tragedy of the protagonist and the collective tragedy of the people, in that age as in any age; and it is a twentieth-century, not a nineteenth-century, sensibility at work.

The opening section depicts the public holiday and the excitement of the mob at the imminent arrival of Razin, brought in chains to Moscow for his execution. It is breathtaking music, worthy to stand beside any of Musorgsky's crowd-scenes: it has a tigerish energy, superb rhythmic drive, strong and simple material which builds into monumental ostinati and compelling repetitions. The chorus, used with much more colouristic variety than in Symphony No. 13, projects the essence of the drama, climaxing in great shouts set to fierce upward-sweeping glissandi.

After all this turmoil, the noble restraint of Razin's mono-logue, beginning with the soloist's words *On molchal* (he was silent), is all the more impressive. Yevtushenko's self-doubting, self-condemning Razin is very far from the cardboard revolu-tionary saint of conventional Soviet hagiography, and one must speculate again at Shostakovich's choice of text: did the words awake an echo of identification? '*I was a rebel – half-way,/ and should have been – to the end . . .* I am guilty, as a foe of serfdom,/ of being in the least degree a serf./ I am guilty of wanting to fight/ for a good tsar./ *There are no good tsars . . .*' As Razin is led to the place of execution, the opening music comes back, but utterly changed: pianissimo, wonderfully and icily transfigured on muted, much-divided strings, celesta, and bells. From the world of Musorgsky we seem suddenly to be transported into that of Ingmar Bergman: the effect is weird, hallucinatory in its fragile intensity, and prepares the way naturally for the work's central, dreamlike revelation – among the undifferentiated, animalistic 'mugs, snouts, muzzles' of the mob, Razin begins to discern FACES (so capitalized in Yevtushenko's text), indi-vidual human beings to whom his life, and his death, will speak. He knows then that he has not lived in vain. The cryptic, clenched motifs of the work's opening flower here into a tender, lyrical stream of melody.

The ferocious drum-rolls and staccato brass chording of the actual beheading give way to another uncanny inspiration: the crowd is struck dumb, refuses to rejoice to order. A frenetic reedy dance-music strikes up, clarinets and E flat clarinet in raucous unison, *fff*: but it is unable to quicken a response from the rest of the orchestra. The strings, muted, *sempre pp*, divided in nineteen parts, hold a frozen, neutral chord built up of two sets of crushed semitones a fourth apart: simply hold it, unmoving, until the woodwind sputter into silence, and then return to the earlier hallucinatory lyricism, while xylophone chords depict how 'in the deathlike silence/ the fleas jumped over/ from the smocks of the poor/ to the furs of the rich'.

Solemn bells toll for Razin, awesomely scored in deep octave
C-sharps on bass clarinet, double bassoon, timpani, tam-tam,
tubular bell, harps (the score specifies 'not less than two'),[8]
piano, cellos, and pizzicato basses. Compare the Memoirs'
account (p. 181) of how Shostakovich scored the bell-sounds in
the Prologue to *Boris Godunov* – and the accompanying comment
chimes with this passage in *Stepan Razin*: 'When the bell tolls,
it's a reminder that there are powers mightier than man, that
you can't escape the judgement of history'. In the final
moments of Shostakovich's cantata, that judgement is turned
against the Tsar by the eerie laughter of the decapitated head,
which laughs 'brutually, not hiding its triumph'. In Yevtushenko's poem, Razin literally has the last laugh after his
death. Did Shostakovich hope the same for himself, when he
cloaked that grisly triumph in such super-charged music?

Shostakovich's interest in provocative word-setting continued in the succeeding years. The *Five Romances on texts from
'Krokodil' magazine*, op. 121, a cycle for bass and piano, appeared
in 1965. With their gentler, but no less mordant commentary on
the slight imperfections of life as it is lived in contemporary
Russia, they are a kind of lightweight footnote to the Thirteenth
Symphony; and a different sort of footnote, rather more
unsettling, is the little song written in 1966 with the curious title
*Preface to the Complete Collection of my Works, and Brief Reflections on
this Preface*, op. 123. The text in this instance is Shostakovich's
own, except for the brief 'Preface' itself, which is a four-line
paraphrase of a Pushkin poem. It runs as follows:

> I scribble a page in a single breath.
> I listen to my whistling with an accustomed ear.
> I torment the ears of the world around me.
> Then I get into print, and bang into oblivion!

Such a preface could have been written not only to the complete
edition of my works, but also to the complete edition of the works of
very many other composers, Soviet as well as foreign. So here's the
signature: Dmitry Shostakovich, national artist of the USSR, and
recipient of many other honourable titles: first secretary of the
Union of composers of the RSFSR, and secretary of the Union of
composers of the USSR. He also has many other very responsible
commitments and obligations.

This is so deadpan that it allows of shades of interpretation, from the absolutely straight to the satirical. It's left to the music to define the sense in which we should hear and understand the text. It's odd stuff: the 'Preface' spluttered out by a bass voice in staccato style against an accompaniment of rapid, banging chords, and then the 'Reflections' set to wryly lilting music that *dares* us to try and take the words at their face value. This latter section proved to be replete with musical allusions. In fact, it's largely based on Shostakovich's musical 'signature' DSCH (in our notation D, E♭, C, B), which emerges apt and undisguised in bare octaves for the actual setting of his name; and this quite naturally admits allusions to some of the many works in which he has used that monogram, not least the Tenth Symphony and Eighth String Quartet. But the piano part twice makes a brief, mocking, fanfarish reference to the Thirteenth Symphony – to 'A Career' (very suitable among this parade of 'honourable titles' received), and specifically to the *i Tolstogo* passage I referred to earlier.

So there are at least three levels on which *Preface to the Complete Collection* can be heard. The first would be to take it literally, as a formal musical superscription for inclusion in an edition of his works. The second, the middle way, would be to think that Shostakovich is self-deprecatingly having some gentle fun at his own expense, trotting out all his high-flown official honours to such perky, irreverent music. The third layer of meaning, triggered by the reference to Symphony No. 13, isn't funny at all: it reminds us that such honours are often the rewards for compromise, if not worse. The question is raised (and it is surely infinitely to Shostakovich's credit that he could raise it): if Shostakovich is like Tolstoy, is he more of a Lev or a Count Alexei?

All the works so far discussed strike me as fundamentally optimistic: whatever their bitternesses and ambiguities, their thought is turned outward, positively, and Shostakovich uses music and text, however obliquely, to suggest the need for and possibility of reforms of attitudes in the outside world. There seems little doubt that word-setting in turn stimulated his purely musical invention. The principal orchestral works of this period, the Second Cello and Violin Concertos, are less direct in expression than their respective predecessors – and received a bad press in the West for that reason at the time of their first appearance – but they are emotionally as complex (in the case of the Second Cello Concerto, more so), and their rejection of familiar bold concertante gestures does not render them the less satisfying in the long run. There is haunting beauty in the Adagio of Violin Concerto No. 2, and a kind of defiant courage in the finale's jerky cheerfulness and fusillade of tom-tom entries; while the bittersweet finale of the Cello Concerto No. 2 seems to me one of Shostakovich's finest inspirations, pitting a warm, heart-easing cadential figure against the mechanistic chatter of the percussion, so reminiscent of Mandelshtam's line about 'Eternity beating on stone clocks'. In both works, the soloist's role is not so much that of a contestant against the orchestra but as the most important voice among many: it may be that Shostakovich revisited the concerto form with some new attitudes derived from his more recent vocal works.

In about 1967, however, another change seems to come over his output, a change which it is perhaps not inadmissable to connect with his worsening health. (His first heart-attack occured in March 1966, and he seemes to have been failing gradually ever afterwards, with all hope of recovery finally abandoned in 1973.) His works become more inward-looking, bleaker, tinged with despair; the flash of wit is dimmed, the warmth of expression loses its heat. This development seems to be signalled by the beautiful, but achingly depressive *Seven Romances on Poems of Alexander Blok* for soprano and piano trio (written after the Second Violin Concerto, despite its lower opus-number): the turn to Blok's anxious poems of emotional suffering and doubt is perhaps significant in itself. And of course the archetypal work of this last period is the Fourteenth Symphony, apparently conceived as a 'continuation' of the Musorgsky *Songs and Dances of Death*, with its array of eleven carefully-chosen and eloquently-grouped poems from Lorca, Apollinaire, Rilke, and Küchelbecker – gall and wormwood all. Few would deny the obsessive power of this music, its heart-rending emotion and stark directness of expression. Some, especially in Russia itself, have attempted however to deny its bone-deep despair. Marietta Shaganian, in a frequently-quoted article[9] tries to claim, for instance, that Shostakovich is not obsessed with death *as such*, but only with sudden, unnatural, violent or premature death. This is a forced interpretation. No ray of light pierces the Symphony's eleven movements, and the final Rilke setting is specifically about death as a *universal* evil. Seldom is there even an echo of the more positive qualities of the Thirteenth or *Stepan Razin*: perhaps the bitter scorn of 'The Zaporozhian Cossacks' Reply to the Sultan of Constantinople' – which the Memoirs (pp. 139–140) claim is directed at the memory of Stalin. One values the piece for its extraordinarily resourceful use of string orchestra and percussion, and the *tour-de-force* of fantastic narrative in music that distinguishes the setting of Apollinaire's 'Lorelei'; personally, one regrets, even if one can understand and sympathise with, the death-obsession it reveals as a whole. It is the dark night of the composer's soul, whose gloom also envelops the Thirteenth and Fifteenth String Quartets. For the most part, in these last years, the positive forces of his earlier music appear again, if at all, in shadowy guise, wry questionings of the prevailing mood of desolation.

In 1971, however, Shostakovich – in the same way that he had previously orchestrated *From Jewish Folk-Poetry* – returned to his even earlier *Six Romances to Verses by English Poets* and produced a new version for voice and small orchestra which he designated his op. 140. It is one of his most refined orchestrations, for a couple of woodwind, two horns, timpani, percussion, celesta, and a small body of strings, and brings dark and subtle 'late-period' hues to these brief and often poignant settings of Raleigh, Burns, Shakespeare, and Anon. One gets the feeling that the orchestration was intended to make the cycle performable in context with any of his late vocal works, where its frequent vein of intense personal lyricism could offset their comparative ambiguities and acerbities; and it may have helped to usher in a last important group of three vocal cycles.

Three works – the *Six Poems of Marina Tsvetaeva*, op. 143, the *Suite on Verses by Michelangelo Buonarroti*, op. 145, and the *Four Verses of Captain Lebyadkin*, op. 146 – were all originally written for voice and piano, but Shostakovich then orchestrated the first two, the Tsvetaeva setting for a similarly small ensemble to that used in the 'English' songs, the Michelangelo Suite for a full-sized symphony orchestra, though used with the characteristic spareness, even attenuation, of his very late manner.[10] It was his last orchestral work. All three works date from 1973–4, which is to say immediately after his return from his last visit to America in June 1973, during which American specialists had confirmed that there were no further grounds for hope of recovery and that his remaining life-expectancy must be very short.

It is therefore surprising that the extreme negativity which, for this writer at least, renders a work like the Fourteenth Symphony almost intolerable, is no longer present – bleak and sombre though the first two of these cycles mainly are. Or perhaps not surprising: the imminence of death, as Dr Johnson tells us, wonderfully concentrates the mind – and though the Tsvetaeva and Michelangelo cycles are only half turned again to the outside world, one receives the impression of Shostakovich striving finally to sort out and identify the essential issues and attitudes which will help him approach death, rather than railing against it. The choice of texts by Tsvetaeva, a suicide and an otherwise embarassingly tragic figure in Soviet literature,[11] take on added significance in this light; and indeed the Tsvetaeva set is maybe the most intimately personal of all Shostakovich's song-cycles, even in its orchestral version. 'Whence such tenderness?' is a pure love-song – a very rare thing in his output – and shows the utmost delicacy of feeling. Elsewhere in the cycle there is sometimes brightness, but little warmth. 'Hamlet's dialogue with his conscience' is a presentation of the sense of personal guilt in a confused, disordered, wandering mind, trying desperately to excuse itself: in this song, tonality itself becomes a vocabulary of disconnected fragments, jerky, alienated interjections which are unable to form long lines or lead anywhere harmonically.

The other four songs are concerned with affirming the ultimate validity of creative work: the first concludes that 'My poems, like precious wines,/ will have their day'. Shostakovich, who interestingly enough uses a 12-note melodic line as the basis of his setting, may well be invoking this Tsvetaevan guarantee for his own works. 'Poet and Tsar' and 'No, beat the drum' revert to the familiar theme of the creative artist ranged against the tyrant – Pushkin against Nicholas I. The brilliant toccata (for strings and xylophone in the orchestral version) of 'Poet and Tsar' echoes the stinging rebukes of 'The Zaporozhian Cossacks'; and 'No, beat the drum' evokes Pushkin's death and burial: 'Who was this then who was carried by thieves. . . A traitor? No! This was Russia's wisest man'. And the final song celebrates another great poet, nearer in time, a close friend of Tsvetaeva's and deeply admired by Shostakovich himself: Anna Akhmatova,[12] who died in 1966. It is the longest song of the cycle, measured in its tread and reverberant with tolling bells, a great paean to the poet as Unacknowledged Legislator of the World: 'Hundreds of thousands swear allegiance to you, Anna Akhmatova' – the name prompts a loud, ceremonious sequence of repeated chords which one would expect to be triadic, but which prove dissonant, tritonal, affirmative only at the expense of pain. This music expresses a kind of stony pride, but not triumph. 'Anyone who is wounded by your fate becomes immortal': such immortality is no matter for simple rejoicing, and the song ends in a mood of impersonal justification rather than with any hint of comfort.

The Michelangelo Suite pursues the same themes as the Tsvetaeva set, but at greater length, on a larger scale, and in even more austere style. It is a strange work, curiously bodiless for all its large (45-minute) dimensions, full of a crabbed yet impressive eloquence from which all trace of rhetoric has been purged away – musically almost self-effacing, as if the simple communication of the sense behind the words has become the overriding consideration. Counterpoint or even textural complication of any kind is strictly avoided, and even in the version for large orchestra the extent to which the voice may be accompanied simply by grave string chords, or a wandering bass line, is remarkable.

The eleven poems are grouped in such a way as to highlight what seem, by this stage, to have become for Shostakovich the perennial verities. Three love-poems, Nos. 2–4, two of which are set to darker-hued and more troubled music than Michelangelo's texts would seem to imply, are framed between two sonnets (Nos. 1 and 5) against a tyrannical ruler – here Pope Julius II – who surrounds himself with flatterers and 'keeps mercy under lock and key'. Nos. 6 and 7 praise another great poet, Dante, 'whose works are misunderstood by the ungrateful crowd'. No. 8, the most violent and complex song, compares the writer's artistic creativity (should we understand that of

Michelangelo or Shostakovich?) to God's creation of man. The exquisite No. 9, 'Night' – evocatively scored in the orchestral version for strings, harp, the celesta of which Shostakovich has fair claim to be considered the greatest master, and a muted horn-call that refers back obliquely to the finale of his Fourth Symphony – contrasts Giovanni Strozzi's conventional praise of Michelangelo's figure of Night with the sculptor's world-weary reply: 'Sleep is dear to me; and still more being made of stone/ When shame and crime are all around:/ It is a relief not to feel, not to see'. This leads naturally to the tenth song, 'Death', to the most disillusioned of all the poems ('There is no hope; gloom covers everything;/ and falsehood reigns, truth hides its eye'). Here we are back on the emotional quicksands of the Fourteenth Symphony, though with its solemn framing fanfares and Musorgskian intensity of vocal expression, this is an undeniably impressive song.

It might have been the end of the Suite (the fanfares derive from the work's very opening, apparently closing a circle), but it is not. Instead, there follows an eleventh song, 'Immortality' (all these titles are Shostakovich's, not Michelangelo's) – and it is a surprise: a cheerful little Allegretto which promises that 'I am not dead, though buried in earth . . . I live on/ in the hearts of all loving people'). It even has a carefree, whistleable tune, the only one in the entire work – and strangely familiar: the quotation from Beethoven's *Moonlight* Sonata in Shostakovich's very last work, the Viola Sonata, has received much attention, so it is surprising that (at least to my knowledge) no-one has pointed out that this song's main theme is an even more blatant borrowing (Example 4).

Example 4
a. Shostakovich, 'Immortality'

Just what Shostakovich means to convey by this final song is far from clear. It turns Beethoven's great C major triumph theme into a perky little ditty in F sharp; it has something of the

lilt of 'A Career'; like that song, it eventually takes a turn into
more spacious seriousness before the end, a soft, regularly
pulsing triad of F sharp major, with (in the orchestral version)
interpolated figurations from the celesta, like the chiming of
some delicate clock. There could be many levels of irony here,
but it is difficult to feel them. Maybe it is another version of
'having the last laugh' after death. One wonders, however,
whether the material of this song, Beethoven and all, is not too
lightweight to seem convincing after the gloom of the ten
preceeding movements; whether in reaching for the 'immortality' promised in Michelangelo's poem Shostakovich is not at
the end simply adopting a comforting formula. What hope for
'all loving people', left in a human predicament where 'falsehood reigns'?

But this, too, is not the end. There was one further vocal work
to come,[13] one last song-cycle for bass and piano: Shostakovich's penultimate composition, the *Four Verses of Captain Lebyadkin,*whose texts are taken from Dostoevsky's novel *The Devils*
(sometimes also known as *The Possessed*). This, in some ways the
oddest and most opaque of Shostakovich's late works, seems to
me a last, unexpected flare-up of the defiant double-edged wit
of pieces like 'Humour', 'A Career', and *Preface to the Complete
Collection*. In its truly Russian grotesquerie it also looks much
further back, to the gleefully satirical Shostakovich of *The Nose*
and the First Symphony. It is always salutary to remember that
his early reputation in Russia was made not as 'the Soviet
Beethoven', but as 'the Soviet Rossini'.

The 'Lebyadkin' songs are, on a casual perusal of the music,
simple and straightforward to a reckless degree. They carry the
general idiom of the late cycles to an extreme bordering on
caricature. The textures are spare to the point of dessication,
the harmony almost entirely limited to bare octaves, with the
occasional buzzing dissonance or triadic gesture, the voice-part
'unvocal' in its register, narrow compass, and doggedly syllabic
setting, but subtly and effectively harnessed to the speech-
rhythms. The spirit of Musorgsky looms ever more clearly – but
Musorgsky refracted through some very murky glass. In this
stark artlessness it seems that everything is left to the interpretative powers of the singer and pianist. It's certainly true
that the performers carry a heavy interpretative responsibility –

but *not* because there is anything sketchy or incomplete in Shostakovich's conception. On the contrary, this little song-cycle is a veritable Chinese box of ambiguities and double meanings – most of them text-related – where nothing is quite what it appears.

Yet again the choice of texts is hardly uncontroversial: Dostoevsky's reputation in the USSR has been the profoundly ambiguous one of a respected 'reactionary', ever since the strong criticisms of him made by Maxim Gorky. And of all his novels, *The Devils* is the most disturbing to the Soviet literary and political establishment – since it's essentially a damning critique, from a religious viewpoint, of the kind of intellectual revolutionary conspiracy which helped to bring modern Russia into being.[14] Shostakovich, therefore, was casting light on a somewhat shady area of Russian literature. And that he should turn, after Tsvetaeva and Michelangelo, to the doggerel of Captain Ignaty Lebyadkin, looks like an irreverent negation of Soviet ideas on High Art. Lebyadkin is a minor character in *The Devils*, and a wholly disreputable one – a buffoon, a drunkard, a scoundrel, whom Dostoevsky describes in terms of ridicule. With his clumsiness, his absurd ambition, his alcoholic muddle-headedness and his atrocious verses, he's a helpless tool of the real revolutionaries, who cast him aside and murder him when he's served his purpose.

Lebyadkin is also referred to as the licensed fool or jester to Stavrogin, the most corrupt of the conspirators. He might, therefore, be seen as the last, rather shabby, representative of the long line of jester-figures who touched a responsive chord in Shostakovich, from the Fool in *King Lear* (whose songs he set for a Leningrad production in 1941, in his most pungent manner), through Macpherson, to 'Humour' in the Thirteenth Symphony. This concern with jester-figures argues a certain degree of identification between composer and subject. So, when Shostakovich chose the lucubrations of Captain Lebyadkin for his last song-cycle, he may have felt more in common with his disagreeable mouthpiece than at first meets the eye. His only reported comment on the cycle implicitly acknowledges the disturbing ambiguities of his settings: 'I think I've managed to capture the spirit of Dostoevsky . . . Lebyadkin is of course a buffoon, but from time to time he becomes terrifying.'[15]

For Lebyadkin's verses are the most interesting things about
him. They come out as half-nonsense, half-satire, and it's
difficult to know how seriously they might be meant. They can
easily set the hearer searching for hidden significances, and in
fact Dostoevsky specifically tells us that one of Lebyadkin's
rudest squibs – which turns up as the third of Shostakovich's
settings – is received by some of its audience in a quite different
spirit from the Captain's apparent intention: not as a lampoon,
but as 'the truth . . . verses with a political tendency'. So, are
Shostakovich's apparently simple settings of ambiguously
awful doggerel by a doomed fool who is one of the more
unsavoury characters in Dostoevsky's most controversial
novel, 'just a lampoon', or something more serious?

At any event, nothing here is as straightforward as it seems –
not even the constitution of the texts themselves. The words of
the first song, 'The Love of Captain Lebyadkin', are actually
stitched together from four separate passages in Dostoevsky's
novel. They aren't confined to the Captain's literary efforts,
either, but include passages of prose from the main text in
which the drunkard breaks off to explain things to the narrator.
Shostakovich incorporates these into the song, and the effect is
a distancing one, adding another layer of ambiguity to the
whole design: who is commenting on whom? This kind of
'double focus' extends further in the second song, 'The
Cockroach', which is a kind of mock-ballad, a beast-fable of the
sort made popular by Ivan Krylov (c. 1769–1844).[16] In the
novel, Lebyadkin has difficulty getting started in his recitation
of this nonsense, because his hearers keep interrupting him –
and Shostakovich faithfully sets the resultant altercation,
beautifully rendering the Captain flying off the handle and
controlling himself with difficulty.

The third poem, which Shostakovich calls 'The Benefit Ball
for Governesses' (this being the function at which it is recited in
the novel) is an ill-mannered lampoon: but perhaps the most
ambiguous of the lot is the final song, 'A pure Soul'. In *The
Devils*, this particular piece of versifying isn't actually attributed to Lebyadkin, and some of the characters take it quite
seriously as a bit of seditious revolutionary propaganda which
expresses hope in a coming, world-reforming revolution. But in
fact, Dostoevsky is showing-up the character of the poem's

protagonist, the 'Pure Soul' who would be a revolutionary
leader – a student, for whom the Russian people are imagined
to be waiting 'from Smolensk to Tashkent', who preaches
'brotherhood, equality and freedom' and tries to whip up
rebellion from abroad, well out of reach of 'the whip, the
thumbscrew and the executioner'; who seduces the people into
believing all will be rosy in the future, as soon as estates have
been made common property and they have abolished the
church, marriage, and family ties – 'those triple bonds which
deceived the human mind in the old, evil world'.

Whereas the other three songs are open-ended and con-
tinuously-developing in their structure, this last one is a simple
strophic song, with a pawky little refrain on the piano (Example
5*a*). It seems to me that that scrap of tune looks back – for the
last time – to Shostakovich's Thirteenth Symphony; and again
to that enigmatic autobiographical song 'A Career', with its
similarly cheery bassoon refrain (Example 5*b*).

Example 5
a. 'A Pure Soul'

b. 'A Career'

Is Shostakovich hinting here, in blandly merry music that
underlies mock-serious words, that paying lip-service to
Revolution and social justice without actually doing anything
about it, or taking any risks, is as cushy a way of having a career
as any? That is just one of the questions which this last,
marvellously acid and eldritch song-cycle poses for us.

Notes

1. *Testimony: the Memoirs of Shostakovich* as related to and edited by Solomon
   Volkov (London: Hamish Hamilton 1979), p. 140. Translated by
   Antonia W. Bouis. Since the authenticity of this book, in whole or in part,
   is still hotly disputed, my citations of it in the present article have been
   couched in such locutions as may avoid the suggestion that it *automatically*
   has final authority.

2. ibid., p. 107.

3. 'There was a time when I considered the Eleventh my most "Musorg-skian" composition' – ibid., p. 186. A reasonable view, considering that symphony's epic sweep and Eisenstein-like evocation of crowd-scenes. It is the very mastery of the Eleventh – still, possibly, an underrated symphony in the West – that makes the rather confused and contradic-tory Twelfth so disappointing: the more so as Shostakovich had clearly not lost the ability to write such music. It flares up again in the score for the film *God kak Zhizn'* (*A Year is like a Lifetime*, also sometimes called *Karl Marx*), op. 120, of 1965, which harks back, often compellingly, to the tremendous rhythmic energy and massed effects of the Eleventh.

4. Shostakovich's own comments, as reported in Dmitri and Ludmilla Sollertinsky, *Pages from the Life of Dmitri Shostakovich* (London: Robert Hale, 1981, trs. Graham Hobbs and Charles Midgely), pp. 157–8, are germane: 'Initially I wrote a sort of vocal and symphonic poem to Yevgeni Yevtushenko's poem "Babi Yar". Then I thought of continuing the work by setting other verses by the same poet. . . The poem "Fears" was written by Yevtushenko with my symphony specifically in mind. . . There is no thread linking the subject matter of these poems. They were published at different times and are concerned with different themes, but I wanted to give them a musical unity. I was writing a symphony, not a set of individual musical tableaux.' (The source of this statement is not given.) The same book suggests that the Symphony was essentially conceived in 1961.

5. In his collection *Vzmakh Ruki* (1962), though the poem dates from 1957.

6. Not, for instance, that literary ornament of the early Soviet state, the 'Red Count' Alexei Nikolayevich Tolstoy, famous less for his novels than his adroitness in political manouvre – and for receiving a slap in the face by the poet Osip Mandelshtam after Tolstoy, as president of a Writers' Court, had let off scot-free a novelist who had assaulted Mandelshtam's wife. Shostakovich and Tolstoy had been in the same circle in pre-Revolutionary St Petersburg (cf. D. & L. Sollertinsky, op. cit., p. 12).

7. *Testimony*, pp. 117–18.

8. In Symphony No. 13, the requirement is for '2–4' harps. Most performances I have heard of these two works convince me that the larger number is not extravagant: indeed, they are necessary for effective balance of sonority.

9. Cf., for instance, D. and L. Sollertinsky, op. cit., p. 197. Presumably the same Marietta Shaganian who makes such an unedifying appearance in Nadezhda Mandelshtam's *Hope Abandoned*, pp. 173–177.

10. Howard Skempton, prompted perhaps by his own experience of compos-ing piano pieces simple enough for Benajamin Britten to play during his last illness, has suggested to me that the extreme bareness of Shostako-vich's late keyboard writing may reflect the limitations imposed on him as a performer by his physical condition: limitations he turned to advantage. The accompaniment to the fifth song of the Tsvetaeva set, for instance, can be played with one hand.

11. Her husband was executed in 1939 and her daughter sent to a labour

camp, two years before Tsvetaeva hanged herself. A close friend of Mandelshtam and Akhmatova, her poetry was not widely published in the USSR until 20 years after her death.

12. For Shostakovich's and Akhmatova's mutual regard, see D. & L. Sollertinsky, op. cit., pp. 211–212 (confirming *Testimony*, p. 213). The 'living conscience' of Soviet literature and a woman of magnetic personality, Akhamatova was virtually proscribed for the first 30 years of the USSR, and was abused by Zhdanov and expelled from the Writers' Union in 1946, despite her great undergound popularity. A somewhat bowdlerized edition of her poetry was eventually published in the USSR a year before her death: it omits the fine long poem *Requiem* commemorating her first husband (the poet Gumilëv, shot by the Bolsheviks in 1921) and her son (who spent 20 years of his life in a forced labour camp). According to the Memoirs, Shostakovich particularly esteemed this poem, which circulated widely in typescript and was set to music by his pupil Boris Tishchenko.

13. If we except the orchestration he made for Yevgeny Nestevenko of Beethoven's setting of Goethe's *Song of the Flea*, which was his last vocal work of all: an instrumentation with all the characteristic mordant qualities of his own songs to similarly satirical, anti-authoritarian texts.

14. The Memoirs (p. 209) have Shostakovich commenting on the fact that even in the early 1970s the chapter 'Stavrogin's Confession' was still suppressed in Soviet editions of *The Devils*. Nadezhda Mandelshtam (*Hope Abandoned*, pp. 171–2) recalls her astonishment when told in 1956, that a Complete Edition of Dostoevsky's works was planned. 'If they were talking of a complete Dostoevsky, it really must be the beginning of a new era. He had been under a ban for more years than I could remember. An exception was made for *Crime and Punishment*, but *The Devils* provoked gnashing of teeth.'

15. D. and L. Sollertinsky, op. cit., p. 231.

16. Shostakovich's earliest acknowledged vocal work is a setting of two of Krylov's fables for mezzo-soprano and orchestra (op. 4, 1922).

Bernard Stevens

Shostakovich and the British Composer

The English musical public has taken the music of Shostakovich to its heart, ever since the First Symphony became widely performed in the 1930s. But what has been the attitude of English composers?

Benjamin Britten acknowledged his indebtedness to Shostakovich's Fifth Symphony in the late 1930s and this is certainly to be observed in his works of this period, particularly in the 'Frank Bridge' Variations and in the 'Sinfonia da Requiem'. This indebtedness was to be reciprocated in the 1960s when the two composers became close friends. The Fourteenth Symphony is dedicated to Benjamin Britten, but this is no mere formal acknowledgement; much of the poetic imagery is reflected in musical motives that recall Britten's 'Serenade' and 'Nocturne' songs with chamber orchestra and in the Fourteenth Symphony he borrows Britten's favourite method of bringing together poems of several poets to present varied and contrasting aspects of one subject. The melodic inflections in Britten's settings of Pushkin in the original Russian recall the intervals and rhythms of Shostakovich's Jewish songs; here Britten uncharacteristically avoids the Purcellian melismatic style of his English settings. Shostakovich was quoted in the 1960s as saying that he considered Britten to be the greatest living composer.

However, apart from Britten, there are few examples of the direct stylistic influence of Shostakovich on the work of English composers. Does this mean that English composers do not share a love of his music with the English musical public? There can be few who do not respect the fertility of his invention, his individuality and consistent technical command. Most have admired his resilience in the face of public and private suffering. In discussing my own attitude, as a composer, to Shostakovich's work I hope to stress those aspects which are shared by other composers of my generation.

I was nineteen when I first encountered Shostakovich's music in 1935, the same age as Shostakovich had been when he composed his First Symphony in 1926, and that was the work I heard. At that time I was a pupil of Edward Dent, the first President of the International Society of Contemporary Music. I had been composing for about five years, starting in the style of Vaughan Williams, followed by a brief flirtation with Schönbergian atonality, and had arrived at a sort of modest lyricism that owed more to Fauré than to any more recent composer. I had little respect at that time for any modern symphonic composer except Sibelius and then only for his more concentrated works such as the Fourth Symphony. This was hardly the mood in which to accept Shostakovich's First Symphony, particularly the third and fourth movements, which seemed hardly better than Hollywood film-music (particularly the 'fate-knocking-at-the-door' timpani motif). The first movement was by far the most original, with sudden changes of mood and avoidance of conventional 'bridge-passages'. The First Symphony is certainly a remarkable work for a nineteen-year-old, although not as mature as the First Symphony of the twenty-year-old Kurt Weill, written six years earlier.

I heard no other Shostakovich until the Fifth Symphony in 1938, by which time I had undergone a considerable change in aesthetic, philosophical and political outlook, largely through the impact of the Spanish Civil War. If I had heard the Fifth Symphony at the time of its first performance in 1937, I would have been incapable of appreciating its epic character as anything other than demonstrating pompous self-importance; but, on the eve of the Second World War, I and many others of

my generation had matured sufficiently to be able to recognise
the wide range of human experience reflected in that work. We
were ready to accept the composer's stated reasons for
withdrawing his Fourth Symphony when such self-criticism
could be so obviously beneficial to his creative development
and could make possible the achievement of such a masterpiece. This opinion was confirmed when the Fourth Symphony
was eventually heard in the early 1960s. Like most composers of
his generation, Shostakovich had tried to break away from the
German Romantic tradition of thematic development that the
older Russian composers, particularly Tchaikovsky had followed. In the first movement of the First Symphony he had
replaced this by episodic treatment of the thematic material
that has much in common with the Soviet film-music of the
period, particularly that of Edmund Meisel in his music to
Eisenstein's *Potemkin* of the previous year. The second movement uses the simple binary form of the Classical period. In the
third and fourth movements, however, he attempts thematic
development in the German tradition but relies too heavily on
predictable melodic and harmonic sequence.

That he was aware of this weakness is shown in the Second,
Third and Fourth Symphonies. During this period he stated
that it was very difficult to find new way of composing
large-scale movements. (It is interesting to note that Holst in
England at about the same time said 'Development is dead!').
Unfortunately, in the Second and Third Symphonies, it seems
to me that Shostakovitch took the easy course by avoiding
distinctive thematic material, relying on mechanical figuration
and atmospheric orchestration to give formal cohesion. These
works are brief and appear to have been written in haste. The
choral finales are somewhat trite both in words and music, a
pale reflection of the choral finale of Scriabin's First Symphony
and not very successful attempts to reach a wide audience.

The Fourth Symphony, however, is at once an advance and
retrogression, containing elements that were to be more fully
developed in the Fifth. It is surprising that the two works have
so much in common in respect of thematic style, bearing in
mind Shostakovich's criticism of the earlier. The Fourth is a
great advance in that it is the first large-scale work in which he
achieved real organic integration of material and structure

without recourse to the predictable sequences of the First. It is backward-looking, however, with regard to style as it frequently reverts to nineteenth-century German harmonic language and even Viennese 'ländler' which seem to have little relevance in the post-Revolutionary USSR, unless we are expected to interpret this style as a parody of 'bourgeois' music. This raises the question of the satirical element in Shostakovich, very prevalent in the '30s and '40s. If we are to consider it as political comment, it is far less telling than that of Satie or Weill. Fortunately, it gradually disappears in his later work, except for the powerful example of the second movement of the Thirteenth Symphony.

Symmetrical four-bar phrases and predictable sequences that had been a weakness of his early work become gradually transformed into over-lapping and odd-number barred phrases from the Fifth Symphony onwards. Musorgsky probably gave the impetus to this development, although in other respects Musorgsky's influence does not appear until his last works. A remarkable example is in the finale of the Sixth Symphony where the rhythms themselves are obvious enough but which achieve a remarkable kaleidoscopic effect through the over-lapping of phrases, suggesting a film-camera scanning a May-Day crowd in Red Square. This is one of the few really satisfying finales in modern symphonies, one which comes nearest to a modern equivalent of a Haydn finale. The Sixth, as a whole, is one of Shostakovich's finest works and is strangely neglected; it is also important in his development as is his first symphony in which the over-all structure is derived from a literary source, namely Mayakovsky's poem 'Lenin'. It recalls Berlioz in the skill with which the events of the poem are integrated into the musical structure. The language also develops more fully than hitherto the use of Classical motives, as in the Bach-like 'cantilena' of the first movement and the second subject of the finale, which closely resembles the opening of the finale of Mozart's Fortieth Symphony.

The 'ricochet' figure of the first subject of the finale may well be an unconscious reference to the similar figure in Rossini's 'William Tell' Overture; (the direct quotation from the Rossini in the first movement of the Fifteenth Symphony was stated by Shostakovich to refer to that piece having been his earliest musical recollection).

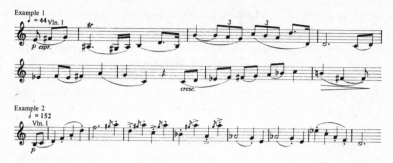

Hearing the Piano Quintet for the first time in 1941, during the first great Nazi assault on the USSR, was for me a profoundly moving experience. I realised the greatness of a musical mind that could speak in such simple and direct terms. It seemed to me to embody the new 'classicism' that Busoni had envisaged in his 'The New Aesthetic', not to be confused with the 'neo-classicism' of Stravinsky and 'Les Six'. With this work Shostakovich spoke with a universal voice. No longer would the understanding of his music be in any way dependent on knowledge of and sympathy for its Soviet background. This explains why musicians as opposed in their philosophical and aesthetic outlook as Schönberg and Rubbra express their admiration for it. It helped composers to return to the mainstream of European music from the various fashionable tributaries of the '30s but without reverting to that of German Romanticism. The slow movement in particular shows how original thought can be expressed through traditional technique:

Not all musicians, however, saw the Quintet in this light. For some it represented a cowardly retreat into a safe haven and a deliberate avoidance of controversy. Prokofiev, for instance, expressed his disappointment that such a young composer should write so unadventurously. Hitherto, Prokofiev and Shostakovich shared some stylistic features, notably the satirical element already mentioned. Satire became much less marked in the later works of both composers, but the avoidance of the 'expected' in Prokofiev's lyricism seems to me to have a self-conscious quality, whereas the originality of Shostakovich's later work arises out of the compelling logic of the thought process itself. In this respect it is significant that Prokofiev's son is reported to have said that when his father had first drafted a passage he then considered how it could be made more 'interesting'.

Nothing shows more clearly the range of expressive power that Shostakovich had acquired by the early 1940s than the contrast between the quiet subtlety of the Quintet and the almost overwhelming strength of the Seventh Symphony, the next major work. At first I was distrustful of the extreme length and huge orchestral resources, suggesting a return to nineteenth-century German mannerisms. However, after the emotion generated by the tragic events associated with its composition and first performance could be recollected in tranquility, it became possible to wonder at the truly epic nature of the work, in the Aristotelian sense of 'out of time and space'. Even the notorious motif of the first movement that is said, understandably, to have annoyed Bartók in his last days of poverty and sickness, was shown to be the generating element in a structure of almost Beethovenian strength.

The beautiful and relaxed second movement seems to contain a hint of the BACH-like motif, DSCH that was to become such an enriching element in the composer's melodic and harmonic language from the Tenth Symphony onwards.

The Twenty-four Preludes and Fugues of 1951 are a rich store-house of seeds that were to germinate in many of

Shostakovich's later works as well as to become a stimulating influence on other composers in causing them to reconsider the meaning of Classical fugal procedure in present-day terms. They invite comparison with Hindemith's 'Ludus Tonalis' but, in my opinion, are much more resourceful both in technique and in imagination and, although not didactic in purpose as is the Hindemith, nevertheless open up many new avenues of contrapuntal thought, as Edmund Rubbra has stressed in his perceptive treatise 'Counterpoint'. The variety of style in the subjects alone is very great, ranging as it does from the consistent diatonism of the First (the whole fugue being on the white notes of the keyboard), to the almost twelve-note chromaticism of the Fifteenth.

Example 6   ♩. = 138

The Seventh is a tour-de-force of rhythm, the subject consisting entirely of the notes of the triad of A Major.

Example 7   ♩ = 92

Several of the subjects have the character of folk-songs from non-European countries. The Eighth is like a negro spiritual. The Sixteenth consists of highly elaborate decoration and the Nineteenth features the augmented second interval of the 'Gypsy' scale. Never before to my knowledge, have themes of such improvisatorial character been subjected to such sustained contrapuntal concentration and resource, unlike Rimsky-Korsakov and Borodin, who often treat folk-songs fugally but in short episodes only.

Several of the Preludes as well as some of the longer Fugues seem like preliminary sketches for later symphonic movements, concertos and string quartets. The last Fugue is the most extended and developed of all and has much in common with the first movement of the Tenth Symphony; not only is the over-all rhythmical shape very similar (even to a very close speed indication), but the second counter-subject is almost identical with that of the Symphony and grows out of the texture in the same way. The Prelude of the Twelfth is a passacaglia of which the ostinato bass is very similar to that of the second movement of the First Violin Concerto, particularly in the repeated notes at the ends of phrases; the superimposed melodic lines also have the same impassioned and sustained lyricism. Similar parallels with the later string quartets may be observed, particularly in the more intimate and capricious preludes. For me, these Preludes and Fugues are a never-ending source of ideas and possibilities, almost as rewarding as Bach's 'Forty-eight'.

From the time of the Preludes and Fugues there begin to appear more discernible Russian characteristics in Shostakovich's melody, harmony and instrumentation. This development seems to coincide with his growing interest in setting Russian texts, the Cantata 'The Song of the Forests', the 'Ten Poems by Revolutionary Poets' and the 'Jewish Folk-poems', as well as his editing and completing Musorgsky's operas for performance on film. In addition to the non-European features already mentioned, the Preludes and Fugues contain many European Russian elements; the interval of the fourth (rather than the triadic fifth), a very ancient feature of Russian folk-song, is a strong characteristic of many of the fugue subjects. There is much modality and several Preludes recall Musorgsky's orchestral sonority, for example the spacious, almost liturgical opening of the Twentieth Prelude. This seems to be a sketch for the first movement of the Eleventh Symphony ('1905') which is his most consciously nationalistic symphony. Not only are the opening themes almost identical (transposed from Dorian C to G) but also the subsequent ruminating melodies.

It is not surprising that Shostakovich's melodic style should have become more national as a consequence of setting Russian texts. There are many parallels in other nationalities, notably Debussy, Janáček, Vaughan Williams and many other English composers. This is particularly noticeable in those composers who have set their own language extensively only in their later work, such as Alan Bush, Ronald Stevenson and myself. It should perhaps be stressed that this recent nationalism in Shostakovich in no way diminishes his international stature.

Shostakovich was nearly fifty before he produced a major work in concerto form, but in the following twelve years four remarkable examples appeared, of which the first for violin and the second for 'cello rank with the greatest ever written for their instruments. The third movement of the First Violin Concerto, the passacaglia already mentioned, is one of his most sublime utterances and is, as far as I am aware, the only example of this form to be found in a concerto, although the chaconne in Rawsthorne's First Piano Concerto is a close parallel and one of that composer's finest achievements. The playing of Oistrakh and Rostropovich inspired these works; it is therefore surprising and to be regretted that Shostakovich was not similarly inspired to write a comparable piano concerto for Richter, attractive as are his two light-weight examples of the form. In fact it is surprising that, apart from the Twenty-four Preludes and Fugues, he wrote no solo works in his maturity for the instrument of which, as a young man, he was such a brilliant exponent.

That the string quartet should grow in importance in his last years is to be expected, not only because of the ease and naturalness with which he first approached the medium in 1938 but even more because of the growing seriousness and concentration of his mature thought. It is fashionable to describe the Symphonies as 'public' or 'official' Shostakovich and the Quartets as containing his 'private' or 'uncensored' thoughts. This view is as erroneous in respect of Shostakovich as it is of Beethoven (concerning whose symphonies and quartets similar comparisons are often made), because it minimises the epic element in the symphonies, which is as personal and deeply felt as is the subtlety and poignancy of the quartets. It is true that there are many daring innovations of harmony and form in Shostakovich's later Quartets, particularly in the Twelfth, which are not to be found in the Symphonies but it is probable that they would have become gradually involved in a wider context had he lived to explore and develop them. Some of them, indeed, are to be seen in the Fourteenth Symphony. The short Eighth Quartet, said to have been composed amid the ruins of the bombed city of Dresden, is perhaps his most personal statement, not only because the material is derived from his own initials and from earlier works.

As already mentioned, there are hints of twelve-note chromaticism in the Twenty-four Preludes and Fugues and this aspect of his language is developed in the Quartets and the Fourteenth Symphony but in a manner very different from that of Schönberg. As with Frank Martin, far from this device destroying tonality, on the contrary, it builds up harmonic tension through a series of compound appogiaturas that make the final resolution all the more compelling. Particularly vivid examples are the opening of the Twelfth Quartet and the third and fifth movements of the Fourteenth Symphony. Many composers (including myself) have found that this use of twelve-note chromaticism, following the examples of Martin and Shostakovich, opens up new possibilities of tonality that avoid the cul-de-sac into which Schönberg's serialism led both himself and his followers, notwithstanding the fine works achieved on the way. In spite of Schönberg's prediction that his method would perpetuate the hegemony of German music for the next hundred years, there is, in fact, an almost total absence of his method of composition in use at the present time.

Closely related to Shostakovich's chromaticism in his later works is the frequent appearance of his initials DSCH. Although there is undoubtedly some symbolic significance in this feature, it must not be exaggerated. I have not heard of such significance attributed to BACH, not even by Albert Schweitzer, who was given to this kind of interpretation of the inner meaning of Bach's music. Most composers have tried out the musical possibilities of their own names or those of their friends; sometimes it is rewarding but, as Hanns Eisler has said, it is fortunate we were spared fugues on the name HANDEL! It is tempting to attribute symbolic significance to the large number of thematic cross-references that occur in Shostakovich's music but to carry this sort of analysis too far would reduce the works to mere 'anecdotal' significance. Obvious examples are the scherzi of the Second Piano Trio and the Eighth Symphony, themes from 'Katerina Izmailova' and the 'Jewish Songs' re-appearing in several later instrumental works. It is surely understandable that a composer might wish to develop further aspects of themes that would have been inappropriate in the original work, without thereby endowing them with extra-musical significance. Others, like the similarity between themes in the first movement of the First Cello

Concerto, the last movement of the Eighth Quartet and the third movement of the Fourteenth Symphony, are probably evidence that the themes have been assimilated into the composer's general consciousness rather than intended to be intentional quotations. Analysts have also found such similarities in Beethoven's last three Piano Sonatas.

I see the significance of Shostakovich's use of DSCH principally in the rewarding possibilities of harmony and counterpoint it offers. It belongs to that group of short patterns of intervals at the primal source of melody that composers find inexhaustible.

Example 8
    Dies Irae   B A C H   'Jupiter' Symph.   D Es C H   Quartet, Op. 28 (Webern)
                                            (Mozart)

Just as BACH has inspired other composers than Bach himself, so DSCH has inspired Ronald Stevenson in his great 'passacaglia', one of the few masterpieces for the piano of this century, as well as his beautiful 'Recitative and Air' in memory of Shostakovitch, and there is no reason to think that its possibilities have been exhausted.

The final fugue of the Eighth Quartet contains the most concentrated use of the DSCH motif but its influence is present even where it does not occur in complete and identifiable form. Its minor third and semitone features permeate the first movement of the Tenth Symphony, although it does not appear as a rhythmical unit until the third movement, contributing to the remarkable organic unity this work conveys. In my opinion, this is Shostakovich's greatest symphonic movement and I find it puzzling that Shostakovich should have publicly criticised it as failing to be a truly symphonic Allegro. Schönberg formulated his principle of 'developing variation' as the best means of achieving a large-scale and unified symphonic movement. I agree with this view but I believe the first movement of Shostakovich's Tenth Symphony demonstrates this principle better than any of Schönberg's own works. I must confess to some disappointment in the two Symphonies that followed the Tenth; the second movement of the Eleventh ('Ninth of January'), is certainly on a level with its great predecessor but in other respects the revolutionary songs are not always integrated into the structure and they lack, in spite of their length, the epic quality of the Sixth and Seventh.

The Thirteenth and Fourteenth Symphonies suggest that, if he had lived, Shostakovich might well have turned again to opera. It is to be regretted that there are no stage works of his maturity. 'Katerina Izmailova' has moments of great power but lacks vivid characterisation. The early 'The Nose' has the rather mild satire characteristic of other works of the period. The second movement of the Thirteenth Symphony ('Humour'), shows how much he learned from editing Musorgsky. The irony here is altogether more powerful than in the early operas; the matching of musical and speech rhythms is worthy of Musorgsky himself. Even more telling is the third movement ('Loreley'), of the Fourteenth Symphony. This is a complete operatic 'scena' in the dialogue of the Bishop and the Witch. The characterisation of the latter is particularly telling.

The last works of Shostakovich and Britten reflect their awareness of the proximity of death and this knowledge inspired some of their finest music – Britten's *Death in Venice* and the last movement of the Third String Quartet and Shostakovich's Fourteenth Symphony and Viola and Piano Sonata. Shostakovich's setting of Rilke's 'Death of the Poet' in the tenth movement of the Fourteenth Symphony is very beautiful, particularly the 'chorale' that occurs three times, intertwined with the 'De Profundis' theme of the first movement, to which the voice is added with the third statement.

Example 9

Shostakovich stands for me as not only a very great composer but as a constant encouragement to other artists. I disagree both with those who see him as a tragic figure fighting a lonely battle against overwhelming odds and with those others, particularly in the Polish 'avant-garde', who dismiss him as 'irrelevant' to Twentieth Century music in having discarded artistic integrity, meekly obeying his powerful masters in order to gain comfort and material reward. One could wish that he had been more outspoken in his condemnation of Stalinism at the time of the Twentieth Congress of the Communist Party in 1955 and of the Congress of Soviet Composers in 1957. But, more important in my opinion, he always showed resilience in his composition by grasping and developing the positive elements that existed even in the most unpromising situations in which he found himself in 1936, 1948 and 1957. Unlike many of his Soviet colleagues Shostakovich never retreated into mere conformity or abject epigonism. His work demonstrates the truth of Lenin's view of the relationship between artists and socialism, expressed in a letter to Clara Zetkin:

> It goes without saying that literary activity is least of all subject to mechanical equalisation and levelling, to domination of a majority over a minority. It goes without saying that in this sphere it is absolutely necessary to ensure larger scope for personal initiative and individual inclination, full play for thought and imagination, form and content.

Boris Pasternak's thoughts on the poet Mayakovsky, in his autobiography *Safe Conduct*, apply with equal relevance to Shostakovich: 'The novelty of the age flowed climatically through his blood. His strangeness was the strangeness of our times of which half is as yet to be fulfilled.'

Christopher Norris

Shostakovich: politics and musical language

Shostakovich died in August 1975 after a long-rumoured illness
and a series of 'late' compositions which seemed increasingly to
brood on images of death and finality. His passing was
nevertheless hard to acknowledge, perhaps because those same
last works – the quartets, symphonies and vocal settings – had
broken new ground and looked forward, as it seemed, to a
period of intense creativity. What made the fact still more
difficult to accept was Shostakovich's curiously intimate place
in the public awareness of his music and its background history.
His various crises over the years had been those of (in Oscar
Wilde's premonitory phrase) 'the soul of man under socialism'.
In the case of Shostakovich this meant an artistic temperament
which had come to accept, and gradually to forestall, the edicts
of Soviet cultural policy. Shostakovich was often in the public
eye, whether as a hero of the new Soviet music or – more
commonly – as a chastened heretic set up to atone for his own
past faults.

Ironically it was his wartime compositions which caused
least trouble with the Party mentors. Works like the *Leningrad
Symphony* had a rousing directness of purpose and a nobly-
suffering pathos which yet managed to resist – as occasion
required – the forbidden ethos of 'tragic individualism'. In
retrospect the *Leningrad* may seem to harbour distinct ambi-

guities of meaning and programme. Recent commentators
(including Robert Dearling in his essay for this volume) have
tended to look behind the music's surface rhetoric for a hint of
divided loyalties or cryptic double-statement. Indeed, if one
credits the Volkov *Memoirs* – and their authenticity is, to say the
least, open to doubt – Shostakovich was perfectly aware of
composing a work whose hidden anti-Stalinist message would
one day be heard for what it was.[1] But such interpretations
after-the-event are at best highly speculative, seeking out
complexities of motive which perhaps Shostakovich himself
was pleased to discover in retrospect. They don't alter the fact
that here, most unusually, Shostakovich found a theme and a
musical idiom perfectly suited to the demands of public
occasion. One need not doubt the testimony of a witness at the
First (Leningrad) performance, where the impact of this music
'was felt not only by the listeners but also by the performers who
read the music sheets as if they were reading a living chronicle
about themselves. . .'.[2]

All this is familiar enough, along with the way in which the
Symphony took hold as a symbol of wartime hope in America
and elsewhere. If the epic quality in art depends upon a sense of
large-scale uncomplicated public involvement, then the *Leningrad* certainly achieves that status, despite all the riddling
ambiguities of hindsight. But Shostakovich's popularity at this
time, among both the Soviets and the Western Allies, was really
a simplified and unrepresentative version of his role as
citizen-composer. For the greater part of his life Shostakovich
could rely upon no such external aids to musical acceptability.
His struggles to attain a workable socialised aesthetic, and
moreover to square it with a sensitive musical conscience, are a
matter of public record (though no doubt the record is
ambiguous and shrewdly selective). More important, the music
itself bears witness to the crises of commitment, the ideological
conflicts and the often self-alienated character of Shostakovich's life-in-music.

In this instance, therefore, the composer's biography has a
more than usual relevance. What we learn, say, of Mozart
through Einstein's biographical account is connected with the
music mostly in an ad hoc, occasional way. Circumstances
sometimes suggest just how and why a work was composed, but

on the whole we are more impressed by the distance which Mozart managed to preserve between his emotional life and the demands of his music. With Beethoven – and even more with a composer like Mahler – the biographical connection is of course more suggestive, and the music often seems to convey a heightened or idealised version of the composer's lived experience. Thus Beethoven's cosmic optimism and Mahler's fatalistic brooding both enter strongly into the musical complexion of their respective last symphonies. An appeal is always open from the work to the life, not merely by way of anecdotal interest but because the two spheres overlap at various points and make up a single imaginative project, at least from the standpoint of interpretative hindsight.

In Shostakovich, the relation of Life and Work is at once more profound and more difficult to interpret. There is of course the history of public reprimands (most notably those of 1936 and 1948), and of answering self-criticisms on the composer's part; a depressing story, none the less so for Shostakovich's own description of his Fifth Symphony as 'a Soviet artist's reply to just criticism'. But there is also a task for the musical critic, working with the usual tools of analysis and description but recognising, where the music eludes his methods, that the cryptic suggestiveness of Shostakovich's idiom often takes on a quite extraordinary depth and complexity. With this composer it is impossible to apply T. S. Eliot's well-known critical dictum, that 'the man who suffers' must always be treated as separate from 'the mind which creates'. Shostakovich's sufferings of artistic conscience are 'there' in his music, and the critic who ignores them – or regards them in purist fashion as matters of 'extra-musical' interest – is closing his mind to an important aspect of the music's meaning and form.

This is to suggest (as Sartre does in his massive study of Flaubert) a new and more valuable form of artistic biography. The aim is not merely to draw a vague parallel between life and work, but to specify precisely how the work took shape as an active and determinate part of the subject's life-history.[3] Sartre believes that such questions can be posed with a degree of conceptual rigour far removed from the old, impressionistic style of creative biography. What were the conditions or self-imposed choices of social role within which the artist worked out his personal destiny? How far did those choices find themselves reflected and (perhaps) implicitly questioned in the art which they produced? What is the relation, in short, between art and ideology where the latter is dictated by political fiat but subject also to the ruses and obliquities of artistic expression? Such an approach might account for at least some of the deep ambiguities which listeners find in Shostakovich's music. It would concentrate on aspects of form and style which leave something to be explained when musical analysis of the traditional kind has exhausted its powers of description. Indeed it is often the case – as Norman Kay remarks in his brief but perceptive study[4] – that Shostakovich's music somehow defeats the methods of even the closest and most sensitive formal analysis. There are passages, especially in the string quartets, which possess a complexity and depth of feeling oddly unrelated to anything 'there' in the music's simple, almost neutral style. This curious effect of expressive self-distancing, as if by an act of willed withdrawal, is perhaps another symptom of Shostakovich's complex predicament. It suggests once again how the critic must treat the 'life' in constant relation to the 'work'.

Of course it is true that composers have always had to find themselves – to work out their intentions and their creative self-image – in terms of an existing social order with its norms and expectations. For Haydn and Mozart in an age of patronage, the relation amounted to a form of implicit contractual agreement as to how the composer should best fulfil his social-aesthetic obligations. For Beethoven and his Romantic successors, the artist assumed a more complex and isolated role as the individual genius pitted against the forces of social and cultural conformity. The modern avant-garde had its roots in this Romantic ideology of lonely achievement and alienated genius. Yet the conflict remained an essentially *productive* source of tension, fostering the energies and self-assertive passion of so much romantic and modern music. It is present in Shostakovich, albeit in a more self-conscious and defensively ironic form. Officially the Soviet composer has little use for the tragic intensities and isolated selfhood of late-romantic fashion. Shostakovich was on safe ideological ground when he expressed, in 1931, an antipathy for Scriabin and his 'bourgeois-decadent' aesthetic. 'We consider Scriabin as our bitter musical enemy. Why? Because his music tends toward unhealthy eroticism. Also to mysticism, passivity and a flight from the reality of life.'[5] A ringing affirmation, one might think, of Shostakovich's belief in the socialist-optimist creed. Yet all these charges were soon to be laid at his own door, including the taint of 'unhealthy eroticism' detected (not without reason!) in the opera *Lady Macbeth*.

The problem for criticism lies in explaining precisely how and where the pressures of commitment impinge upon the processes of musical thought. It may be useful, at this point, to distinguish different levels of convention and individuality in what normally counts quite simply as a composer's 'style'. That term is I think best reserved for the deep-grained and perhaps biological traits of expression which make up his individual voice. Although of course subject to changes and development – sometimes of a radical kind – style remains basically a given, indelible part of the composer's identity. It subsists through his music as a sense of (sometimes elusive) continuity, a kind of involuntary selfhood dense with its own prehistory and character. With Shostakovich it is not at all difficult to recognise this personal register of style. The signs are to some extent 'primitive' and sub-thematic, like the penchant for obsessive dotted rhythms in a sharp, toccata-like pattern or the semitonal brooding on germinal motives in a vein of dark introspection. These 'fingerprints' are obvious enough, while others are remarked upon by several of the authors in this volume. At a higher level of stylistic consciousness one finds those repeated self-quotations and thematic cross-references which abound in the later works. Sometimes the effect is virtually that of a *retreat* into style, so that movements like the opening Allegro of the Fifteenth Symphony have a well-nigh impenetrably cryptic character. These riddling gestures often sound like a defence built up around the private places of memory, the mind forced back upon the stoical limits of repetitive auto-suggestion.

This implies a distinction between *style*, as the matrix of individual expression, and the *language* within which that style develops and discovers its identity. Literary critics have always relied upon some such idea of what distinguishes an author's performance from the currency of language in his time and place. With music this line is more difficult to draw, but it plays a vital part in our feeling for a composer's individual voice and relation to his age. Even the most radical break with tradition depends on this sense of background expectation against which to make its point. Thus one can say of Shostakovich that his musical language is a product of various shifting and competing tendencies. His early receptiveness to Western modernist influence (Stravinsky, Hindemith, Milhaud) gives way under pressure to a language of conservative retrenchment and simplified emotion, epitomised in the Fifth Symphony of 1936. Musorgsky later became a dominating presence, though not – it seems clear – for reasons of nationalistic fervour. Indeed his influence deepened the strain of fatalistic brooding and death-haunted reverie in the Fourteenth Symphony and later quartets. In fact Shostakovich's musical language was a constant facing-about between different attractions. Some proved ideologically dangerous, while others were acceptable but – one senses – constrained and personally unfulfilling.

Shostakovich's relationship with Musorgsky is the topic of a lengthy passage in the Volkov *Memoirs*. Whatever their proportion of interpolated spleen, these pages do at least suggest the profound kinship – temperamental as well as musical – between the two composers. That Shostakovich took comfort in Musorgsky's clear-eyed pessimism, that he found in it a refuge from the cruder manifestations of socialised art, is hardly to be doubted. (He or Volkov – one can never be sure – makes joyful play with a statement by the critic Asafiev, defining Socialist Realism as 'an all-healing feeling of the ultimate rightness of reality'.)[6] The point is that temperamental sympathy expressed itself in the choice of musical language, and this in turn was imbued with political meaning. Musorgsky's was an influence which, like others at an earlier stage, Shostakovich could only take on with an attendant weight of implied ideology. The presence of Mahler in his Fourth Symphony – albeit refracted through a welter of conflicting moods – was likewise a risk, and one which led to the music's twenty-year span of enforced cold storage.

Roland Barthes has some interesting reflections on 'style' and 'language' as related to the politics of literature.[7] Their relevance to music, and especially to Shostakovich, will I hope be fairly evident by now. Style, according to Barthes, is at root a 'vertical and lonely' dimension, a medium of deep-grained habit 'biological or biographical' in nature and to that extent 'indifferent to society and transparent to it'. Language can likewise be seen as a neutral or 'indifferent' medium, in the sense that it conditions and preexists the artist's choice of expressive idiom. It forms, Barthes suggests, 'a kind of natural ambience wholly pervading the writer's expression, yet without endowing it with form or content. . .'. It is *between* these two fixed destinies, the private and the communal, that literature (or music) has to work out its individual terms of freedom.

For Barthes there is a third dimension which he calls a 'mode of writing', and which might be translated into musical terms as 'practice of composition' or 'mode of development'. As he puts it:

> A language and a style are blind forces; a mode of writing is an act of historical solidarity. A language and a style are objects; a mode of writing is the relationship between creation and society, language transformed by its social finality, form considered as a human intention and thus linked to the great crises of history.[8]

It is at this level, I would argue, that Shostakovich's music pursues its difficult path amid the thorns and brambles of commitment. Barthes takes the events of 1848 as a kind of political watershed, after which no French writer could practice an 'innocent' or neutral style. To cultivate aesthetic self-absorption, like Flaubert, was itself a quite specific avowal of attitude. The same might be said of Soviet music in the wake of 1917. There is no musical language immune to ideology, or free of the associative traits and suggestions bound up with its specific prehistory. Hence the rather frequent adjustments of attitude, on Shostakovich's part, to the various composers whose musical stock went up and down with the changes of Soviet cultural policy. Stravinsky and Schoenberg are the obvious examples, but others – including Musorgsky – became touchstones of opinion at certain crucial points. Schwarz quotes an article of 1960, published in *Pravda* under Shostakovich's name, which singles out a strange assortment of talents for praise and support. Bartók, Britten, Milhaud, Villa-Lobos,

Weiner and Orff are among those commended for their fearless resistance to the creeping evil of modernism. The article appeared, hardly by coincidence, just a month before the endorsement of Shostakovich's application for Communist Party membership.[9]

George Steiner has remarked that ideological tensions in art can often bring about 'a dissociation of identity very like that suffered by the protagonist in tragic drama'.[10] What one seems to hear in much of Shostakovich's music is the drawn-out and complex drama of a style in search of an acceptable public language. Indeed his whole career could be seen as a tightrope-walk between opposed temptations, whether those of *Proletkult* and the avant-garde, as in the early Leningrad years, or between private musing and public display, as so often in the middle-period symphonies. The music enacts a drama of choice every bit as rooted and compulsive as the temperamental conflicts of a Mahler or Tchaikovsky. To understand these wrenchings of mood one has to appreciate how the iron of self-criticism has entered into Shostakovich's soul, and how apparently *pre-conscious* are those elements in his music which come to forestall the effects of public judgement.

These purgings of musical conscience take various forms at different stages of Shostakovich's career. Sometimes they are signalled by a willed suppression of individual style in the effort to achieve a more accessible and 'public' language. The most obvious move in this direction came with the Eleventh and Twelfth Symphonies, both composed for state occasions and programmed explicitly to celebrate the events of 1905 and 1917. In the Volkov *Memoirs* one finds – predictably – an attempt to undermine and recast this programmatic content. The Eleventh is recalled as a desolate reflection on the period which produced it (1957), rather than a grim portrayal of the first, abortive revolution. The Twelfth is explained as a failed attempt – 'the material put up resistance' – to celebrate Stalin's heroic virtues. (Since by all accounts the intended subject was Lenin, not Stalin, one can only assume a momentary lapse either in Shostakovich's memory or in Volkov's otherwise well-oiled machinery of slanted reconstruction.) At any rate the Eleventh and Twelfth Symphonies were well enough received at the time and represented a partial solution, or line of appeasement, in Shostakovich's struggle for a workable public language.

Other attempts were less successful and ran into the various problems and paradoxes which are, perhaps, inherent in the concept of Socialist Realism. The Ninth Symphony is one such case, a work of (on the face of it) impeccable good humour and accessible emotion. Root cause of the trouble, apparently, was that Shostakovich had been expected to compose a large-scale programmatic work, celebrating the victory of 1945 and resolving the war-weary tensions of the Eighth Symphony. (It was also to have been a tribute to Lenin, though Shostakovich/ Volkov again cast Stalin in the role of disgruntled non-recipient.) As it turned out the Ninth was a fluent and self-possessed work, high-spirited and plangent by turns, but much too lightweight to satisfy such grand expectations. The old charge of 'formalism' was again in the air, and Shostakovich lost the favour he had gained with his rousing wartime productions.

There is an irony in the fact that this symphony achieved such a happy directness of mood, and was yet held up to censure on grounds of formalist deviation. It is a paradox which indeed lies close to the heart of the Soviet-Marxist aesthetic. That programme required – and one should not underestimate its hold on Shostakovich's thinking – a music which revolved around the major triad, effectively equating tonal vigour and simplicity with the aims of socialist optimism. In practice, however, the equation proved more difficult to balance. The Ninth with its classicist, at times almost Haydnesque vein was seen as a culpable retreat from the march of historical events. Shostakovich's striving for a simplified language failed to engage with the specified sense of *occasion* – the explicit revolutionary programme – which loyalty required. Roland Barthes again provides a suggestive parallel in his comments on Gide, whose writing Barthes admires for its studious avoidance of 'style'. Gide, he reflects, 'is the very type of an author without style . . . whose craftsmanlike approach exploits the pleasure the moderns derive from a certain classical ethos, just as Saint-Saëns has composed in Bach's idiom, or Poulenc in Schubert's'.[11] There is a similar harking-back to the 'classical ethos' at several points in Shostakovich's career, often in the wake of some large-scale programmatic effort. Thus, as we have seen, the masterly Piano Quintet followed closely upon the *Leningrad* Symphony, while the *24 Preludes and Fugues* of 1933 marked a chastened withdrawal into problems of style and technique at a time when tensions were perhaps already building toward the *Lady Macbeth* furore.

It seems, in short, that Shostakovich repeatedly ran up against trouble in his efforts to square the demands of socialist realism with the clear-cut emotional pattern of a 'classical' language. Oddly enough, it is in the Twelfth Symphony – in many ways the least convincing of the cycle – that classical form is most closely bound up with programmatic content. The opening movement (as Schwarz wryly notes) is a worked-out sonata-allegro of the type that Shostakovich had always been anxious to create. The subsequent Adagio, Scherzo and Finale are in an equally traditional mould, albeit overlaid with a rhetoric of alternating pathos and bravado. That the symphony fails to convince – that it leaves an impression of brashness and misdirected energy – is a symptom of the problems which confronted Shostakovich in his search for a programmatic language. This sense of dislocated purpose in the music reflects a deeper tension in the premises of (old-style) socialist realism. Herbert Marcuse has analysed this tension in his study of Soviet ideology and its ethical-aesthetic implications. Marcuse points out that socialist morality tends to assume a convergence between the real and the ideal, such that any hint of romantic 'transcendence' becomes either false or merely gratuitous. 'The *promesse du bonheur* which, being beyond reality, constituted the "romantic" element in art, now appears as the realistic concern of the policy-makers – realism and romanticism converge.'[12] To Marcuse this signifies the negation of art in its active, critical role. The aesthetic realm retains its dignity and meaning 'only in so far as it preserves the images of liberation'.

Marcuse, like his intellectual mentor Adorno, goes too far in his theory of art as the 'determinate negation' of everything pertaining to social reality. His overreaction can be judged from his (surely desperate) view that the 'bourgeois anti-realists and formalists' are more committed to political change than their social-realist counterparts. Nevertheless there is an aspect of his argument which touches directly on the problems implicit in Shostakovich's music. It emerges in what I have described as the composer's struggle to combine revolutionary content with a largely conventional or handed-down language. 'Transcendence' is restricted to the evocation of an ideal society *already achieved*, or in imminent prospect of achievement. Revolutionary content is therefore prescribed, but not – emphatically – the kind of revolutionary language or form which might imply a continuing process of change. Shostakovich was liable to charges of formalist abstraction whenever his music approached the realm of transcendent (or non-programmatic) ideals, as defined by Marcuse.

This conservative aspect of Soviet thinking was much in evidence during the Stalin years, and affected many areas of cultural debate. In linguistics and philosophy, for instance, there was an effort to counter extreme formulations of the base/superstructure model, theories which held that the very foundations of language and thought must change with the coming of a new social order. Such 'leftist' deviations erred by placing too much weight on the socio-economic base, and ignoring the relative autonomy of certain privileged cultural forms. Language and logic, Stalin decreed, were themselves prime determinants of thought and not to be treated relativistically as 'mere' components of the superstructure. Dialectics was defined as a higher, more powerful application to social realities of a process of thought which still needed to obey the ground-rules of classical logic. With language likewise, a line was to be drawn between the changeable manifestations of social time and place and the deeper continuity of a national culture. Style and content might be socially conditioned and undergo radical transformations from stage to stage in the historical process. There remained, however, a bedrock of linguistic tradition impervious to such shifts and far out-reaching the various periods of economic change.

Marcuse sees this philosophy as one of conservative retrenchment, reflecting the Soviet need both for coexistence with the West and for compromise measures to boost the internal economy. What it clearly led to, in cultural terms, was a call for the artist to confine his experiments to matters of 'relevant' content, and not to interfere with the primary resources of medium or language. Gone was the heady post-revolutionary climate of the 'twenties, when radicalism in art could claim a close kinship with the process of political change. The resultant paradox – 'revolutionary' art in a conservative mould – was one which dogged Shostakovich's attempts to reconcile musical argument with programmatic content.

This is not to say that Shostakovich rejected the very notion of programmaticism, or pretended to accept it while in truth undermining its claims. (Such is Volkov's repeated implication, but his 'alternative' programmes are too neat and consistent by half.) Shostakovich offered several public statements on the subject, some of which at least have a genuinely pondered and strikingly unorthodox import. Schwarz quotes an article of 1951, 'On Real And Alleged Programme Music', wherein Shostakovich sets out to tackle these thorny problems on the margins of music and ideology. Musical content, he argues, 'consists not only of a subject stated in detail but also of a crystallised idea or the sum-total of ideas'.[13] Programmaticism is at one point simply identified with 'cogent content', an equation which could be stretched to accommodate even the most resistant musical forms. Since this article appeared between the Ninth and Tenth Symphonies, perhaps it is a reasonable guess that Shostakovich was tentatively feeling his way toward a new, more flexible aesthetic.

His problems were no doubt intensified by the constant talk, in Soviet aesthetics, about 'form' and 'content' as if these were distinct and separable aspects of artistic endeavour. Such distinctions are of course artificial at root, and indeed represent the heresy of 'formalism' in its pure, aboriginal guise. Ironically, the whole anti-formalist thrust of Soviet discussion tends to perpetuate this drastic dualism by implying that 'content' is something the composer can profitably work at while 'form' should somehow look after itself, or at least not get in the way. One can see why the question of programme-music became for Shostakovich a test-case and a matter for earnest speculation. It offered a focus and a public forum for debates which were otherwise conducted in the solitude of his own imagination.

The difficulties Shostakovich faced are in some sense echoed by the tortuous pronouncements of Soviet critics responding to his music. Thus Khubov, a prominent commentator, writing on the Fifth Symphony in 1937:

Shostakovich took the criticism of his formalism quite seriously. For two years he worked stubbornly at a new creative development of gifts . . . recognising the impossibility of any such growth unless he abandoned his formalism, Shostakovich chose the line of greatest resistance: that of organically overcoming his errors by intense internal struggle. . .'[14]

One notices the forced, paradoxical quality of thought and language alike: the oddity of 'working stubbornly' at a 'new development of creative gifts', and of the term 'organic' applied to a conscious effort of will. These puzzles are all a part of the Marxist determinist aesthetic, the implications of which are frequently at work in Shostakovich's development. They tend to reproduce in critical thought the same basic conflicts of instinct, motive and will as are manifest in the music itself. To give 'organic' this curious deterministic force, as opposed to certain rooted individualist temptations, is to prescribe a dialectics of musical content which can hardly fail to have a complex, self-alienating effect. Understanding Shostakovich is often a matter of sensing this conflict between musical impulse and various kinds of extra-musical imperative. The critic Martynov finds himself on the same paradoxical ground in his talk of 'optimistic tragedy', of the virtues of artistic conservatism in the cause of revolution, and of Shostakovich's early 'innovations' as mere distracting foibles.[15] It is often depressing to read these tortuous mixtures of pure hagiography and confidently handed-down abuse. They do, however, give an added sense of the contradictions which beset Shostakovich and are lived through, at a certain level, in the composition of his music.

Much of this debate naturally centred on the Fifth Symphony, this being of all Shostakovich's works the most avowedly 'correct' and self-reforming. The symphony was planned to represent 'the maturing of a human personality', passing from private or neurotic discord to a reaffirmation of purpose, identified of course with social progress at large. The catch here, to sceptical Western ears, lies in that last equation; and to many listeners the closing pages of the symphony, with their insistent optimistic build-up, betray a collapse into programmatic bombast. Volkov in the *Memoirs* has Shostakovich wearily protesting that here, as with the *Leningrad*, his intentions were double-edged and satirical from the start. He reviles a certain conductor 'who considers himself its greatest interpreter' (Volkov suggests Mravinsky) for regarding the Fifth as having failed to achieve its 'exultant' finale. 'I think that it is clear to everyone what happens in the Fifth. The rejoicing is forced, created under a threat, as in *Boris Godunov*.'[16] Like so much in the *Memoirs*, this strikes a false note not because it seems foreign to our experience of the music, but because it squares so perfectly with what a Western ideologue would want to say. No doubt many critics will congratulate themselves for having arrived by pure intuition at what the *Memoirs* now place on public record. That the record is so shrewdly, consistently slanted should at least give them pause for thought. In the case of the Fifth Symphony, any such clear-cut 'alternative' programme can only seem as crude and wide of the mark as the original, official version. Intentions are at best an ambiguous matter, complicated both by the distance of hindsight and the often intractable demands of musical form. Revisionist interpretations are subject to the same kind of doubt and ultimate undecidability as marked almost all Shostakovich's dealings with programme music.

Criticism, like good deeds, is known by its fruits; so that only a detailed analysis of the music can justify the kind of conjectural method here put forward. Musical criticism in this sense partakes of the 'hermeneutic circle' beloved of literary theorists: the fact that our experience of the work as a whole depends on our detailed understanding of its parts, while such local understanding can only be achieved through some basic or intuitive grasp of the whole. A composer's biography becomes relevant when, as I have argued, it cuts across this suggestive relation of parts to whole. No artist can say, like Shakespeare's Parolles, 'simply the thing I am shall make me live'. At either of two extremes it may be almost possible: for a man like Haydn whose genial style is largely what the age (or patronage) demands, or for a composer like Mahler whose suffering ego contracts the whole world into its own subjective limits. Both examples are relevant, since Shostakovich's musical language has often veered between a Haydnesque classical lightness and a brooding intensity reminiscent of Mahler. But in his case the result is an obscure and cryptic music, its personal style increasingly set off against its public aspirations. With composers who lived (or live) in strongly individualist and liberal cultures, such symptoms lead back mainly to *private* states of conflict – for instance, the kind of neurotic psycho-biography which we infer, by common understanding, from the symphonies of Mahler. These habits of response are by no means timeless or 'natural'. They are a matter of advanced cultural adjustment, as much subject to historical change as the evolving patterns of harmonic and tonal language. In Shostakovich we have the paradigm of a new, essentially *political* form of complex inward adjustment, one which in turn requires a new kind of sympathy and habit of extended response.

But perhaps it is time to return from these speculative regions and look more closely at the music itself. What compositional traits can one point to by way of arguing this intimate relation between 'life' and 'work'? First, and most basic, is the extreme *nervous* quality which runs through so many of Shostakovich's scores; the impression one has that lyrical instinct has been somehow displaced or deflected by an almost hyper-active conscious alertness. Symptomatic in this way are the prolonged *ostinati*, the obsessive toccata-based movements (Eighth and Tenth Symphonies) and the vein of edgy nervous brilliance which marks so much of his music. One also remembers those repeated self-quotations which increasingly suggest a mood of protective introvert withdrawal.

That conscious and unconscious functions have an unusual relation in Shostakovich's music is, I think, a point of some importance. Freud tells us that the conscious mind, with its structure of memory and expectation, exists partly as a safeguard against the barrage of impressions which would – if not thus prevented – cause total psychic disruption. In modern times (and especially, perhaps, in a post-revolutionary climate) the shocks of novel experience come ever more quickly, and consciousness assumes a more complicated role in countering the stream of events. One can hear this mood of tensed expectation in the Second Symphony, where Shostakovich briefly indulged a taste for *outré* experiment and musical shock tactics. There is a kind of high-pitched nervous excitement which tries to get on terms with outside events (revolution and the march of industrialisation) by outdoing them in sheer audacity.

Add to this the constant fear of public condemnation, often for the most contradictory reasons, and it becomes clear that a certain protective heightening of consciousness is almost inevitable in Shostakovich's music. These possibilities are explored by the critic Walter Benjamin in his classic essay 'Some Motifs in Baudelaire'. Benjamin discusses the modern history and background of lyric poetry, and asks whether the pure contemplative mode can possibly survive this preternatural sharpening of awareness. In Baudelaire, poet of the huge anonymous city, Benjamin finds a model and precursor of the new defensive lyricism, painfully alert and forced into a posture of perpetual expectation.

> The greater the share of the shock factor in particular impressions, the more constantly consciousness has to be alert as a screen against stimuli. . . Baudelaire made it his business to parry the shocks, wherever they might come from, with his physical and spiritual self. He indicated the price for which the sensation of the modern age may be had. . .[17]

These remarks apply strikingly to the music of Shostakovich, where the place of lyrical instinct has been threatened and to some extent invaded by the pressures of strategic self-awareness.

Examples of his curiously tortured lyricism are not hard to find. Take the *Lento* theme of the First Symphony's slow movement; a melodic outline of genuine beauty and pathos, yet characterised by a desolate chromaticism, and by wide melodic leaps which sharpen one's reactions against any too easy emotional empathy. The same is true of the impressive second subject which so dominates the opening movement of the Fifth Symphony (fig. 8*ff*). Its effect of a strangely thwarted lyricism comes of its closeness to a pure singing line, disrupted by leaps of up to an octave-and-a-half; arming its emotions with an offbeat, slightly recalcitrant quality which again precludes a straightforward sense of involvement. One could find many similar examples, all pointing to the sources of tension at the heart of Shostakovich's music.

With the later works this screening of emotional impulse

becomes a kind of second nature, a deep-lying habit of thought. This is particularly true of the string quartets, where Shostakovich's language shows a steadily deepening obscurity and privacy of utterance. It is not exactly a matter of *emotional* depth, since the Eighth Quartet – the most popular of the sequence – has a charged intensity of feeling which comes across clearly enough to the listener. Its use of the famous *DSCH* motive (D-E flat-C-B) may have some kind of riddling private significance, but here the effect is one of direct and powerful self-expression. The Eighth is also, paradoxically, the most 'public' of the series, with its literal evocation of the Dresden bombing and its screaming rehearsal of fragments from the wartime compositions. In this work for once Shostakovich achieved a perfect communicative balance between the private and the public dimensions. Elsewhere the quartets are more reticent and cryptic, sometimes to the point of virtual isolation in a world of eerie echoes and half-caught allusions. In the Fifth Quartet the DSCH motive again turns up, but this time in various changed and often distorted guises, the effect of which is to question and parody the emotional sources of the original theme. The Ninth is remarkable likewise for its remote tonal idiom, the fragmentary treatment of its themes and the tenuous, almost disjunct progress of its five contrasted sections. It occupies a realm of contradictory emotions, epitomised by the E flat major Adagio (fourth movement), which veers alarmingly from quiet meandering to a wild and unprepared-for pizzicato outburst.

Critics have spoken in general terms of the 'modernistic' elements in these later quartets, judging probably by the twelve-tone patterns audible in Nos. 12 and 13. More to the point – since the music remains very distinctly tonal – is the way in which these conscious devices of order provide yet another retreat, or protective outwork, for Shostakovich's feelings. In the long run, perhaps, the conflict of impulse and commitment in his music produced a late style which was close in some respects to the character and ethos of serialism. The philosopher Anton Ehrenzweig has argued that serial techniques – along with certain other developments in modern art – have the primary purpose of baffling and thus re-defining our perceptions of ordered significance.[18] This reordering takes place at a pre-conscious level where instinct and awareness are related in ways unfamiliar from normal experience. Such I believe is the case with Shostakovich's music. It is audible in works like the Twelfth Quartet, where the second-movement Scherzo is full of such disruptive effects, and the overall impression is one of strangely oblique intensity. This sense of dislocated feeling might be called the equivalent, in psychological terms, of the formal *dérèglement* achieved by serial procedures.

I have been trying to suggest how a heightened self-consciousness in this later music parries and deflects the dangers of public exposure. Shostakovich meets criticism more than half-way; his music anticipates, appeases and often implicitly *expresses* the tensions of exacted commitment. A detailed history of the music's reception would bear increasingly on its actual character, on the way in which Shostakovich's language grew to fit the contradictory self-image given back by a watchful public. Good intentions were by no means a definite safeguard, as we have seen in the twists of popular and critical fortune which met so many of his works. Typical in this respect was the opera *Katerina Ismailovna* (originally *Lady Macbeth of the Mtensk Region*), a work which helped to bring about the first of Shostakovich's lapses from grace. The opera is, on the face of it, a quite unexceptionable piece of post-revolutionary theatre. It is the story of a spirited woman bored beyond endurance by her bourgeois-merchant husband, so that eventually she takes a lover and, forced by circumstance, connives at the husband's murder. Like Janáček's *Katya Kabanova*, the opera suggests a close liaison between parental tyranny (in this case Katerina's boorish father-in-law) and the old property-based system of a near-feudal society. In its first two years the work had more than a hundred performances in Russia, and was well received when Rodzinski took it to New York. Then, in January 1936, *Pravda* came out with its famous attack on Shostakovich, and *Lady Macbeth* was henceforth dropped from the Soviet repertory. The article reproved Shostakovich for (among other things) the raucous character of his satire, the incoherence of his musical language and – above all – the sympathy shown to his hapless heroine.

The effect of these criticisms on Shostakovich's mind – on his sense of what counted toward a revolutionary art – can only be guessed at. *Lady Macbeth* was like the Fourth Symphony, a work conceived in the spirit of revolt and iconoclastic zeal which marked the early, exciting phase of Soviet cultural life. Hence the vein of grotesque caricature and the musically-explicit eroticism which set out to shock (and succeeded all too well). One finds the same attitudes, more defiantly pitched, in the life and poetry of Mayakovsky. The artist who tries to live up to the revolution, who makes his art a constant affront, a challenge to all received dignities – such a man is forced in the end to view himself ironically and stage his life as a running satire. Revolution becomes a kind of private romp, a self-advertising drama set up to project the artist's grudge against society in general.

Russian art after 1917 produced its fair share of these Byronic individualists, combining a high-romantic zeal for self-expression with a taste for the extremes of destructive satire. Shostakovich's Fourth Symphony is in many ways a product of this ethos, switching as it does – sometimes within the space of a few bars – from Mahlerian anguish and intensity to raucous, self-lacerating humour. In this sense there was, one can see, a measure of clear-sightedness in the disapproving edict of 1936. The censors were right to find something more subversive than revolutionary in the romantic-satirical vogue *pour épater le bourgeois*. But for Shostakovich, who had invested such youthful energies in the earlier phase, this official turn-about to Socialist Realism must have come with all the shock of a personal disinheritance. Implicit in *Lady Macbeth* was the hopeful, affirmative view: that music could serve society by destructively satirising the old, repressive order while at the same time preserving, in the midst of this violence, the image of suffering humanity as a value to be redeemed. With the repudiation of these ideals, so forcefully announced by *Pravda*, Shostakovich embarked upon that long painful process of adjustment which made up the course of his private-public career.

We are now perhaps in a position to distinguish the subdued *structural* irony of the later music – especially the quartets – from the indulged romantic irony of works like *Lady Macbeth* and the Fourth Symphony. The pre-1936 compositions struck a note of extravagant satirical relish and personal revolt which seemed to romanticise the business of revolution. The later compositions, where their mood is most complex, also bear the marks of a deeply politicised aesthetic, but now in a vein of cryptic understatement and defensive irony. On the other hand there *is* a continuity present from the earliest works and carried over, through subtle transformations, into the 'final' phase. It lies in that habit of self-deflating humour – caustic, ironic or mildly benevolent – which runs through the whole of Shostakovich's music. In an article of 1934 one finds him publicly extolling the virtues of laughter in music, and declaring against the monopoly held by the earnest, the solemn and the tragic.[19] This accords with the strong satirical bent of the early works. It forms the active principle of that feeling which he elsewhere expressed as a hatred of Scriabin and his musical values: a rejection of everything tending to mysticism, passivity and other-worldliness.

This element of subterranean laughter in Shostakovich's music is aptly figured in his choice of Gogol's story *The Nose* for operatic treatment. The score is a downright satirical romp, poking fun at bumbling officialdom and using all manner of crude musical devices (the role of the Nose is directed to be sung through pinched nostrils!). What gives all this freakish humour a certain representative value is the fact that it survives, in a muted and subtilised form, into much of Shostakovich's later music. It foreshadows the touches of grotesque self-parody which lurk behind passages in even his most 'personal' and deeply-felt works. In the Fifth Symphony, for instance, ideas from the finely-wrought first and third movements are carried over, crudely transformed, into the rousing finale; a process of more-or-less conscious deformation which reflects ironically on the music's idealistic programme. The Fifteenth Symphony is the furthest advanced along this path of baffling allusiveness and self-conscious parody. Its manifold associative hints and quotations (including the snatches from Wagner and the *William Tell* overture) make up a kind of serio-comic brooding on the oddities of musical tradition. Yet the Fifteenth contains, in its slow movement especially, passages of a rapt intensity and strangeness as powerful as anything in Shostakovich's music. Again one has to recognise the unsettling coexistence of a deep lyrical impulse with a reflex desire to mock, subvert or defensively cover the sources of emotion.

This turn to the grotesque, as a means of debunking

high-flown ideals, was much in evidence during the formative years of Shostakovich's youth. It was recognised by a group of literary theorists – the so-called 'Bakhtin circle' – who erected their insight into a generalised theory of the 'dialogical' or many-voiced text.[20] This school took issue with the formalist strain in Soviet poetics, but also opposed itself to the cruder, more reductive forms of socialist realism. It was therefore placed, like Shostakovich's music, on the critical ground where new ideas tried to make their peace with the demands of political commitment. Bakhtin and his colleagues objected to formalism in so far as it treated the work of art as a timeless, autonomous creation, divorced from historical events and answerable only to the laws of aesthetic form. They were quick to perceive how such ideas related to the *avant-garde* movements in art – Symbolism, Futurism and their various offshoots – which flourished during those years. The stress on matters of device and technique went along with the doctrine of 'defami-liarisation', the idea that art achieved its best effects by deliberately skewing or subverting our perceptions of reality. Formalism was thus in league, not only with the more abstract kinds of experimentation, but also with the futuristic cult of machine-age violence which one hears in the Shostakovich Second Symphony. Bakhtin has both 'deviations' in view when he criticises the formalist notion of *ostranenie* (defamiliarisation or 'making it strange'). His remarks on the concept as applied to literary language are in much the same vein as contemporary attacks on abstract or futuristic trends in music. Far from 'enriching the word with new and positive constructive mean-ing', the doctrine of *ostranenie* 'simply emphasises the negation of the old meaning . . . the novelty and strangeness of the word and the object it designates originate here, in the loss of meaning'.[21]

Such imputations of artistic 'nihilism' were also levelled at Shostakovich's music, the critics objecting (like Bakhtin) to an attitude which devalued existing reality without putting any-thing 'constructive' in its place. His response, as we have seen, took various forms, some of them bowing to public demand while others assumed a more complex and refractory guise. What is even more striking is the parallel shift, of theory and ethos alike, which occurred in the poetics of Bakhtin and his colleagues. Despite his criticisms, Bakhtin went on to argue that the Formalist method had its positive uses, chiefly that of focussing attention on the detail and specific workings of literary language. He envisages a dialogue of viewpoints, a fruitful exchange whereby Marxist Realism might refine and sharpen its analytic tools, while the Formalists in turn might perceive the importance of social and historical context. The two schools of thought are in need of each other as spurs to the new and higher form of criticism which Bakhtin calls a 'sociological poetics'.

This need for present dialogue on matters of method is projected back, as it were, into Bakhtin's view of literary history. He argues that certain kinds of text (especially novels) are 'dialogical' in the sense that they offer not a single, authoritative 'voice' but a multitude of codes for interpretation. Such texts are typically produced in a period of radical change or social instability when values are open to question and authority subjected to the unsettling voices of satire. These ideas were put to work in Bakhtin's brilliant study of Rabelais, whose technique he characterised as a mocking subversion of all the codes, religious and political, which made up the image of authority. And of course there were examples nearer home – Gogol and Pushkin in particular – to underline the message for Soviet readers.

What is remarkable about this school of criticism is the way in which it managed to express its own problems – the pressures and conflicts of ideology – in universal terms. That the connection was partly conscious is implied by a passage in one of Bakhtin's essays where he speaks of the modern 'scholarly article' as (rather surprisingly) a typical case of 'dialogical' discourse.[22] He goes on to describe 'the present age' (writing in 1928) as one which lacks a commanding system of values, and which therefore lies open to the productive interplay of codes and meanings. This doubtless reflects the period of freedom and cultural licence which went along with Lenin's New Economic Policy. But it also implies – and more pointedly, in the light of subsequent events – that political power when firmly established can still produce such wayward and subversive undercurrents of meaning. Indeed it is a main contention of Bakhtin's theory that 'dialogical' attitudes tend to develop in the face of monolithic or highly institutionalised cultures. He argues powerfully against any form of criticism – be it formalist, Marxist or whatever – which would seek to 'monologise' literary texts, or reduce them to a single, conformable order of meaning. One can see how such a theory might reflexively apply to those very constraints and pressures of commitment which were soon to overtake Soviet intellectual life. Literary criticism found itself, as usual, in the thick of these disputes since it represented the most advanced and articulate form of cultural self-awareness.

The bearing of all this on Shostakovich's music can only be gauged indirectly, through the shifts and obliquities of style which I have tried to describe. It is, on the other hand, a matter of historical fact that he was caught up in many of the same dilemmas and cross-currents of influence as affected the Bakhtin circle. Leningrad, the centre of Shostakovich's musical training, was also the homeground of all the more 'advanced' artistic trends during the period when such options were still officially open. Later it witnessed a growing hostility between the westward-looking modernists and the *proletkult* adherents of music for the masses. Shostakovich was undoubtedly tugged both ways, as can be heard in his *May Day* Symphony (No. 3), at once the most brashly programmatic and oddly non-commital of the sequence. Leopold Stokowski – who conducted the earliest American performances – described the Third as a unique example of 'music written to a Bolshevik programme', radical in message but not, most certainly, in musical idiom. Gerald Abraham has written with some justice of the histrionic element in this symphony: 'one cannot help feeling that the composer is playing a part . . . he tries to be Marxian but a fantastic Gogolian humour keeps breaking in'.[23]

Such intrusions and perhaps involuntary twists of impulse are, as we have seen, a persistent feature of Shostakovich's music, by no means confined to this early phase. A subversive irony continued to play beneath the surface, creating (as Bakhtin might have said) a 'polyphony' of muted, ambivalent voices. To 'monologise' this music in the service of any single message or ideology is to find it once again eluding one's grasp. Straightforward standards of meaning, truth or sincerity scarcely apply to Shostakovich's intentions, stated or imputed.

One is struck by the irrelevance of Schwarz's statement, however well-meant: 'there is an aura of incorruptible sincerity about Shostakovich which does not admit of any sham. . .'.[24] The record, documentary *and* musical, is too full of puzzles and downright contradictions to admit of any such pure-minded faith. The one central truth to which everything bears witness is that Shostakovich, in Nietzsche's words, suffered the destiny of music in his time 'like an open wound'. That destiny presented itself in squarely political terms, and it is hardly surprising that judgements on the music so often partake of a covert or explicit ideological slant. Volkov with his cold-war interpretative tactics will go down as part of the music's peripheral history, along with the unseemly wranglings of the Zhdanov period. Shostakovich's greatness and his fortunes as a Soviet citizen-composer are inseparably bound up together.

Notes

1. *Testimony: the memoirs of Shostakovich*, edited by Solomon Volkov (London: Hamish Hamilton, 1979), pp. 118ff. The authenticity of this passage, like so much in the book, is open to question on various factual and ideological grounds.

2. Quoted in Boris Schwarz, *Music and Musical Life in Soviet Russia, 1917–1970* (London: Barrie & Jenkins, 1972), p. 180.

3. Jean-Paul Sartre, *Search for a Method*, trans. Hazel Barnes (New York: Alfred A. Knopf, 1963).

4. Norman Kay, *Shostakovich* (London: Oxford University Press, 1972).

5. Shostakovich's remarks appeared in the *New York Times*, 20 December 1931. Quoted in Schwarz, p. 62.

6. Volkov, p. 187.

7. Roland Barthes, *Writing Degree Zero* (London: Jonathan Cape, 1967).

8. Barthes, p. 20.

9. Schwarz, p. 335.

10. George Steiner, *Language and Silence* (London: Faber, 1967), p. 193.

11. Barthes, p. 17.

12. Herbert Marcuse, *Soviet Marxism: a critical analysis* (Penguin, 1971), p. 110.

13. Schwarz, pp. 338–9.

14. Quoted in foreword to score of Symphony No. 5 (Leeds Music, 1974).

15. I. Martynov, *D. D. Schostakowitsch* (German-language edn., Moscow 1946).

16. Volkov, p. 140.

17. Walter Benjamin, 'Some Motifs in Baudelaire', in *Illuminations*, trans. Harry Zohn (London: Collins/Fontana, 1973), p. 165.
18. Anton Ehrenzweg, *The Hidden Order of Art* (London: Paladin, 1970).
19. Quoted in F. K. Frieberg, *Musik in der Sowjetunion* (Cologne, 1962), p. 110.
20. P. N. Medvedev & M. M. Bakhtin, *The Formal Method in Literary Scholarship*, trans. Albert J. Wehrle (Baltimore: Johns Hopkins University Press, 1978).
21. ibid, p. 136.
22. M. M. Bakhtin, 'Discourse Typology in Prose' (first published 1929). Reprinted in translation by Matejka & Pomorska (eds), *Readings in Russian Poetics* (Massachusetts: M.I.T. Press, 1971).
23. Quoted by Schwarz from Gerald Abraham, *Eight Soviet Composers* (London, 1943), p. 18.
24. Schwarz, p. 83.

Robert Stradling

Shostakovich and the Soviet System, 1925–1975

> Thus conscience does make cowards of us all;
> And thus the native hue of resolution
> Is sicklied o'er with the pale cast of thought.
> (*Hamlet*, Act III Sc. i)

The 'character' of Hamlet held great significance for Dmitry Shostakovich. In many ways, this essay consists of variations on this theme which in a manner analogous to that of the musical form attempts to present the subject prior to exploring and analysing its characteristics, as it undergoes various changes of time and environment. Of course, a number of Shostakovich's predecessors concurred with Coleridge's 'discovery' of *Hamlet* as being 'about' the frustrations of the Romantic Artist – Berlioz, Liszt, and Tchaikovsky, to name only a few. Unfashionable as it may now be among literary critics, the view of Hamlet as an intellectual caught in the toils of political struggle clearly attracted Shostakovich, who twice (in 1932 and 1964) composed music to accompany productions of the play. So much of the output of the man seems to concern itself with a similar theme – the ambiguous relationship of the artist to a society in ferment of change – that critics have been led to comment (if somewhat cryptically) on the appropriateness of *Hamlet*.[1] The general frame of reference of Shostakovich's music is naturally much wider than this. It is safe to say that no composer since Beethoven has been so central to the history of his time, or has so consistently sought to express the sufferings and aspirations shared by millions of his contemporaries. His experience has at some point been that of every twentieth-century human, a fact reflected in his overt and documented obsessions. The list reads like the syllabus for a course in modern political and social problems: war, revolutionary change, individual freedom, antisemitism, the role of women in society, dictatorship and disillusionment. In terms of the universal value of Shostakovich's music, nevertheless, all this refers back ultimately to the composer's own psyche and to its Hamlet-like characteristics.

It would perhaps be useful to make clear at the outset that the present writer regards Shostakovich, in the absence of any convincing evidence to the contrary, as a lifelong communist and an intense Russian patriot. This given, he believes that there existed, in some elemental way, a profound bond (in both senses of the word) between the composer and his society, which enabled him to survive, to work, and to develop, whatever his external circumstances. This element is to the fore in those passages of his music, occurring even in the most stressful works, which are suffused with an almost ecstatic calm. In any case, it is impossible to discuss Shostakovich at all without reference to his historical context, and critical study of his work is a test-case of the increasing need for musicology to borrow approaches and techniques from the historian. Though actual access to the composer's artistic and biographical relics is restricted, enough is known to provide a fairly continuous narrative (with commentary where called for) of the relationship of his creative life to the development of the Soviet system.[2]

The artistic career of Dmitry Shostakovich covers exactly the two central quarters of the twentieth century. He began composing – indeed he began thinking – in the unprecedented political and intellectual atmosphere of the 1920s. The chaos of postwar Europe, accompanied as it was by the breakdown of old social relationships, saw the widespread questioning of authority and tradition, in which for many the overthrow of long-cherished taboos and prejudices became a way of life.

'Isms' proliferated as never before or since; many artistic prophets turned eagerly to revolutionary Russia, where the break with the past seemed more complete and more conducive to experiment than in Western Europe. This was the period of Lenin's famous New Economic Policy, when a flexible attitude was adopted to small-scale capitalistic development, particularly on the land, complemented by a series of commercial agreements with bourgeois countries, especially Weimar Germany. The mixed socio-economic structure epitomised in Bukharin's exhortation to the peasants to 'enrich yourselves', had its spiritual counterpart in the new worlds of experience opened up to the intellectuals under the benign aegis of Anatoly Lunacharsky, the Commissar of Education and the Arts. It was above all in Leningrad that the avant garde held sway, with many performances of Stravinsky, Hindemith, Krenek, and even Berg. This pragmatic reversion to liberal modes, involving as it did a relaxation of strict Marxist principles, was not to endure. It was later to be felt that in the world of culture, attitudes had formed that were basically heretical and inimical to a socialist society.

To the Western observer, Shostakovich's activities in these early stages of his career seem perfectly consistent with involvement in a revolutionary ideal. For one thing, his compositional language moved rapidly from one pole to another in the two years which separate the First Symphony from the Second (1925–27). His gravitation to the world of the theatre was equally swift and total, and in collaboration with innovators like Meyerhold, he took a full part in the movement to popularize the stage and heighten social awareness. Operas, ballets, film scores on revolutionary themes, poured from his pen. In his hands even the symphony became overtly representational and exhortatory in nature. Though the guiding influence of the eminent musicologist Boris Asafiev was important, few artists can have struggled as wholeheartedly as Shostakovich to achieve the intrinsic relevance of his work to his social environment.

Unfortunately, things were not as straightforward as all this might indicate. In the years following the death of Lenin in 1924, an intense struggle was joined between Stalin, on the one hand, and his rivals (especially Zinoviev and Trotsky) on the other, for control of the Soviet state. One would be wrong to imply that only the prize of supreme power was involved, for serious and honest disagreement over ideological-economic issues was also present. At any rate, Stalin's control of the Communist Party itself proved decisive. From our present standpoint, an important element in his victory, more or less complete by 1928, was the triumph of the party apparatus centred in Moscow over the resistance of Leningrad, 'soul' of the revolution, where Zinoviev was Commissar. To many historians, the emergence of Moscow, the capital of traditional Russian nationalism, and the consequent relegation of Leningrad, historical location of the country's 'window to the West', is richly symbolic of the direction the Soviet system was to take under Stalin.

In Leningrad, Asafiev had formed the Association of Contemporary Musicians, to which Shostakovich belonged in company with the majority of his colleagues. The rival Muscovite organisation, the Russian Association of Proletarian Musicians, was nothing like as popular among professionals, who regarded it as maintaining the *proletkult* movement of crude debasement of the arts in the interests of mass-consumption. The RAPM, in its turn, looked upon the Leningraders as elitists who withheld Culture from the people. With this view the Kremlin increasingly agreed, becoming especially suspicious of the tendency to absorb 'alien' influences. Moreover – and this was a characteristic to be found to an acute degree in Shostakovich's work – the ACM seemed to be given over to the use of a free-ranging satirical humour, which, though perhaps useful at an earlier stage, was now in danger of encouraging contempt for authority itself. Such criticisms came to assume a pressing importance as the 1930s approached, a period when Stalin's policy was to mobilise the full resources of the Russian state and people. In his view only 'socialism in one country', based on a planned economy, could create a system strong enough to defend itself against the reactionary West. The result was the first Five Year Plan, launched in 1929, which transformed the whole material and spiritual basis of Soviet society. Associated with what one historian has called 'the third Russian revolution' was the wholesale collectivisation of the countryside (put through by a military operation which

amounted to large-scale civil war) and the massive programmes of industrialisation and urbanisation.[3] The clampdown on
remnants of 'bourgeois' activity also encompassed artistic
spheres, and a more rigid supervision of intellectual life can be
seen as developing alongside the perfection of Stalin's personal
dictatorship. All the gears of the 1920s were thus thrown into
reverse, and it was in this period that the Soviet system
assumed the introverted and monolithic features that have
since been commonly attributed to it. It is not the place of this
essay to expound on the validity or necessity of all this, but
simply to note that it elevated one man, Joseph Stalin, to a
position in which he assumed the unique arbitration of
intellectual taste and opinion.

The first outward sign of Stalin's inward grace came in 1929
itself, when the Party officially recognised the Moscow-based
RAPM. This move involved the 'reform' of the latter's
constitution, which now clearly stated its regret that:

> the proletariat, which exercises hegemony in social policy and
> general economy, does not exercise this hegemony in cultural
> pursuits, and, in particular, in the arts.[4]

It went on to point to the formation of a fifth column amongst
Soviet artists, 'actually serving enemy ideology' by its use of
forms and techniques which were incomprehensible to the
masses. This aberration was specifically attributed to the NEP;
and Asafiev's group was accused of being 'sustained by the
penetration into the USSR of bourgeois influences from
capitalist countries'. This was a warning shot fired across the
bows of progressive music; but in art (as in much else) the
Kremlin had no very exact idea of what it wanted in the place of
the ruling philosophy of the previous decade. Just as the first
Five Year Plan was 'a leap into the dark' in material life, so its
concomitant 'cultural revolution' was equally speculative. For
the moment, therefore, the RAPM constitution concluded that,
'it is imperative to exercise tolerance towards the intermediate
ideological forms, patiently helping them to form comradely
relationships with the cultural powers of communism'.

At this point we encounter the first difficulties of identifying
motive in the assessment of Shostakovich's development. The
major signpost, as Norman Kay points out,[5] is the Twenty-

Four Preludes for piano (1932), which seems an attempt at an almost ritual expunging of more extreme 'formalistic' techniques. However, if Shostakovich was merely (and purely) taking heed of the straws in the political wind, 1932 would seem rather late for the fact to be registered. On the other hand, to suggest a completely autonomous crisis of creativity is surely stretching coincidence too far. Whatever their relative proportions, both factors clearly existed. The composer's exercise in self-reform was a limited one, as the Fourth Symphony was to show – indeed, to the constant irritation and exasperation of Soviet critics, the reform was never at any point in Shostakovich's life to be definitive. But the Fourth Symphony was composed alongside the first full-scale, and eminently 'approachable' chamber work, the 'cello sonata (1934). These two pieces are the first of many opposed pairs, or grouped pairs, of compositions which illustrate the profound duality in the artistic personality of our subject.

It may be instructive to compare Shostakovich in this period of uncertainty and adjustment to another musician caught in the tightening vice of a totalitarian system. The Russian composer had been influenced by Paul Hindemith to a greater degree than by any other contemporary. Not only the language, but the aesthetic style of his First Symphony – designed (as I believe it was) as an anti-symphony, a 'deconstruction' of the grandiose and decadent statement favoured in 'First Symphonies' by such bourgeois musicians as Sibelius, Rachmaninov, and even Stravinsky – were indebted to Hindemith's method. In 1929, Hindemith produced his 'anti-opera' *The News* (with its 'hate duet' and 'divorce march'), the same year as Shostakovich's iconoclastic diversion *The Nose* (after Gogol). Both artists quickly matured from this youthful debunking of convention in the atmosphere of the 'thirties; the former's opera *Mathis der Maler*, and the latter's *Lady Macbeth of Mtsensk* (both produced in 1934) were statements of a considerably more responsible and profound nature. Indeed, Hindemith's concern was explicitly with the artistic predicament with which he, like Shostakovich, was confronted; and though Mathis recoils from the violence of revolutionary struggle, the opera concludes that the artist cannot survive by retreating into a private creative world, but must come to terms with the socio-political problems of his day, however bitter the experience.[6] The humanism and tragic lyricism of *Lady Macbeth* demonstrates Shostakovich's similar acceptance of this maxim.

By 1934, the period of 'toleration' was over. Maxim Gorky produced the formula of 'socialist realism' as the objective of all Soviet art. This was not quite pulled like a rabbit out of a hat, as many commentaries suggest. In the late 'twenties, Lunacharsky had evolved a very similar principle, by the use of the classic Marxist dialectic of thesis, antithesis, synthesis. In his view, the struggle of 'socialist realism' with 'pessimistic romanticism' gave rise to 'vital romanticism'. Lunacharsky, one of the Leninist old guard, died in 1933. At the end of the following year (once again in Leningrad) Stalin's series of political purges began. Gorky's tag was sufficiently vague to mean anything that the Party – or rather Stalin – might wish. In the musical sphere it shortly became clear that the prescription eschewed formal, technical, or harmonic advances which had taken place since *Tristan* and *Parsifal*. The ideal language of 'socialist realism', as exemplified for the 'thirties in the work of composers like Dzerzhinsky and Kabalevsky, was that of Rimsky-Korsakov or of Saint-Saëns. Only in these familiar and unproblematical wrappings could the message of socialism be presented to the masses. To this there is an important rider; since the message was one of optimism, the tragic muse was to be discouraged, or at least (in order to stress the need for struggle and sacrifice) utilised in a strictly functional way, as representing an adversary invariably overcome. It should be understood, therefore, that for the Soviet critic, 'revolutionary' or 'new' music equalled 'socialist realism', more or less as defined above – that is to say music that his Western counterpart would glibly refer to as 'conservative'. This paradox effectively spelt the end of experiment, and the proscription of all the 'progressive' elements in the work of the previous generation. From now on, the criterion of success was to be basically, if not crudely, utilitarian. In later years, Shostakovich himself was to prefer a description in terms of 'Soviet humanism': 'formalism we call that art which does not know of love for the people . . . which takes into account only form and denies content'.[7] It will be appreciated from this how mutually antipathetic were the trends in Marxist art and criticism nurtured in Soviet and Western intellectual circles.

As the series of purges began which were to consume millions of victims before 1941, Shostakovich was in a very vulnerable position. He more than any other prominent artist had been influenced by 'decadent' Western trends, the effect of which had 'carried him away from the natural path of development of Soviet art'.[8] Though this 'natural path' had only just been discovered, and was by no means clearly marked, this did not prevent *Pravda* from censuring Shostakovich's ballet music *The Limpid Stream* in 1934. This event – coming two years before the *Lady Macbeth* affair – was particularly worrying for Shostakovich. The ballet was an explicit piece of propaganda on behalf of collectivisation, but in portraying the idyllic life of the *kolkhozy* the composer had apparently been too light-hearted and comic. The situation was certainly far from comic for the newly-married composer. Thousands of people in state service and public life – categories which in the Soviet system include professional artists and intellectuals – were now falling victim to the great purges. Liquidations took place without prosecution or trial (until 1937) and on the mere suspicion of offences which were no more specific than that which had now fallen on Shostakovich. Charges, when made or hinted at, almost invariably mentioned 'alien influences' or 'bourgeois contacts'. Many eminent figures in political and military life, well-known in the West and with long records of service, simply disappeared. It cannot now be believed that Shostakovich's survival was assured; on the contrary hindsight should not condition us to feel that he could never have met the fate of Isaac Babel and others. The years between *The Limpid Stream* and the Fifth Symphony were unquestionably years of immense physical danger.[9]

With the suppression of *Lady Macbeth*, a full-scale opera which had already entered the Russian repertoire and obtained productions all over the world, this crisis reached its peak. The reasons for its official unpopularity seem fairly clear. I cannot agree with Bernard Stevens's suggestion that the opera's 'satire . . . had almost reached the point where humanity itself, not merely bourgeois society, was ridiculed'. It is true that many of the incidents portrayed are essentially bitter and destructive in comment, but the humanist inspiration at the work's core can hardly be questioned. Norman Kay, on the other hand, exaggerates in maintaining that *Lady Macbeth* was an excellent example of 'socialist realism' and that the censure is a puzzling matter.[10] For one thing the plot is unrelievedly pessimistic; for another one can be fairly certain that the original score contained more distinct traces of 'bourgeois formalism', the 'infantile disorders' disseminated by Stravinsky, Berg (*et al.*) than survive in the revised version of 1963.[11] At any rate, the fact that the infamous *Pravda* article 'A Muddle instead of Music' appeared only after Stalin had himself attended a performance underlines the importance of the dictator's personal opinion. Whether or not influenced by Molotov (who was after all a reasonable amateur fiddler and Scriabin's nephew to boot), for Stalin the opera was a painful experience. Doubtless he found the music unpalatable, but possibly also something in his own past helped to inspire reaction against the subject-matter. According to the picture of Stalin given by both his daughter Svetlana and Khrushchëv, he was not likely to be attracted by Shostakovich's treatment of the feminist theme.[12] Moreover, 1936 was not an appropriate time to remind audiences of the horrors of Siberian labour camps, nor to exonerate the assassination of those placed in authority. If the composer wished to keep his head, his next major work would have to be one in which as few hostages as possible were offered to fortune.

In view of the foregoing, it is salutary to the point of discomfort to record that Shostakovich managed to appease the demands of officialdom with a symphony which, far from being a spiritless hackwork, was his first unqualified masterpiece for orchestra. The Fifth Symphony is rightly regarded, not only as one of the finest of Shostakovich's great series, but as a key contribution to the revival of the genre in the twentieth century.[13] Its dramaturgical outline presents very much the image of Soviet society and its mammoth efforts in the building of a new civilisation, which the Stalinist regime wished to establish and perpetuate. Yet it involved no serious compromise of aesthetic principle on its composer's part. In this difficult act of resolution of very real political and musical problems the uses of adversity seem to have been sweet indeed. Nevertheless, an important reservation must be expressed as regards the composer's celebrated statement that the symphony represented 'a Soviet artist's response to just criticism'. Whilst one would certainly not wish to equate this remark with the numberless 'confessions' extracted from the less fortunate victims of Stalinist tyranny, it is all the same noteworthy that two important departures took place at this stage of Shostakovich's career. First, the composer whose interest in vocal and theatre music had become no less than central to his output, ceased to write in these areas altogether. He never wrote another work for the stage; for the voice, nothing of any significance until the cycle on Jewish Folk Poetry, which came shortly after the war, but was withheld from publication and performance until the mid-fifties. These facts seem to hold an inescapable political significance; but in a way even more striking is the resort, at this juncture, to the medium of the string quartet. His first, extremely sunny, essay in this form, represented the modest inauguration of a stupendous series, and was composed alongside the Fifth Symphony. The quartet, perhaps above all other exercises, provides a refuge for the private psyche of author and audience, proof against the inscrutable and temperamental 'interpretation' of officialdom. It was no accident that the tendency of Soviet composers generally in devoting too much attention to chamber music was later noted and attacked by Zhdanov. Such developments were also part of Shostakovich's 'response to criticism'; as it happened, in his case, the line of least resistance was also a line of genius and of permanent value.

If the Fifth Symphony represented a struggle for resolution, its successor proclaimed a new-found stability and mastery. The Sixth is an assured masterpiece which has not yet received sufficient recognition, particularly for its profound aesthetic.[14] It supremely illustrates Shostakovich's ambiguous approach to his work, and seems to me the key example of the bond or contract between composer and society referred to earlier. The symphony presents with vivid honesty two aspects, private in the first movement, public in the finale, linked with nice judgement by an enigmatic scherzo, instinct with delicacy of feeling, the shadowy world between the two 'sides'. Thus Shostakovich makes use of a kind of 'bilingualism', one strain of which accepts the social function demanded of him, and performs it with genuine joy and superlative skill, whilst the other asserts the survival of his autonomous personality. As in true bilingualism neither language takes precedence, but they exist as equal partners, constantly informing and cross-fertilising each other. Only this can explain the unique and otherwise disjunctive formal structure of the Sixth Symphony. A similar duality is to be observed, expanded on to a vastly larger canvas, in the two different – but surely not separate – 'war symphonies', the Seventh and Eighth. In the last analysis, this compromise was not acceptable to the Soviet authorities, though for a decade it provided a working relationship rewarding to both parties. In dealing with the compositions of this period, the major Soviet biographer, Rabinovich, is constantly obliged to explain away his subject's frequent lapses from ideological purity back into the sinful habits of adolescence – dissonance, chromaticism, motor-rhythms. Whatever deviates from the utilitarian and optimistic simply will not do, even for such a valuable and symphathetic advocate, while the idea that there can be any *distinction* (much less, *tension*) between citizen and artist is patently absurd.

The decisive phase of the anti-Nazi war produced a very different relationship between composer and state. Shostakovich, as is well known, contributed towards the defence of Leningrad and hymned the city's determination and sacrifice in the symphony which came to epitomise the worldwide struggle against Fascism. This resulted in a period of relatively relaxed supervision, in which a series of deeply-felt and even experimental works were produced and performed. However, Russia's return to isolation during the cold war, accompanied by Stalin's increasing paranoia, put an end to this harmonious state of things. As early as 1946, 'Soviet composers were warned that the authorities were taking a dim view of the trend . . . towards chamber music, a genre not felt to be so immediately accessible to the masses'.[15] As the Greek civil war was swiftly succeeded by the other explosions in the chain-reaction which led to the cold war, the return to strict vetting of the arts was inexorable. Once again, Shostakovich found himself in a particularly exposed position. He had failed to produce the great 'Victory Symphony' which had been expected – on the contrary, the Ninth was inappropriately lightweight, even displaying a regression to satirical characteristics. In manuscript he had completed two works which could easily be construed as unhelpful. The songs to Jewish texts were a strong condemnation of antisemitic attitudes, of the kind which permeated the camarilla surrounding Stalin. The Violin Concerto – his first for a stringed instrument – was a seminal work in his personal development, since (inter alia) it introduced his obsession with the motto theme (D, E flat, C, B). These notes, which comprise the composer's initials in the *German* spelling of his name, may have been hit upon accidentally, but could easily have been considered a prime example of the tendencies which were now singled out for opprobrium. In Stalin's Russia, there was room for only one 'personality cult'.

The *Zhdanovshchina* (Zhdanov's purge) when it came in 1948–9 was extremely thorough and wideranging – little less than an intellectual terror, launched against all institutions of creativity, criticism, and higher education. In January, 1948, Zhdanov peremptorily summoned members of the Union of Soviet Composers to a conference which proved, in effect, an elaborate show-trial of the main offenders.[16] His technique was to encourage the younger element (led by Tikhon Khrennikov) and the embittered mediocrities (represented by Vladimir Zakharov) to turn against their senior or more successful colleagues. In his opening speech, Zhdanov clearly identified the targets – those who had failed to reform themselves since 1936, and in particular those composers whose work was appreciated in the West. Then he sat back and allowed jealousy and ambition to do their work. The result was like a senior common-room with the collective super-ego somehow removed. Shostakovich, Shebalin, and Khatchaturian were obliged to listen to a series of slanders, vicious and petty by turns. By far the greatest number of darts were aimed at Shostakovich, whose music was indicted as being the preferred listening 'of nobody except foreign bandits and imperialists'. But neither Prokofiev (absent through illness) nor Miaskovsky (who was on his deathbed) were allowed to escape censure. To his lasting credit, Khachaturian fearlessly defended Shostakovich, and was followed by others, most effectively by Visarion Shebalin. Shostakovich's own contribution to the 'debate' was understandably bewildered; virtually his last words were 'and now, I suppose, instructions will be given'.

Indeed. A month later, Zhdanov issued his decree, singling out for condemnation precisely those major figures who had either defended Shostakovich or had absented themselves from his 'trial'. 'Socialist Realism' was underlined as the only permissible aesthetic, and all the shibboleths of the mid-thirties were resurrected. Confessions, retractions, and atonements followed rapidly. Prokofiev issued a humble apology to the Party,[17] Shostakovich, at least outwardly, conformed. From this period date some of the latter's most meretricious scores, such as the feeble cantata *Song of the Forests*, and (more notably) the single work which can be viewed as a tribute to Stalin himself. I refer here to the film music for *The Unforgettable 1919* (1951), an opus which certainly belies its name to an embarrassing degree. The film itself portrayed Comrade Stalin's (partly fictional) exploits as a dashing and heroic Red Army commander during the civil war against the Whites. During his last years, Stalin comforted himself with repeated showings of this hagiography,[18] and one may assume that it helped to ameliorate the wrath of the Party. To aid this process, Shostakovich agreed to act as Soviet representative at various conferences (including one at New York in 1949), where he obediently mouthed platitudinous condemnations of Western tendencies in politics and music. Meanwhile, his creative spring dried up, a phenomenon unconvincingly attributed by Rabinovich to his paralysing fear of Western belligerence and a third world war.[19]

As a result of the purge, Shebalin was dismissed outright from his academic position at the Moscow Conservatoire, whilst Shostakovich himself, chief among the accused, was only suspended for a short spell. The egregious Khrennikov, former pupil and main persectuor of Shebalin, took over as Secretary of the Union of Soviet Composers, central position of patronage and power. Early in 1949, he opened the plenary congress of that body with a speech in which the new party line was firmly established. By this time, however, Commissar Zhdanov was already dead, poisoned (it was later claimed) by his Jewish physicians. This event was the origin of the so-called 'Jewish Doctor's Plot', characterstic of the synthetic pretexts for purges which dominated Stalin's last, feverish and frightening, years of

supreme power. The victims were finally condemned only
weeks before the dictator's death in March, 1953. The sense of
relief at the latter event amongst Stalin's closest associates was
as profound as the sense of loss amongst the wider population.
Shostakovich immediately began work upon his Tenth Symphony, which to some extent reflects both these emotions, but is
mainly compounded of that mixture of self-congratulation and
guilt which marked all the 'survivors' of Stalin's indiscriminate
blood-letting. Though the Tenth Symphony wonderfully
expressed the feelings of hundreds of Soviet artists and
intellectuals, it was not accompanied by any verbal explanation
– the composer resisting attempts to foist 'programmes' upon it
with unusual energy and finality. Since the deaths of Prokofiev
and Eisenstein, Shostakovich had inherited the mantle of the
most distinguished living Soviet artist. He proved unable,
however, to take the decisive action that moral leadership
required, Hamlet-like hesitation and apprehension vitiating
the resolve and integrity so often present in his music. It was
left, once again, to Aram Khachaturian to make the first public
protest against the maintenance of the Zhdanov-Khrennikov
policy.

Khachaturian's criticism appeared simultaneously with the
initial signs of a 'thaw' in the official attitude. This came out in
the pages of *Pravda*, interestingly enough shortly after the arrest
of Laurentia Beria, Stalin's omnipotent police-chief and puta-
tive successor whose disgrace seemed to remove the last serious
threat of renewed dictatorship. It was after Beria's execution
(December 1953) that Shostakovich supported his Armenian
colleague. In February 1954, the official musical journal,
Sovestkaya Muzyka, carried his article, roundly deploring the
concentration on ideological (as opposed to musical) merit in
the assessment of new works, criticising Khrennikov's
bureaucratic attitudes, and the attempts to force all creative
work into a 'a single, fixed pattern, even though it be the best. . .
The sooner we reject these levelling tendencies (he added) the
better it will be for the development of Soviet art'.[20] These
remain Shostakovich's most forthright remarks on the subject
of basic artistic freedoms, and display an extremity of utterance
that one suspects was only forced from him by the mindless
excesses of the Stalinist era. This is not to suggest that it was

wholly isolated. During the periods of the so-called 'collective leadership' (1953–56) and the government of Nikita Khrushchëv (1956–64), Shostakovich was frequently to be heard in defence of the right of younger composers to absorb, and even to experiment with, the 'new methods' of the West – including even serial composition, which, by its very 'objectivity' and 'obscurity' remained the turnip-ghost of Soviet officialdom. Equally often, however, he extolled the 'civic responsibility' of the artist, accepting the overall supervision of the Party and condemning experimentation for its own sake. In 1960, for example (during the most liberal phase of Khrushchëv's premiership), he unleashed a tirade against 'avant garde' music in the pages of *Pravda* of which Khrennikov himself would have been proud, and just at the time when his application for membership of the CPSU was being considered.

Duality and ambiguity were not, therefore, restricted to the music. Indeed for nearly ten years after the death of Stalin such a tension is not often present in his scores. During this period the composer seems to have been at his most settled and stable, the relationship between art and environment at its most productive. A series of pieces flowed from Shostakovich's pen which were the most rewarding examples of 'Socialist Realism' yet to have been heard, and will certainly stand as unsurpassed in the genre. The Eleventh and Twelfth Symphonies, the Second Concerto for piano and the first for 'cello (along with other major works), attested the fact that, when informed by genius, the most procrustian of limitations can be the mother of invention. (Or, to put it another way, 'I could be bounded in a nutshell and count myself a king of infinite space').[21] None of these works is without merit, some are masterpieces, all are entirely characteristic of the composer. Such compositions brought to fullest fruition Shostakovich's acknowledgement and deep appreciation of the positive achievement and the enduring qualities of the Soviet system. What, by a complete set of criteria, they lack in purely musical terms, they more than compensate for by their importance in the history of aesthetics and indeed in history itself. On the other hand, in these years the string quartet was explored with an intensity which at times seemed obsessive. The Fifth in the series (1952) is generally regarded as the first masterpiece, and no fewer than five others were to follow by the time of Khrushchëv's fall. It is notable, however, that none of these illustrates a frame of mind which modifies the above remarks. Though it is true that the Seventh and Eighth Quartets are tragic in conception neither seems susceptible of an interpretation connecting them with a wider dissatisfaction or profounder disease; and the Sixth and Tenth are redolent of 'Socialist Realism' at its most fertile and satisfying.

Even more striking, even paradoxical, is the fact that this period of strongly conservative retrenchment in Shostakovich's work was that which witnessed his breakthrough on to a higher plane of critical esteem in the West. 'Peaceful Coexistence' was marked by a grand exchange of musical emissaries, individual and collective, between Russia and the outside world. Shostakovich's Tenth Symphony entered the normal orchestral repertoire of the major Western ensembles (the first to do so since the Fifth), and the success of the Eleventh in particular was gratifying to Soviet critics, who regarded it as its composer's greatest effusion to date. In addition, the sustained advocacy of Benjamin Britten, along with the sudden and radical revaluation of Gustav Mahler (whose music was, of course, a seminal influence on both) helped advance Shostakovich's popularity among critics and audiences in the West; a phenomenon which (with perhaps the single exception of Rachmaninov) was unprecedented for a living twentieth-century composer.

At the time and often since, it has seemed to outside observers that the premiership of Khrushchëv was an era of sweetness and light. In the collective memory Nikita Sergeyevich belongs to that same period of new-born hope which embraced his contemporaries Pope John XXIII and John F. Kennedy – the trinity of benign influences which led the world out of the Cold War. In later years the fallen premier was naturally anxious to perpetuate this impression in his memoirs. On the *Zhdanovshchina*, for example, he writes

> I think Stalin's cultural policies, especially the cultural policies imposed on Leningrad through Zhdanov, were cruel and senseless. You can't regulate the development of literature, art, and culture with a stick or by barking orders. You can't lay down a furrow and

then harness all your artists to make sure they don't deviate from the straight and narrow. If you try to control your artists too tightly, there will be no clashing of opinions, consequently no criticism, and consequently no truth. There will just be a gloomy stereotype, boring and useless. Not only will this stereotype fail to encourage the people to benefit from their art; it will poison and kill their relationship to art.

At first glance this seems to accord with Khrushchëv's well-known attitude towards Stalin, which culminated in the sweeping denunciation at the Twentieth Party Congress of 1956. This is partly illusory; Soviet intellectual life, and the nature and degree of its contact with external influences, continued to be carefully monitored. Permissiveness was, and was accepted as, a strictly limited and conditional – above all a changeable – attitude. Not long after Khrushchëv's 'Secret Speech' exposing Stalin, Zhdanov's *obiter dicta* on cultural matters were officially disavowed. But within a short space, there was another reversion of policy, associated with the political setbacks of the early sixties (the Sino-Soviet dispute, the Cuban missile crisis, and especially the failure of agriculture) which would ultimately lead to Khrushchëv's removal. Conforming to what is a clearly identifiable pattern of cause-and-effect, *Pravda* announced a crackdown on 'deviationism' in the arts, and Khrushchëv himself addressed the musical world in his own inimitable fashion:

> We stand for melodious music with content, music that stirs people and gives rise to strong feelings and we are against cacophony. . . You can meet young people who try to prove that melody in music has lost the right to exist and that its place is now being taken by 'new music' – 'dodecaphony', the music of noises. It is hard for the normal person to understand what the word 'dodecaphony' means, but apparently it means the same as the word 'cacophony'. Well, we flatly reject this cacophonous music. Our people cannot use this garbage as a tool of their ideology.[22]

As it happened, it was at this time that Shostakovich was working on two major works of a controversial nature, the revision of his opera *Lady Macbeth* (eventually produced, as *Katerina Izmailova*, in 1963), and the Thirteenth Symphony, to poems by Yevtushenko. The latter, his first serious address to

large-scale textual composition since the opera, was also the
most daring in terms of its subject-matter. In the Thirteenth
Symphony, the dual sources of inspiration which had been
developed *sua generis* since Stalin's death again achieved the
kind of fertile reunion which (to my mind) is the hallmark of
Shostakovich's most universally valuable compositions. It is
not surprising that this tour-de-force of trenchant comment on
Soviet life was difficult for Khrushchëv to stomach. However,
although the symphony was banned following a couple of
performances (reappearing later with enforced textual
changes) the action was not, on this occasion, compounded
with public criticism of the composer himself. Perhaps Shostakovich had at last reached the point of immunity, that privilege
granted to so few in the Soviet system. By now he had been
awarded every conceivable civic honour; all his output was
published, performed, and even (by the 1970s) recorded. New
work still had to be submitted to the peculiar Soviet ritual of
professional discussion, but in Shostakovich's case a position of
strength had been achieved from which it was possible to
negotiate with the authorities. Maybe this was an heretical and
dangerous precedent; but Dmitry Shostakovich had become a
'special case'.

This development had little general effect during the years of
relative reaction which followed Khrushchëv's fall. Neither did
Shostakovich's elevation to a sort of divinity prevent his
turning, as age increased and health diminished, to a morbid
and isolated world in which death – or rather the prospect of
personal mortality – increasingly dominated his thoughts. This
process, which centred upon the Fourteenth Symphony, and
which embraced among other works the last five string
quartets, involved a loss of interest in public concerns. In 1968,
he surrendered the secretaryship of the Russian 'national'
branch of the USC. In the same year, the events in Czecho-
slovakia and the subsequent scandals associated with the rise of
the so-called *Samizdat* movement of dissident intellectuals,
considerably diminished the prestige which the Soviet Union
had gained in the West since the mid-fifties. Shostakovich's
apparent indifference to these affairs led to the unfortunate
disturbances at the London Proms in August 1968, ironically at
the opening of a performance of his Tenth Symphony by the

visiting Leningrad Philharmonic under Svetlanov. Circumstances had clearly altered since – only a few years previously –
many had spoken with radiant enthusiasm of Shostakovich's
idealist revolutionary commitment. In 1974, the year before his
death and that of the exile of Solzhenitsyn, he was moved to
deplore action taken against the physicist Andrei Sakharov by
the Soviet government. The rest is silence.

In retrospect, it may well be that future generations will
conclude that Shostakovich was never fully nor directly
engaged in an altruistic struggle for the principles of intellectual
freedom. On the other hand, it can hardly be denied that,
unlike his counterpart Richard Strauss, his consciousness of
their importance is a central and essential element in his
musical life's work. Moreover, it is clear that Shostakovich's
revolutionary training and socio-political commitment *itself*
encouraged this awareness to a crucial degree, a paradox which is
one of the most positive and residually encouraging aspects of
applied Marxist ideology. Certainly one ought not to compile a
crudely quantitative balance-sheet of works (e.g. entering the
cantata *Stepan Razin* against the Thirteenth Symphony, both on
texts by Yevtushenko). Such an exercise, sometimes attempted
in professional journalism, falls into two traps; the ideological
pitfall which tends to exaggerate beyond all true proportion the
socio-political dimension in the qualitative valuation of a great
artist, and the equally seductive error of presuming that some of
Shostakovich's work was written (as it were) *pro* and some *contra*
the Soviet system. Further, it seems to me self-evident that the
degree of physical self-sacrifice, the martyrological urge if you
like, in an artist's make-up cannot be the *sine qua non* of genuine
stature. This is as true of Strauss as it is of Shostakovich. The
romantic ideology of doomed, suicidal genius is a potent but
very partial myth.

None the less, an essay of this kind cannot be complete
without some attempt to analyze the manner in which Shostakovich approached and mediated his environment through his
work. This, after all, is one way of interpreting the mark of
genius. Essentially, the composer's attitude to the socio-moral
problems of his time was derived from that part of the Marxist
tradition which might loosely be termed the liberal-humanist.

The cynic (especially if he is a radical cynic) might respond that Shostakovich's social views were thus as quaintly old fashioned as his compositional methods. So be it; but it remains true that a commitment to such values is, more often than not, a distinguishing mark of universality. It is this, as much as anything else, which connects Monteverdi with Mozart and Mozart with Stockhausen. (In his last symphony, Shostakovich quoted from Wagner one of the great exceptions to this rule.) The themes which concerned Shostakovich (of the kind which are usually but inadequately called 'extra-musical') are stated in the opening paragraph of this essay. These concerns were not discrete and watertight, but connected and overlapping, united at base by the thread of violence and oppression. Much of his output is a kind of passacaglia on this ground bass. The Thirteenth Symphony is a miraculous synthesis of these moral interests, and may thus be utilised as a focal point, establishing some coherence in what might otherwise tend to become a formless discussion.

Revolution: It has been claimed that the Thirteenth Symphony belongs with its two immediate predecessors, thus forming a 'triptych' of revolution, a documentary chronicle of the Russian peoples' struggle to achieve a true communist society.[23] There is a point to this, for the symphonies do treat, in historical sequence, of the themes of the pre-revolution (in the Eleventh, 'The Year 1905'), the October Revolution itself (the Twelfth 'The Year 1917') and lastly the Stalinist aberration and its overthrow in number Thirteen. One must be careful, however, not to make *too* close an identification between the three symphonies, for the last of them stands a way apart by virtue of the fact that it operates both on a much deeper level and wider plane. The music of the Thirteenth is as gripping and ultimately satisfying, particularly in the first movement, as anything its composer has written, and moreover displays solid development of harmonic language and formal technique in the 'true' symphonic tradition. This is not to belittle nos. 11 and 12 as shallow or insincere, for both are well-made, enjoyable, and at times impressive works, far greater in conception and execution than anything else belonging to their genre. They certainly justify *The Times*' front-page comment at the time of

Shostakovich's death, that the composer was 'a committed believer in communism and Soviet power'.[24] True as this is, the Thirteenth shows that it is not the whole truth, that belief in revolution is not simply a matter of homage to its history and pantheon of heroes, but of constant renewal and defence of its principles in the here-and-now. This is the burden of Yevtushenko's lines set in the fourth movement, entitled 'Fears':[25]

> Today this has become something remote.
> Now it's even strange to remember
> The secret terror of someone informing,
> The secret fear of a knock on the door.

The same feeling inspires the exhilarating celebration of the place of humour – the allegorical artist – in the second movement. Having survived innumerable executions under the Tsarist regime:

> Coughing and spitting
> like the rank and file
> rifle in hand
> he marched upon the Winter Palace
> singing a popular song.

Expression of this kind also links backwards across time with the early 'revolutionary' symphonies, as well as with the poetry of Mayakovsky which struck such sparks from the young Shostakovich. The Second and Third Symphonies (like the Fourth) were resuscitated during the Khrushchev period, and proved of exceptional interest in musical terms, well worthy of taking their place in an unparalleled tableau of historical documentation.

War: In the Soviet experience, war is virtually inseparable from revolution. The traumatic years of 1914–21 witnessed Russia's involvement in World War and civil war as well as revolution, a desperate syndrome of catastrophe, bloodshed, famine, and devastation in which some 25 million lost their lives. Even greater losses were suffered in 1941–45, during the 'Great Patriotic War' against Nazi Germany, whilst it now seems not unlikely that a further 10–15 million Soviet citizens were victims of Stalinism, an endless procession stretching from collectivisation (1929–30) to the atrocities of the 1940s. The effects of 'Operation Barbarossa', Hitler's invasion of the Soviet Union, were particularly appalling: 80% of human losses were males of mature age, whilst the Western and most fertile areas of Russia were laid waste both by the retreating Soviets in 1941–42 and the retreating Germans in 1943–44. In 1945, 25 million citizens were homeless, 31,000 factories and 40,000 miles of railway had been destroyed. The almost unprecedented demographic holocaust meant that the Russian population had been literally decimated twice over within thirty years.

Shostakovich's reaction is perhaps the best-known aspect of his career. The awful endeavours of the siege of Leningrad in which he participated can now be seen as the central experience of Shostakovich's life. The Third Reich's ruthless attempt to wipe out the Soviet system both sharpened and confirmed the composer's fundamental loyalties, an attitude that therefore was made proof against all the disillusions of Stalinism. In this he was representative of millions, inside and outside the Soviet Union, whose doubts and reservations were dissipated in the defence of basic principles of behaviour and belief. The Seventh and Eighth Symphonies, therefore, will always stand as a supreme spiritual monument to the struggle of peoples and individuals (respectively) against the violent intimidation of barbarism. But Shostakovich had also grown up in an atmosphere of life-or-death conflict against Germany and German-assisted military reaction. This earlier experience doubtless came into play during the composition of his first film score, *The New Babylon* (1929). The subject of the film was the first great irruption of the German problem in European politics, Bismarck's war against France in 1870. It portrayed the march of Prussian militarism, the siege of Paris, and the bloody suppression of the Paris Commune. These events were a peculiar kind of dress rehearsal for those which were to overtake Shostakovich in 1941. It is notable that after 1917, Leningrad was widely regarded as having succeeded to the tradition of the Paris Commune, taking over the torch of revolution which had been kept burning in Paris since 1789. Like Eisenstein and Prokofiev, collaborators in *Alexander Nevsky*, Shostakovich could hardly fail to see the historical implications of the siege of Leningrad by enemies who were the lineal descendants of the Prussians as of the Teutonic Knights. It is not surprising therefore to find actual musical connections between the Seventh ('Leningrad') Symphony and the accomplished film score of a decade earlier. Moreover, it may be pointed out that the latter contains useful evidence that Shostakovich's Fifteenth Symphony (1971) is, at least in part, a retrospective comment upon the experience of war. For in addition to explicit quotations from the Seventh and Eighth Symphonies, the Fifteenth also refers back at certain important structural points to the music for *The New Babylon*.[26]

Three significant chamber works also address themselves to the problem of war. Of these, the Third Quartet is perhaps of limited interest, having overtones which are purely Russian and nationalistic, and the Piano Trio will be dealt with in a different context. The Eighth Quartet is another matter, being almost as fertile a point of central reference as the Thirteenth Symphony. Written as a result of a visit to Dresden, the city destroyed by bombing on one horrific night in 1945, the quartet illustrates a major emotional breakthrough, for it shows the composer now able to feel for the sufferings of the German enemy – or rather, perhaps, the German civilian-comrade. (It is worth remark that it is contemporaneous with Britten's *War Requiem*).

Antisemitism: The Thirteenth Symphony was deliberately omitted from the foregoing section despite the fact that war figures prominently in its cogitations, because it does so indirectly, through the theme of anti-Jewish persecution. The Second World War is inextricable from anti-semitism and inexplicable without reference to it. The onslaught against European Jewry was one of the most dreadful setbacks in the history of Western civilisation, and one suspects that Shostakovich realised this sooner than many people apart from the victims themselves. It is only recently that historians have come to recognise – and the tardiness is understandable – that Hitler's war was, intrinsically and inseparably, a war of extermination against Judaism. Auschwitz, as well as Stalingrad, was a logical outcome of the Nazi New Order. Even before the full revelations of the major Death Camps emerged, Shostakovich paid tribute in his Piano Trio (1944) to those slaughtered by the SS at Majdanek in the Ukraine. Both here, and in the Eighth Quartet (where the 'Majdanek' theme is quoted) the resistance to oppression is made identical with the struggle against antisemitism. These works are linked, in basic inspiration if nothing else, by the song-cycle on *Jewish Folk Poetry*, already referred to. But the Thirteenth Symphony is the *locus classicus* of the composer's concern. In its intense and moving opening movement, Yevtushenko's reaction to 'Babi Yar', a place of mass-murder not far from Kiev, finds a fresh dimension and consummate recreation. It is a joint affirmation by two generations that no freedom can be fully achieved while antisemitism persists. This uncompromising manifesto was, in the circumstances of 1962, impermissible to the authorities, bearing as it did implications not only for Soviet society but also for the foreign policy of the USSR. The consequent attempt at censorship was nevertheless performed with little conviction, and rarely can imposed textual changes to a major work have missed the point so completely.

Women:

> These women are our honour and our judgement
> They have mixed our concrete
> They have ploughed and reaped
> They have endured anything
> And will endure everything.

Thus Yevtushenko, in his poem 'At the Store' which forms the third movement of the Thirteenth Symphony, proclaims the female contribution in revolution and war. In placing the feminist cause side by side with the other aspects of his credo, Shostakovich echoed a sense of injustice which had preoccupied him since his earliest maturity. In the opera *Lady Macbeth of Mtsensk* (dedicated to his first wife) his resentment at the exploitation of women stands out sharply as the main theme of the work. The opera was designed, be it noted, as the first of three such treatments of this theme. The composer himself deliberately shifted, even distorted the balance of social comment in Nicolai Leskov's original story:

> It is mainly with Katerina [he stated] that there is a departure from Leskov's story. He described Katerina as a cruel woman, depraved. I refused to take such a course and presented her as a clever woman, gifted and interesting. . . Aside from Katerina, there is no positive character or hero in this opera.[27]

Thus the heroine is made in every instance the victim of oppressive circumstances; indeed, it is her very attempt to vindicate her sex by a trial of strength with the egregious Sergey, which ends in seduction, and the slippery slope to murder, arrest, desertion, and suicide. Even at this ultimate point, she betrays her congenital weakness by dragging with her to perdition not the author of her woes, her lover Sergey (for whom Shostakovich developed a deeply personal loathing), but his new fancy and rival for her slavery! Doubtless, Katerina does not evoke the sympathy amongst modern feminists that belongs to her predecessor, Carmen, or her contemporary, Lulu. But she does have her strengths; as she sings in an aria, the music of which crops up again in the significant context of the Eighth Quartet:

> a woman
> Sometimes feeds the whole family,
> Don't you know
> How women sometimes
> Have fought the enemy in wartime?
> Other times women
> For their husbands and loved ones
> Have laid down their lives.[28]

The artist and society: Two movements of the Thirteenth Symphony are explicitly confessional in nature, together constituting a kind of *apologia pro vita sua*. Both have a direct relevance to the central dilemma dealt with in this essay, on the general as well as the personal level. The first of these concerns the subject of perhaps the most semantically authentic *scherzo* ever written, 'Humour'. The composer's relish in jokes of all kinds had always been an almost irrepressible characteristic, obtruding into all but his most grave and pessimistic pieces. His levity is somewhat portentously condemned by his biographer, Rabinovich, as a major weakness for a serious composer. As we have seen, it was often the cause of official disregard; on the other hand, Martynov (a critic later condemned for his pains in 1948), viewed Shostakovich's sense of fun as 'possibly the most valuable aspect' of his early output.[29] Though at one time he was obliged to repent these sins of his youth, in the Thirteenth Symphony he positively asserts and affirms the role of humour in the necessary subversion of authority, especially arbitrary authority. Far from being inimical to Marxism, this quality in life is (as we have seen) genuinely revolutionary. Yevtushenko adds that the amusing is as important an aspect of creativity as the reflective or prophetic – aspects which Shostakovich combines so naturally in works like the Sixth, Ninth, and Fifteenth Symphonies. Perhaps only Stravinsky among all his contemporaries shared this infectious addiction, and it is notable that in the course of this uproarious movement Shostakovich seems to acknowledge this fact. Strongly influenced by the great expatriate in his youth, he later (in accord with official thinking) turned strongly against Stravinsky, especially excoriating the latter's turning to serialism in the fifties. In 1962, as Shostakovich was working on the Thirteenth Symphony, occurred the famous return visit of Stravinsky to his homeland. In a gesture of reconciliation and respect, Shostakovich's jester makes obeisance by quoting (attenuated and transposed, but none the less unmistakable) a theme from Stravinsky's ballet *The Fairy's Kiss*, highly appropriate because itself based upon original music by their common predecessor, Tchaikovsky. Thus the sharing of origins as well as affections is neatly stressed, as though rising above the ideological chasm between the two composers.

Another composer seems to me to be the real hero of the Thirteenth, however, a figure much less celebrated than Stravinsky or Shostakovich. In the finale, satirical humour is again in evidence, this time of a particularly grim and salutary kind. Yevtushenko's poem 'A Career' has a claim to be the most personal autobiographical text ever set to music by a great composer. For the bitter satire is aimed (in the primary instance at least) at Shostakovich himself. In the poem, two vastly different types of career are contrasted, in a juxtaposition which must surely strike a chord in many thousands of listeners; that of Galileo, who suffered denigration and persecution for the truth, and that of a (fictional) colleague, 'who knew the earth revolved about the sun, but had a large family to maintain' – and acted accordingly. In context, this reference points fairly clearly to the Stalin period by way of analogy. It seems reasonable to suppose that it embodies some form of admission of guilt on the composer's part. Going further along this road, one may hypothesize that if Shostakovich saw himself as 'the other scientist', he saw some other actual person as

Galileo. To my mind, a candidate for this ascription, to whom the (admittedly circumstantial) evidence points most firmly is his lifelong firend, Visarion Shebalin. Shebalin was Shostakovich's first and strongest supporter in the Moscow Conservatoire, holding aloof from the bitter criticism indulged by his colleagues in the thirties. During the witch-hunt of 1948, his was the most uncompromising defence of Shostakovich, including as it did a vigorous counter-attack on the hunters. In the whole Stalin period, Shebalin's own output stands out as making the least concession to the pressures of politics and propaganda.[30] As we have seen, he was duly removed from his professorship in 1949, whilst Shostakovich was merely suspended for a brief period, and only reinstated (in a more junior capacity) four years later. The crisis broke Shebalin's career and his health. His compositions were rarely performed in the 1950s, and at the time of the Thirteenth Symphony he was desperately ill, dying shortly afterwards. If these suppositions are correct, the finale of the symphony constitutes one of the most unusual and devastatingly honest tributes ever paid by one artist to another. Even if they are not, it stands as a statement of the need for integrity which (in our meritocratic age) has a biting relevance far beyond its immediate context.

The art produced in the Soviet Union has recently been denigrated by the historian Hugh Trevor-Roper. In his study of the culture (mainly painting) of the great Habsburg courts of the seventeenth century,[31] he makes a contrast with the art of 'socialist realism', which, in his view, is doomed to extinction because of its failure to give universal expression to the principles which inspire it. Whether Shostakovich's music will help to refute this opinion remains to be seen; it must depend to a large extent upon the treatment of 'socalist realism' by future musicologists, critics and historians. Perhaps the composer's own views are encapsulated, not in the words of Yevtushenko or Leskov, but those of Gogol in the closing sentences of his short story *The Nose*, subject of Shostakovich's early iconoclastic opera:

> The strangest, most incredible thing of all is that authors should write about such things. That, I confess, is beyond my comprehension. It's just . . . no, no, I don't understand it at all! . . . It's no use

to the country whatsoever . . . I simply don't know *what* one can make of it. . .[32]

Like so much of our subject's work, these words seem to carry within themselves the 'answer to just criticism'.

Notes

1. H. Ottaway, *Shostakovich Symphonies* (BBC Music Guides, 1978); I. Martynov, *Dmitri Shostakovich: the Man and his Work* (New York, 1947).
2. None of the above statements is, in my view, substantially in need of modification as a result of the publication of *Testimony: the memoirs of Shostakovich* (ed. S. Volkov, London, 1979). The ubiquitous and cynical resentment of this document is directed against Stalinism and the kind of relationships and behaviour Stalinist society engendered, rather than against the principles of Marxist-Leninism and the aspirations towards them of the Russian people. And in any case – as other contributors to this volume have pointed out – the memoirs as published must be held to be largely tendentious, and are perhaps even spurious. Having said this, however, I must also record my personal feeling that it is difficult to believe that the composer *played no part whatsoever* in their production.
3. A. Nove, *An Economic History of the U.S.S.R.* (Pelican, 1972); the best and most detailed treatment of Russian history in this period is E. H. Carr's now completed *History of Soviet Russia* (14 Vols).
4. N. Slonimsky, *Music Since 1900* (New York, 1951), p. 549.
5. N. Kay, *Shostakovich* (Oxford, 1971).
6. N. Del Mar, 'Paul Hindemith', in H. Hartog (ed.), *European Music in the Twentieth Century* (Pelican, 1960).
7. Quoted by D. Rabinovich, *Dmitri Shostakovich, Composer* (Lawrence and Wishart, 1959), p. 114.
8. ibid., p. 27.
9. The intense and unrelieved fear of apparently reasonless annihilation suffered by Shostakovich and his whole circle in this period is amply illustrated (for what it is worth) in the pages of *Testimony* (op. cit., *passim*).
10. B. Stevens, 'The Soviet Union', in Hartog, op, cit., p. 232; Kay, op. cit.
11. The recording of the original score (by Rostropovich for E.M.I.) appeared too late for use in the preparation of this essay. See the interesting and relevant article and review in *The Gramophone* (May, 1979), which diverge somewhat on their assessment of relative merits.
12. S. Alliluyeva, *Twenty Letters to a Friend* (Penguin, 1968); N. Khrushchev, *Khrushchev Remembers* (Sphere Books, 1971).
13. It is, surely, noteworthy that following the success of the Fifth, Stravinsky turned to the symphony for the first time, and Bartók began to plan a whole series. Neither composer had previously been very attracted to either Shostakovich or symphonic form.

14. Except, perhaps, by Robert Layton in his chapter on Shostakovich in R. Simpson (ed.), *The Symphony* (Pelican, 1967, Vol. 2).

15. Anne C. Lugg, *Dmitri Shostakovich: the Symphony in a Totalitarian State* (Unpublished B. Mus. dissertation, University of Wales, Cardiff, 1976).

16. An almost complete verbatim transcript of the proceedings is printed in A. Werth, *Musical Uproar in Moscow* (London, 1949).

17. Prokofiev's statement is printed in J. Barzun (ed.) *The Pleasures of Music* (London, 1954).

18. Krushchev revealed this titbit in his secret speech of 1956 (op. cit., Appendix 4).

19. Rabinovich, op. cit.

20. D. Shostakovich, 'The Joy of Creative Exploration', quoted by A. Olkhovsky, *Music under the Soviets: the Agony of an Art* (London, 1955), p. 314.

21. *Hamlet*, Act II sc. ii.

22. Quoted by B. Schwarz, *Music and Musical Life in Soviet Russia, 1900–1970* (New York, 1972), p. 418.

23. e.g. by Ottaway, op. cit.

24. *The Times*, 11 August, 1975.

25. The following extracts from Yevtushenko's texts are taken from the English versions on the sleeve of the Everest recording of the live 1965 performance under Kondrashin (SDBR 3181).

26. See the remarks of Rozhdestvensky quoted on the sleeve of the E.M.I. (Melodiya) recording of the New Babylon music (ASD 3381). Also, R. Layton's broadcast talk on 'Shostakovich as Symphonist', B.B.C. Radio 3, 18 April 1979.

27. D. Shostakovich, in his introduction to the original libretto of the opera quoted by Martynov, op. cit., p. 43.

28. From the libretto to the Melodiya recording of *Katerina Izmailova* (SLS 5050).

29. Martynov, op. cit., p. 26.

30. See the *curricula vitae* of various Soviet composers in I. Boelza, *A Handbook of Soviet Composers* (ed. A. Bush, Pilot Press, 1943).

31. H. R. Trevor-Roper, *Princes and Artists: Patronage and Ideology at four Habsburg Courts, 1517–1633* (London, 1976).

32. Penguin ed. (trans. R. Wilks).

Alan Bush

Dmitry Dmitrievich Shostakovich

The Russian Empire of the Tsars may be said to have been established when Tsar Alexis Romanov in 1649 imposed serfdom by edict throughout his domains. Sixty years later in 1709 the army of Tsar Peter the Great finally defeated King Charles the Twelfth of Sweden after nineteen years of intermittent warfare, and Russia came into possession of the Baltic kingdoms of Estonia, Latvia, and Lithuania and parts of Finland. Thus Tsarist Russia became a European state.

Peter the Great died in 1725. Thirty-seven years later, in 1762, after five monarchs had occupied the throne in chaotic succession, Peter the Third ascended it; he had been married for eighteen years to a German Princess, christened Catherine on her entry into the Orthodox Church. Six months after his accession to the throne Peter the Third died 'in a scuffle during dinner', as a guards officer wrote to the Tsaritsa Catherine, whereupon she declared herself Empress and remained so until her death in 1796. She herself had read Voltaire on politics, d'Alembert on philosophy and science, Blackstone on Law, Buffon on natural history and the encyclopaedist Friedrich Melchior Grimm (not Grimm of the fairy tales) on the history of European literature. As Empress she introduced the science, the art and the most advanced political ideas of Europe to the Russian intelligentsia.

Four years after her accession Empress Catherine convened a Great Commission of 564 members from all parts of the Empire; 370 had been elected locally without any class distinction. She was herself responsible for raising before the Commission the question of serfdom and the problems of its abolition through a young delegate from one of the country districts. Following on the initiatives of the Empress Catherine the nineteenth century was a period of almost uninterrupted political turbulence. First came the unsuccessful rising of the Decembrists in 1825. In 1861 the serfs were emancipated by edict of Tsar Alexander II. Peasants had always died of starvation in large numbers on the lands to which they were bound by serfdom. Now, after emancipation, they flocked to those cities where industry was beginning and died in thousands in the streets. Working-class political activity developed in the late nineteenth century and early twentieth centuries. In St Petersburg in 1905 workers on strike marched in a demonstration to the Winter Palace in order to put their complaints and demands to the Tsar; and they were led by priests carrying icons. Troops fired on them without warning and more than one thousand were killed. In 1914 came the First World War and in 1917 the October Revolution.

On 25 September 1906, Dmitry Dmitrievich Shostakovich was born in St Petersburg. His father was a consultant engineer, his mother had studied music at the Conservatoire of St Petersburg and had become a professional teacher of the piano. Many members of the professional classes had become involved in political activities of one kind or another. But some pursued their careers seemingly unaffected by political ideas or events; such were the parents of Dmitry Dmitrievich. There is no evidence that either of them took any interest or part in politics at any time, either at the beginning of the twentieth century or before or after the October Revolution. Dmitry Dmitrievich was the second child of three. His elder sister, Maria, became a professional musician, his younger sister, Zoya, a veterinary surgeon. They all grew up in musical surroundings. The father was an expert amateur singer and amateur string players used often to take part in musical evenings in the Shostakovich house. The mother taught Maria the piano from the age of nine, Dmitry, in his turn, began piano with her. He received his general education at a local day school. In 1916 he studied music at a privately owned music-school, and in 1919 at the age of 14, he entered the Petrograd, now the Leningrad, Conservatoire, where he studied piano and composition, his teachers, being Leonid Nikolayev and Maximilian Steinberg.

While the atmosphere of his home had sheltered him from life, he had evidently become aware as a schoolboy of the explosive political atmosphere. In 1916, the third year of the war, he composed when ten years old a piano piece entitled 'Soldier'. This was followed a year later by a funeral march 'In Memory of those Heroes who fell in the October Revolution'. Such artistic involvement in social and political events was to continue to inspire his creative work for more than fifty years.

As a student at the Conservatoire Shostakovich distinguished himself highly. In 1923, at the age of seventeen, he gave a piano recital, the programme of which included Bach's A Minor Prelude and Fugue for Organ, transcribed by Liszt, the Appassionata by Beethoven and works of his own. In a review published in the Petrograd journal *Zhizn' iskusstva* for 1923 we may read the following:

> A tremendous impression was created by the concert given by D. Shostakovich, the young composer and pianist; he played with a confidence and an artistic endeavour of great fluency, that revealed in him a musician who has a profound feeling for and understanding of his art.

In 1926 he presented for his graduation exercise a Symphony in F minor, his Op. 10. The first public performance took place in Leningrad on 12 May 1926, conducted by Nikolai Malko. It captivated the public of Leningrad and later of Moscow, and was subsequently introduced in Western Europe and the United States. In New York Toscanini conducted it in 1931 in the presence of the composer. In an interview with the New York Times Shostakovich stated the following:

> There can be no music without ideology. . . We, as revolutionaries, have a different conception of music from the composers of other countries. Lenin himself said that 'Music is a means of unifying people'. It is not a leader of the masses, perhaps, but certainly an organising force. . . I think an artist should serve the greatest

possible number of people. I always try to make myself understood as widely as possible, and if I don't succeed I consider it my own fault.

In an article published in January 1940, Shostakovich wrote:

To write a Symphony, dedicated to the memory of Vladimir Ilych Lenin, was my cherished, longstanding wish. As early as 1924 I was thinking about such a Symphony at the time of profound universal mourning.

and later, in a conversation with the musicologist G. Khubov, he said:

My First Symphony was composed during 1924 and was finished at the beginning of 1925. . . I remember it was precisely then that the thought of writing a Symphony to be dedicated to the memory of Lenin occurred to me. . . It goes without saying that I was not able to do it then – I was too young, too inexperienced, not ready for it. But, when working on the First Symphony, I tried to express everything which had overwhelmed my thoughts and feelings.

In 1961 the composer himself has given an assessment of this First Symphony:

It was an attempt at profound content, a picture of a young man, strong, loving life, but who is really beginning to examine the life around him. Although the work is immature it is from my point of view valuable because of the sincere desire to reflect life and reality.

As things turned out it was not until 1961 that his cherished wish was to be accomplished with the creation of the Twelfth Symphony, Op. 112, which bears the sub-title 'The Year 1917'; the four movements of this work were all given names, the third movement, 'Razliv', referring to the place north of Leningrad, from which Lenin directed revolutionary activities while living in hiding in a peasant's hut.

During his years as a student Shostakovich earned money by playing the piano in cinemas and theatres, but after the success of his First Symphony he lived from his compositions, at first from film and theatre music, later from operas and concert music and from 1937 also from fees as a professor of composition in Leningrad Conservatoire.

His large output of works consists of three operas, two completed and one unfinished, fifteen symphonies, eight string quartets, sonatas for violin, viola, cello and piano, of which the sonata for viola and piano was his last work, written in hospital with his left hand after his right hand had become paralysed, shortly before his death in 1976. There is also a large repertoire of solo piano works, including twenty-four Preludes and Fugues and two concertos, together with many songs, including settings of poems by Shakespeare and Michelangelo. In addition he wrote a large number of articles on music, including one, written in 1971 shortly after a severe heart attack and addressed to the delegates of the Seventh Congress of the International Music Council, held in Moscow; in this article he defended the development of music in the Autonomous Republics of the Soviet Union against an attack by one of the French delegates to the Congress, who stated that the development of professional operatic and concert music in these republics had destroyed their indigenous folk music. In fact the exact opposite was the case as was shown in the production for the Congress of two double-sided L.P. records of the 'Folk-music of the Peoples of the USSR'; on these four sides are sixty examples of folk singers and instrumentalists from the central and the most remote parts of every Republic.

Shostakovich took an active part in the organisation, not only of the musical activities of the Union of Soviet Composers and the editorial board of *Sovetskaya Musyka*, but in day to day local politics. In 1933 he was elected a member of the Oktyabrsky District Soviet in Leningrad. On 23 June 1941, the second day of Hitler's invasion of the Soviet Union he volunteered for army service; he was refused on grounds of very poor eyesight. He became an active fire-watcher in Leningrad throughout the siege.

In 1961, at the height of his fame, both inside his own country and throughout the Western world, Shostakovich joined the Communist Party of the Soviet Union. In his address as a candidate he expressed the general principles of Soviet art in the following words:

At the foundation of Soviet art lie the ideas and principles proclaimed by the immortal Lenin. Lenin foresaw much that has become the reality of our artistic practice. He spoke of the spirit of the people and of the Party in art, of the spiritual majesty of art, of its mighty educative power, of its role in the fight for the new man. He called on artists to be in the thick of life, to relate their creative work to the needs of the times.

This statement received total and extreme support in July 1976, from a quarter which many people no doubt found unexpected, namely in the Programme Note from the official programme of the Royal Opera House, Covent Garden, for the production of Hans Werner Henze's opera 'We come to the River', in which the composer and the librettist, Edward Bond, wrote the following:

Writing and performing an opera, creating any work of art in a world of violence and ease, hunger and obesity, could seem to be an act of private withdrawal. But art isn't about itself, it's about how men relate to the world and each other. . . . Asking artists to keep politics out of art it is sensible as asking men to keep politics out of society. An artist doesn't dig down into his private ego, he relates his ego to society in a way which enables his audience to recognise a common, shared humanity.

Dmitry Dmitrievich Shostakovich died in the Kremlin Hospital on 9 August 1975, shortly before his seventieth birthday. In a tribute spoken at a memorial concert held in Moscow on 24 September 1976, the conductor Yevgeny Svetlanov expressed himself as follows:

In August last year Dmitry Dmitrievich Shostakovich ceased to be. His left hand, with which he had trained himself to write since his right hand had become useless, came to rest, having inscribed the last notes dictated by its owner's unquenchable thirst for communication with the world, a thirst, an urge which in the last resort only death could defeat. Shostakovich's last compositions, especially the song cycle to words by Michaelangelo, are the best proof of this. They include the following;

> I am as dead, yet to console the world
> I live with a thousand souls, within the hearts
> Of all who love, and thus am not vile dust;
> Mortality's decay shall touch me not.

The great Italian's words, spoken through Shostakovich's muse, come to us as words pronounced by the composer himself as he addressed us directly for the last time.

Notes on Contributors

Alan Bush is among the most respected and prolific of senior British composers. He received much of his musical education in Berlin in the nineteen-twenties where he was a pupil of Moiseiwitsch and Schnabel. Apart from numerous symphonic and chamber works, he has written four operas – *Wat Tyler* (1951), *Men of Blackmoor* (1955), *The Sugar Reapers* (1960), and *Joe Hill* (1970). He is a Fellow of the Royal College of Music where he was Professor of Composition.

Robert Dearling is a freelance writer on music and co-author (with Roy Blokker) of *The Music of Dmitri Shostakovich* (London, 1979).

Malcolm MacDonald is the author of *Schoenberg* (London, 1976) in the 'Master Musicians' series and of *The Symphonies of Havergal Brian* (2 vols, London 1974, 1978). He compiled the definitive *catalogue raisonné* of Shostakovich's works (London, 1978).

Christopher Norris teaches literature at the University of Wales (Cardiff). He is the author of *William Empson and the Philosophy of Literary Criticism* (London, 1978) and a freelance writer on musical and literary topics.

Geoffrey Norris is a critic and musicologist of wide experience. He has written and broadcast extensively on Russian music and is the author of *Rachmaninov* (London, 1977) and *Shostakovich* (forthcoming), both in the 'Master Musicians' series.

Christopher Rowland and **Alan George** are first violin and violist of the Fitzwilliam Quartet which has done more than any other to establish a British performing interest in Shostakovich's quartets. Shostakovich was deeply impressed by their playing and personally supervised some of their rehearsals in York, in 1975, offering interpretative help and guidance. Their recordings of the cycle have won wide critical acclaim.

Bernard Stevens, Professor of Composition at the Royal College of Music, is a composer in the tradition of large-scale programmatic music close to Shostakovich's own creative temperament. His works include a Violin Concerto (1945) and a 'Symphony of Liberation' (1946). He is the author of 'Music in the Soviet Union' in *European Music in the Twentieth Century*, edited by H. Hartog (London, 1957).

Ronald Stevenson is a Scottish composer, pianist and writer on music. His massive *Passacaglia on DSCH* for solo piano is based on the four-note motif derived from Shostakovich's initials. He is the author of *Western Music: an Introduction* (1971).

Robert Stradling teaches history at University College, Cardiff. He is the author of *Europe and the Decline of Spain* (London, 1981), and writes and lectures on socio-musical topics, especially of the late romantic period.

Index

7